AF269412

ENDORSEMENTS

1 CORINTHIANS — RESTORING A CONGREGATION IN CRISIS
RABBI DR. YOSEF KOELNER

Rabbi Yosef Koelner is a pioneer in the Messianic Jewish movement, as well as a distinguished teacher, scholar, and mentor. This must have commentary on 1 Corinthians clarifies the historical, cultural, and theological issues found in the text.

—Rabbi Alex Yalenga, Senior Rabbi, Zambia Messianic Fellowship, author, international speaker.

To understand Paul's letter to the confused Corinthians, Rabbi Koelner has dug deeply into Jewish Corinth. There, he uncovered the issues that motivated Paul to write his first letter to these new believers. We see these sorts of issues in the Body, even today.

—Paul Wilbur, internationally acclaimed worship artist, song writer, speaker, and award-winning author.

I have known Rabbi Yosef Koelner for forty years. He is a man of great integrity and sound understanding of scripture. This commentary is bound to bring forth great insights into the Hebraic thinking of Paul and the Jewish background of the time in which it was written.

—Chuck Cohen, Director, Intercessors for Israel, Jerusalem

Coming from a traditional Jewish home, immersed in the Hebrew language, Yosef Koelner brings deep insight—what some might call, nuggets—to bible-believers, hungry to understand God's word. His commentary on 1 Corinthians is a great contribution to the Body.

— Ron Cantor, President of *Shelanu* TV, the only 24-7 Hebrew language TV channel sharing the message of Yeshua.

ENDORSEMENTS

2 CORINTHIANS — COUNTERING MESSIANIC MADNESS
RABBI DR. JEFFREY SEIF

When it comes to scholarship and dealing with difficult passages, the word "trust" comes to mind. I have a high level of confidence in the words of Dr. Seif.

— Paul Wilbur, internationally acclaimed worship artist, song writer, speaker, and award-winning author.

His extensive background and knowledge of Messianic Judaism obviously saturates his treatment of 2 Corinthians. I highly recommend Seif's compendium, which strikes a rare balance between multi-cultural scholarship on the one hand and readability on the other!

—Boyd Luter, PhD, Professor Emeritus of Research and Bible, The King's University

As a Jewish believer, and one who has served as a criminal justice professional, like Paul, Jeff has both observed and experienced some of the extremities of the human condition. He brings unique insights to the forefront and is well-qualified to interpret the Apostle's most passionate letter for us today.

— Bill Bjoraker, PhD., US Missions, Assemblies of God

Written in simple language for those of us who are not bible scholars but simply want to better comprehend the scriptures.

—Jonathan Bernis, CEO, Jewish Voice Ministries

A Messianic Commentary

Sha'ul / Paul
God's Shaliach (Apostle)

Corresponds with the

Corinthians

Books in the Messianic Commentary Series

Yochanan (John)
Presents the
Revelation of Yeshua the Messiah

Paul Presents to the
Philippians
Unity in the Messianic Community

John's Three Letters
on Hope, Love and Covenant Fidelity

Rabbi Paul Enlightens the
Ephesians
on Walking with Messiah Yeshua

Matthew
Presents Yeshua, King Messiah

James the Just
Presents Applications of Torah

Jude
on Faith and the
Destructive Influence of Heresy

Acts
of the Emissaries
The Early History of the Yeshua Movement

Paul's Letter to
Titus
His Emissary to Crete, About Congregational Life

A Messianic Commentary

Sha'ul / Paul
God's Shaliach (Apostle)

Corresponds with the

Corinthians

1 Corinthians
Restoring a Congregation in Crisis

2 Corinthians
Countering Messianic Madness

Dr. Yosef Koelner
& Dr. Jeffrey Seif

Lederer Books
An imprint of
Messianic Jewish Publishers
Clarksville, MD 21029

Cover Design by Lisa Rubin, Messianic Jewish Publishers
Graphic Design by Yvonne Vermillion, MagicGraphix.com

Printed in the United States of America

2023   1
ISBN: 978-1-951833-38-1

Published by
Lederer Books
A division of
Messianic Jewish Publishers
6120 Day Long Lane
Clarksville, Maryland 21029

Distributed by
Messianic Jewish Resources Int'l.
www.MessianicJewish.net
Individual and Trade Order Line: 800-410-7367
Email: lederer@messianicjewish.net

CONTENTS

General Editor's Preface

Nearly all Bible commentators emphasize the importance of understanding the historical, cultural, and grammatical aspects of any text of Scripture. As has been said, "A text without a context is a pretext." In other words, to assume one can understand what God has revealed through those who present his Word—prophets, poets, visionaries, apostles—without knowing the context is presumption. To really understand God's Word, it is essential to know something about who wrote it, to whom, what was said, what it originally meant, and when, where, and why it was written.

By now, everyone knows the New Testament is a thoroughly Jewish book, written entirely by Jews, taking place in and around Israel. The people written about—Yeshua (Jesus), Paul, Peter, James, John, etc.—were all Jews who never abandoned their identities or people. The topics covered—sin, salvation, resurrection, Torah, Sabbath, how to "walk with God," the Millennium, etc.— were all Jewish topics that came from the Hebrew Scripture. Many expressions were Jewish idioms of that day. So, to fully understand the New Testament, it must be viewed through "Jewish eyes."

There are commentaries for women, men, teens, even children. There are commentaries that focus on financial issues in the Bible. Others provide archaeological material. Some commentaries are topical. Others are the works of eminent men and women of God. Yet, no commentary series has focused on the Jewish context of each of the New Testament books.... until now.

Some of the world's top Messianic Jewish theologians contributed their knowledge and understanding to this series. Each has written on a book or books of the New Testament he has specialized in, making sure to present the Jewish aspects—the original context—of each book. These works are not meant to be a verse-by-verse exegetical commentary. There are many excellent ones available. The commentaries in this series focus on the Jewish aspects, often missed, along with explaining the book.

Several different authors contributed these commentaries, each in his own style. Just as the Gospels were written by four different men, each with his own perspective and style, these volumes too have variations.

You may see some actual Hebrew expressions or transliterations of Hebrew names in the New Testament. Thus, one writer might refer to the Apostle to the Gentiles as Paul. Another might write *Sha'ul*, Paul's Hebrew name. Still another might write *Saul*, an Anglicized version of *Sha'ul*. And some might write *Saul/Paul* to reflect, not reject, the different ways this servant of Messiah was known.

Another variation is the amount of reference material. Some have ample footnotes or endnotes, while others incorporate references within the text. Some do not have many notes. Some present words in their original languages, either Hebrew or Greek.

So, I invite you to put on your "Jewish glasses" and look at the New Testament in a way that may open new understanding for you, as you get to know the God of Israel and his Messiah better.

Rabbi Barry Rubin
General Editor and Publisher

Introduction

The Jew, Rabbi Sha'ul (Saul/Paul of Tarsus) wrote most of the letters in the *B'rit Hadashah*, the New Testament.

A concerned clergyman, he cared for all the congregations under his spiritual authority as an Apostle. . . and as a Rabbi. Most of the letters were written to people, often leaders, he had encountered in his extensive travels in the Mediterranean world.

The unique thing about this man was that he was an observant, Torah-keeping Jew, a fully credentialed, well-educated, and totally trained, rabbi. The way he interpreted the events he was witnessing and writing about was informed by this background, particularly since Paul was a *talmid* (student) of Gamaliel, one of the leading rabbis of his day.

In this volume, you will find separate commentaries from two educated, well-trained, and experienced Messianic Jewish rabbis, each bringing his own background to the discussion of the weighty matters with which the Rabbi from Tarsus was dealing—immorality, incest, marriage, congregational conflicts, and more. These are many of the same challenges we face today.

As the "Apostle to the Gentiles" (Rom. 11:13), Paul was indeed the chosen messenger to the bring the Word of the God from Israel to the nations of the world.

1 CORINTHIANS

ON RESTORING
A CONGREGATION IN CRISIS

RABBI DR. YOSEF KOELNER

"It is always a good thing to question established theories, as it allows ideas to be tested anew. A consensus cannot mean that the theory is correct but only that most of us have stopped thinking about the matter critically.".[1]

---

1. Yonatan Adler, "Watertight and Rock-Solid Stepped Pools and Chalk Vessels as Expressions of Jewish Ritual Purity," (*Biblical Archaeology Review*, Spring 2021) 45.

ACKNOWLEDGEMENTS

I thank Dr. Daniel Juster both for his encouragement and guidance as I embarked on this journey to write this Commentary on 1 Corinthians. I remember his words: "I didn't know you were a scholar."

Well, whether I am or not will be determined by the readers. I just know that those words by my friend were motivational when I realized the huge task of gathering, organizing, and writing on the often-missing Jewish aspects of 1 Corinthians.

Dozens of my fellow Messianic rabbis cheered me on in this work. There are too many to thank specifically, so I just want to acknowledge and thank those of you who were there for me over the past few years.

But the person to whom I am most grateful is my wife, Marty, who not only has been my beloved for many decades but helped me write, re-write, and edit this book.

To God be the glory.
Rabbi Dr. Yosef Koelner
June, 2023

PREFACE

THE CHALLENGE SHA'UL FACED: RESTORING A CONGREGATION IN CRISIS

After fifty years of leading congregations, it has been my experience that even the most stable and solid groups will face the challenge of having to navigate the tempestuous and murky waters of a crisis. In Corinth, Sha'ul invested eighteen months of his life (Acts 18:11–12), laying a foundation as a wise builder and producing a thriving community of believers (1 Cor. 3:18). He left for Ephesus—circa the spring of 52 C.E.—with the implied assurance that the congregation was in the care of qualified and trusted leaders. While in Ephesus, he received disturbing reports that Corinth had become a congregation in crisis that desperately needed to be restored to its former state (1 Cor. 1:11). He responded to the situation by writing the first letter to the Corinthians—circa 53-54 C.E.

After Saul/Paul left Corinth, the Messianic community began to question his credentials as a *shaliach*/apostle (1 Cor. 9:1–2; 2 Cor. 10:10). The primary issues that Sha'ul addressed were factionalism related to an understanding of wisdom that was at odds with Sha'ul's message of the crucifixion (1:10–4:17), sexuality (4:18–5:12, 6:12–7:40), lawsuits among brothers (6:1–11), idolatry (8:1–33), worship (11:1–14:40), and resurrection/consummation (15:1–58). Similar patterns can be found in Romans 1:21–28, 15:5–16, and 1 Thessalonians 1:9–10.[2]

Mathew Henry, summarizes the situation or crisis:

> He [Sha'ul] wrote this epistle to them, to water what he had planted and rectify some gross disorders which during his absence had been introduced, partly from the interest some false teacher or teachers had obtained amongst them, and partly from the leaven of their old maxims and manners ... Their pride discovered itself in their parties and factions, and the notorious disorders they committed in the exercise of their spiritual gifts. And this vice was not wholly fed by their wealth, but by the insight they had into the Greek learning and philosophy.[3]

Scripture does not indicate if the Corinthian community was ever fully restored, but one could interpret 2 Corinthians 13:11 as implying that the Messianic community was in the process of becoming fully repaired. "Finally, brothers and sisters, rejoice! Strive for full restoration, encourage one another, be of one mind, live in peace. And the God of love and peace will be with you" (2 Cor. 13:11 NIV). I have learned that the "call" to lead any type of congregation is pressure-packed, replete with daily challenges (2 Cor. 11:28). The pressure is exacerbated during the process of restoring a congregation that is in crisis!

---

2 . Roy E. Ciampa and Brian S. Rosner, *The Structure and Argument of 1 Corinthians: A Biblical/Jewish Approach.* (New Testament Studies, 52, 2006), 205-218 doi:10.1017/S0028688506000129.

3. Matthew Henry, *Matthew Henry's Commentary (Vol. VI)* (Old Tappan, NJ: Fleming H. Revell Company, 1960), 719.

REEXAMINING PREVAILING AND ESTABLISHED THEORIES

One of the objectives of this commentary is to examine the text of 1 Corinthians through a new lens by questioning and challenging prevailing and established theories and misperceptions regarding its interpretation. This commentary supports the viewpoint "that rather than reading 1 Corinthians with Greco-Roman rhetorical categories in mind, it is better to use the Tanakh (Old Testament) and Jewish frames of reference as the primary lens that clarifies our understanding of both the form and contents of the letter."[4]

Prior to the emergence of the New Perspective on Paul movement and its subsequent subsets, scholars portrayed Sha'ul as completely rejecting his background in Judaism, and his training as a Pharisee; it was thought that Sha'ul chose to become a "de-Judaized" Jew.

According to the traditional narrative, Paul's revelation of Christ resulted in a radical rethinking of his theology and ethics to the point that he no longer felt responsible to keep the Torah, or at least those aspects of Torah that served as boundary markers of Jewish identity. For the Christian Paul, being a Jew was no longer a matter of election, calling or covenant walked out in Torah observance. By divine design, Jewish identity had been erased, superseded, or revalorized to the point of indifference in Christ.[5]

---

4. Roy E. Ciampa and Brian S. Rosner, 9

5. David Rudolph, *The Circumcised Apostle: Paul and Jewish Identity in 1 Corinthians 9:19-23* (Academia.edu, June 4, 2017, www.academia.edu/33325804/The_Circumcised_ Apostle_Paul_and_Jewish_Identity_in_1_Corinthians_9_19_23.

This contention has fallen by the wayside. Alan Segal aptly states: "Despite the objections of a small but vocal minority, it seems certain that Sha'ul was not only Jewish but also a Pharisee, just as he himself claims."[6]

> But knowing that one part of the *Sanhedrin* consisted of *Tz'dukim* [Sadducees] and the other of *P'rushim* [Pharisees] Sha'ul shouted, "Brothers, I myself am a *Parush* and the son of *P'rushim*; and it is concerning the hope of the resurrection of the dead that I am being tried!" (Acts 23:6).

As Paul wrote to the Philippians,

> Even though I certainly have grounds for putting confidence in such things. If anyone else thinks he has grounds for putting confidence in human qualifications, I have better grounds:
>
> • *b'rit-milah* on the eighth day
> • by birth belonging to the people of Isra'el
> • from the tribe of Binyamin
> • a Hebrew-speaker, with Hebrew-speaking parents
> • regarding the *Torah,* a *Parush* (Pharisee)
> • about zeal, a persecutor of the Messianic Community
> • regarding the righteousness demanded by legalism, blameless.
>
> (Philippians 3:4–6)

Thus, germane to the interpretation of 1 Corinthians is the realization that Sha'ul was a Pharisee with a thoroughly Jewish worldview, recognized as such by Sha'ul's contemporaries. He was a Pharisee who has "rethought and reworked every aspect of his native Jewish theology in light of the Messiah and the spirit."

Elements of Pharisaism frequently appear in Sha'ul's readjusted theology. For instance, Judaism interpreted Deuteronomy 4:6 as equating the Torah with the wisdom of God. "Therefore, observe them;

---

6. Alan Segal, *Paul's Jewish Presuppositions* (James D. G. Dunn, The Cambridge Companion to St. Paul), 159.

and follow them; for then all peoples will see you as having wisdom and understanding. When they hear of all these laws, they will say, 'This great nation is surely a wise and understanding people.'" As a result, Judaism described itself with the Hellenic term "the wisdom of its people." To those in the Greco-Roman world who admired Judaism, it was referred to as the cult or philosophy of wisdom.[7]

Eventually, the Pharisees embraced and incorporated the concept of God's wisdom and its ramifications as well as its manifestations into their systematic theology. Therefore, it is not surprising that in 1 Corinthians Sha'ul extensively addresses this concept. The message of the crucifixion is the wisdom of God which destroys the wisdom of the wise.

> **18** For the message about the execution-stake is nonsense to those in the process of being destroyed, but to us in the process of being saved it is the power of God. **19** Indeed, the *Tanakh* says, "I will destroy the wisdom of the wise and frustrate the intelligence of the intelligent." (1 Cor. 1:18–19)

Messiah Yeshua has become the wisdom of God. It is his doing that unites you with the Messiah Yeshua. He has become wisdom for us from God, and righteousness, holiness, and redemption as well!" (1 Cor. 1:30).

Sha'ul's Pharisaic background is also evident when he expounds upon the following issues:

> Table fellowship which occurred during private or communal meals, whether during ordinary or cultic meals. The rules of table fellowship include the avoidance of consuming ritually impure unconsecrated food as well as proper conduct during a meal.[8] In 1 Corinthians 11:17-33, he chides the Corinthians for improper conduct during the "Lord's Supper" (Passover).

---

7. Jacob Neusner, *Judaism in the Beginning of Christianity* (Philadelphia: Fortress Press, 1984), 51.

8. Jacob Neusner and Bruce Chilton, *In Quest of the Historical Pharisees* (Waco, TX: Baylor University Press, 2007), 325-326.

The admonition to not eat meat sacrificed to idols first appears in Acts 15:29. Sha'ul cautions the Corinthians to use self-restraint when eating meat sacrificed to idols because they may cause a weaker brother to stumble (1 Cor. 8:1–13). He then forbids eating meat that was sacrificed to idols during Pesach [Passover] and by implication all meals because meat sacrificed to idols is meat that has been sacrificed to demons (1 Cor. 10:14–22).

Apocalyptic eschatology was also central to Sha'ul's message. The appearance of the resurrected Yeshua changed Sha'ul's life, and his writings are replete with references to the resurrection from the dead.[9]

For Sha'ul, "The Torah's sacrificial system was incapable of imparting eschatological righteousness (8:3). The answer for both Jews and Gentiles is not the Torah, but the *Evangelion* (Good News) of Jesus and the *Pneuma* (Spirit) that he imparts."[10] Sha'ul believed that he was living in the end times and that the resurrection of the dead was imminent.

> Like many other Jews of the time—including such figures as John the Baptist and Jesus of Nazareth—Pharisees held to a kind of apocalyptic worldview that had developed toward the very end of the biblical period and down into the first century.[11]

Incorporating these insights about Sha'ul's Pharisaic background will enhance one's comprehension of the message of 1 Corinthians.

---

9. Acts 9:1-5; 22:3-16; 26:9-18; 1 Corinthians 15; Galatians 1:16; 1 Thessalonians 1:13-18

10. Mark Kinzer, *Paul and the Torah in Apocalyptic Perspective,* Welcome to Enoch Seminar (October 26, http://enochseminar.org/review/14933.)

11. Bart D. Ehrman, *The Triumph of Christianity: How a Forbidden Religion Swept the World* (New York: Simon & Schuster Paperbacks, 2019), 44.

THE HISTORY OF JEWISH CORINTH FROM ITS INCEPTION THROUGH THE NEW TESTAMENT PERIOD

It is critical to understand the history of the Jewish community of Corinth to comprehend the audience that Sha'ul was addressing. One needs to be aware that the Jewish communities in the Diaspora/Greco-Roman world were not monolithic. Though each community shared many common elements with others, each community had its own unique identity regarding customs (*minhagim*), socio-economic makeup, educational level, as well as its attitude towards the non-Jewish inhabitants of its location.

Corinth had a large mixed population of Romans, Greeks, and Jews. The fact that Jews lived there is attested to by Philo in his book *Legato'd Caium*, § 36.[12]

Although the history of ancient Corinth is abundantly well documented,[13] the amount of information regarding the history of the Jewish community in Corinth from its inception through the Roman period is extremely limited. By integrating a wide range of the available source material, I have attempted to reconstruct the history of Jewish Corinth.

When Sha'ul arrived in Corinth in 51 C.E., it was the most important Jewish community in Southern Greece.[14] The Corinth that Sha'ul saw was a little more than one-hundred years old. Corinth was the capital of the province and five times as large as Athens.

---

12. https://www.jewishencyclopedia.com/articles/4661-corinth

13. Ancient Corinth, Author(s): R. J. Hopper Source: Greece & Rome, Feb., 1955, Vol. 2, No. 1 (Feb., 1955), pp. 2-15 Cambridge University Press on behalf of The Classical Association Stable URL: https://www.jstor.org/stable/642202

14. Hilary Le Cornu and Joseph Shulam, *A Commentary on the Jewish Roots of Acts*, Vol. 2 (Jerusalem: Netivyah Bible Instruction Ministry, 2003), 979.

Strategically located guarding the narrow isthmus that connects the Peloponnesus (as southern Greece is called) to the mainland, it was a powerful commercial center near two seaports only four miles apart. Lechaeum, the western harbor in the Corinthian Gulf, was the trading port to Italy, Sicily, and Cenchreae; the eastern harbor in the Saronic Gulf, was the port for the eastern Mediterranean countries.[15] Smallwood suggests that by Sha'ul's time the Jewish presence at Corinth would be considered a politeuma, i.e., a corporation of resident aliens with permanent rights of domicile and empowered to manage its own affairs through self-appointed officials. Hence, we read of a synagogue ruler (Acts 18:8, 17), and in the ruins of the city a debated inscription [SYN]AGŌGĒ HEBR[AIŌN], "Synagogue of the Hebrews," which may testify to the site of their meeting place.[16] Jewish legal rights in such situations include the right to assembly, permission to send the temple tax to Jerusalem, and exemption from any civic activity that would violate their Sabbath observance.[17]

Corinth was noted for its wealth and for the luxurious, immoral, and vicious habits of the people. Its immorality is attested to in 1 and 2 Corinthians and Jewish literature.

> Pharisaic Judæo-Christians were the cause of much dissension in the young Christian community (2 Cor. 3:1, 10:13, 11:5); for they objected to the celibacy of their Christian brethren (1 Cor. 7:1); and the Christian community was obliged to take a stand against the immorality that prevailed in certain circles (1 Cor. 5:9-11, 6:12-19; 2 Cor. 12:21). These conditions have given rise to the modern hypothesis that the Jewish Book of Jubilees—which insists upon marital fidelity and condemns unchastity—was directed against the immorality at Corinth.[18]

---

15. http://www.abrock.com/Greece-Turkey/corinth.html.
16. Its date cannot be determined with certainty.
17. https://zondervanacademic.com/blog/what-was-the-city-and-church-of-corinth-like-an-excerpt-from-ralph-martins-2-corinthians-wbc.
18. https://www.jewishencyclopedia.com/articles/4661-corinth

The earliest documented evidence of Jews living in Corinth is contained in Agrippa I's letter to Gaius Caligula. King Agrippa, who enjoyed a close friendship with Caligula, was in Rome. Philo was also in Rome at the same time as the head of the delegation of Alexandrian Judaeans. In his book *The Embassy to Gaius (De Legatione ad Caium)*, Philo gives a detailed description of what transpired when King Agrippa became aware of the decree of Gaius regarding the Temple in Jerusalem.

Caligula, more than any Caesar, took his divinity seriously, to the point where he declared himself a god, the counterpart of Zeus. He demanded worship from the people. In the year 39–40 C.E., he ordered Petronius, the legate of Syria, to have a statue of himself erected and placed in the Temple. When Agrippa I heard, he collapsed and was carried out in a coma. The attendants took him to his house where he remained unconscious for thirty-six hours. Upon recovering, Agrippa I wrote a letter to Gaius appealing to him to rescind his order.[19]

King Agrippa I who was revered as a loyal Jew[20] implored Caligula to reconsider and rescind his decision by reminding him that throughout the Roman Empire there were numerous Jewish communities who honored and were loyal to the emperor, including Jews who lived in Corinth.

> Concerning the holy city, I must now say what is necessary. It, as I have already stated, is my native country, and the metropolis, not only of the one country of Judaea, but also of many, by reason of the colonies which it has sent out from time to time into the bordering districts of Egypt, Phoenicia, Syria in general, and especially that part of it which is called Coelo-Syria, and also with those more distant regions of Pamphylia, Cilicia, the greater part of Asia Minor as far as

---

19. "Did Agrippa Write a Letter to Gaius Caligula?" Solomon Zeitlin, *The Jewish Quarterly Review*, Jul. 1965, Vol. 56, No. 1, pp. 22-31, University of Pennsylvania Press Stable URL: www.jstor.org/stable/1453330

20. His close association with the Pharisees is attested in the statement of Josephus that "his permanent residence was Jerusalem, where he enjoyed living, and he scrupulously observed the ancestral laws." Apparently, it is Agrippa I who is referred to in the Mishnah which points out that when celebrating the festival of the first fruits, "even King Agrippa carried the basket [of fruits] on his shoulder" (Bik.3:4)

> Bithynia, and the furthermost corners of Pontus. And in the same manner into Europe, into Thessaly, and Boeotia, and Macedonia, and Aetolia, and Attica, and Argos, and Corinth and all the most fertile and wealthiest districts of Peloponnesus. (282) And not only are the continents full of Jewish colonies, but also all the most celebrated islands are so too, such as Euboea, and Cyprus, and Crete.[21]

From Agrippa's letter it is reasonable to conclude that Jews had been living in Corinth prior to 39-40 C.E.

Migration Patterns

Jews were frequently expelled from Rome, and it is logical to assume that due to Corinth's prominence as a commercial center and its cosmopolitan culture that they would migrate to such a desirable location. Therefore, it is possible that Jews began to settle in Corinth as early as 139 B.C.E., after the praetor Hispanus issued a decree expelling all Jews from Rome who were not Italian citizens.

There is evidence that Jewish exiles from Sicyon, which is northwest of Corinth, may have already relocated there when their city was destroyed in 146 B.C.E.[22]

In 19 C.E., Tiberius also expelled Jews and proselytes, as well as astrologers and Egyptian religions, from Rome (Suet. Tib. 36) [4022]). Four thousand young Jewish men were sent to battle bandits in Sardinia. The Jews who were deported to battle Sardinian brigands according to Tac. Ann. 2.85 were freedmen (former slaves) who were "infected" with Jewish and Egyptian superstition.[23] It is conceivable that these young Jewish men eventually settled in Corinth.

---

21. *The Works of Philo, On the Embassy to Gaius,* www.earlychristianwritings.com/yonge/book40.html.

22. www.zondervanacademic.com/blog/what-was-the-city-and-church-of-corinth-like-an-excerpt-from-ralph-martins-2-corinthians-wbc

23 . John Granger Cook, *Roman Attitudes toward the Christians: From Claudius to Hadrian* (Tübingen: Mohr Siebeck, 2010).

The Book of Acts refers to another expulsion that occurred in 49 C.E. which was ordered by the Roman Emperor Claudius Caesar.[24]

> After this, Sha'ul left Athens and went to Corinth, [2]where he met a Jewish man named Aquila, originally from Pontus but having recently come with his wife Priscilla from Italy, because Claudius had issued a decree expelling all the Jews from Rome. (Acts 18:2)

The Roman historian Suetonius confirms Claudius's edict and adds that Jews were causing disturbances at the instigation of *Chrestus* (Claud. 25), which may be a corruption of "Christ"; the account may reflect tensions created by the proclamations of Jesus' followers.[25]

In 66 C.E., Nero attempted to build a canal in Corinth.[26] Vespasian, after his victory in Galilee, sent 6,000 captive youths to Nero to dig at the Isthmus of Corinth. Josephus records:

> Then came Vespasian, and ordered them all to stand in the stadium, and commanded them to kill the old men, together with the others that were useless, which were in number a thousand and two hundred. Out of the young men he chose six thousand of the strongest, and sent them to Nero, to dig through the Isthmus (Wars, 3: 540).[27]

Some of the 6000 might have escaped and found haven in nearby settlements including Corinth.

---

24. Referred to by Roman historians Suetonius (c. AD 69 – c. AD 122), Cassius Dio (c. AD 150 – c. 235) and fifth-century Christian author Paulus Orosius.

25. Amy-Jill Levine and Marc Zvi Brettler, *The Jewish Annotated New Testament* (Oxford: Oxford Univ Press, 2017), 234.

26. https://www.abrock.com/Greece-Turkey/corinth.html

27. Flavius Josephus, *Complete Works of Josephus: Antiquities of the Jews, the Wars of the Jews against Apion* (New York: Bigelow, 1924).

SOCIAL AND ECONOMIC STATUS IN THE ROMAN WORLD

Conclusive source material has established that by the first century C.E., Jews lived various existences in the Roman Empire and in the city of Rome itself. The exact number and ratio of each is not known; many Jews in Rome were slaves. Though some were lifetime slaves, most were indentured or slaves for a set period. Once they had served their time, they were made free through a process called manumission. Many of Rome's Jews were this type of freed slave. In fact, some were even made Roman citizens upon manumission and there was a large population of Jews who were citizens of Rome in the first century A.D.[28]

Craig S. Keener, as well as E. A. Judge, suggest that both Aquila and Pricilla could have been freed slaves who were granted Roman citizenship.

"As cognomens, 'Aquila' and 'Pricilla' both suggest citizenship. Freed Jewish slaves like them are most likely alluded to in 1 Corinthians 7:22. For the one who was a slave when called to faith in the Lord is the Lord's freed person: similarly, the one who was free when called is Christ's slave."[29]

> Thus, it may not be coincidental that in a letter to Corinth we find the only use in the New Testament of the technical term "freed person" (apeleutheros, 7:22). Some freedmen in Corinth held high civic positions and the Forum was marked by the benefactions of ex-slaves. Sha'ul's words "Let ... those ... who buy [be] as though they had no possessions, and those

---

28. https://study.com/academy/lesson/roman-expulsion-of-judaism-factors-background-events.html

29. Craig S. Keener, *Acts - An Exegetical Commentary - Volume 3* (Grand Rapids: Baker Academic, 2014), 720.

who deal with the world as though they had no dealings with it" (7:29–31) would have been particularly thought-provoking to Corinthians-in-Christ in an urban setting in which buying and dealings with the world were central to civic identity—and in which having been bought and later manumitted were part of the identity of local elites.[30]

In Rome, Jews traded in broken glass for sulfur and worked as lime burners, but most were engaged in low grade occupations, which included craftsmen. It was precisely the low grade of many Jewish occupations and Jewish poverty that evoked the contempt of Roman authors.[31]

There is little research regarding the sub-stratification of the craftsmen. Beechey found evidence that poverty existed in Roman society, primarily in cases of individuals who lacked a profession or a vocation. Stewart claimed that the social status of the artisan correlated with the level of the required theoretical expertise. Thus, design and measurement were considered cognitive skills. The harder the manual labor involved, the lower the status of the artisan. Kehoe points out that there was economic expansion in the provinces of the Roman Empire during the first century C.E., and this advancement would have assisted the artisan and merchant class more than the farmers.[32]

---

30. www.academia.edu/7457182/Chapter_length_commentary_on_1_Corinthians_Fortress_Press_
31. Dora Askowith, *The Toleration and Persecution of the Jews in the Roman Empire* (New York: Columbia University, 1915), 94-98.
32. "The Social Context of Craftsmen in Roman Palestine: 70-250 CE," https://www.researchgate.net/publication/282926465._

JEWISH CRAFTSMEN IN CORINTH

With the information that we do have, we can draw the conclusion that many of the Jews in Corinth were craftsman.

Although there were no direct links between the Jews of Corinth and *Eretz Israel* (the "Land of Israel"), Corinthian products were known in the Holy Land. Josephus (Wars, 5:201) mentions the Corinthian copper that coated one of the Temple gates, the Gate of Nicanor whose special copper is also noted in talmudic sources (Tosefta, Yoma 2:4; Yoma 38a), and he similarly mentions the Corinthian candelabra in Agrippa II's house (Life, 68).[33]

Sha'ul and his coworkers Aquilla and Priscilla, were craftsmen — tentmakers in Rome who continued their profession in Corinth.[34] He would have met them in the Agora where craftsmen plied their trade.[35]

Lea Roth, pointing to Sha'ul, Priscilla, and Aquila as prime examples, posits that the members of the Jewish community were poor and belonged to the lower classes.[36]

Meeks, however, suggests that this couple's background is economically low to middle; their occupation low but not extremely low, and their wealth high based on their ability to make independent

---

33. www.jewishvirtuallibrary.org/corinth.

34. Acts 18:1-3.

35. The Agora, or Roman Forum, was the heart of Ancient Corinth. The Agora was rectangular in shape, measuring 160 meters by 70 meters. It contained shops on the north, west, south, and in the center. www.nomadicniko.com/2018/10/22/ancient-corinth-agora/

As trading was a vital part of Corinthian life, adult citizens often went to the Agora, or public marketplace to trade goods that they made. Some oversaw the money exchange that occurred at Corinth's banks. Corinthians spent much of their time making vases, pottery, and statues. Corinth was a bustling port city, so Corinthians always had many foreign traders to trade goods with. This was very practical as Corinthians were not only traders but excellent craftsmen. This way, they could trade the valuable goods they made for necessary resources. www.sites.google.com/site/ancientgreececorinth/home/daily-life-in-corinth.

36. www.jewishvirtuallibrary.org/corinth.

moves several times (to Rome, then Corinth, Ephesus, and Rome) and to host Paul and Christian gatherings. These observations seem accurate, overall. Those who demur from Meeks's interpretation here may be equally correct—yet, ironically, not so much because of differing on the data itself, but mainly because their definitions of poverty and wealth, based on different standards for comparison, differ from those of Meeks since they compare the couple's economic status with that of different groups. Overall, most urban artisans were poor and despised by the elite but had an independence not available to the agrarian peasants who constituted most of the empire's population.[37] Keener also adds that though several of the Corinthian community's members were affluent, most of its members belonged to a lower socio-economic class (1 Cor. 1:26).[38]

In Alexandria, Jewish people who were craftsman were considered to belong to a lower socio-economic class.

> It has been taught, R. Judah stated, He who has not seen the double colonnade of Alexandria in Egypt has never seen the glory of Israel. It was said that it was like a huge basilica, one colonnade within the other, and it sometimes held twice the number of people that went forth from Egypt. There were in it seventy-one cathedras of gold, corresponding to the seventy-one members of the Great Sanhedrin, not one of them containing less than twenty-one talents of gold, and a wooden platform in the middle upon which the attendant of the Synagogue stood with a scarf in his hand. When the time came to answer Amen, he waved his scarf and all the congregation duly responded. They moreover did not occupy their seats promiscuously, but goldsmiths sat separately, silversmiths separately, blacksmiths separately, metalworkers separately

---

37. *Acts: An Exegetical Commentary: Volume 3,* 692. www.amazon.com/Acts-Exegetical-Commentary-15-1-23-ebook/dp/B00OY906ES, 723-724.
38. *Ibid.* 692.

and weavers separately, so that when a poor man entered the place, he recognized the members of his craft and on applying to that quarter obtained a livelihood for himself and for the members of his family (Sukkot 51b).

Thus, the Talmud also supports Lea Roth's contention regarding the socioeconomic condition of the Corinthian Jewish community.

THE HISTORY OF THE MESSIANIC COMMUNITY OF CORINTH

Prior to Sha'ul's arrival, circa 50–52 C.E., the first believers that are associated with the Messianic community in Corinth are Aquilla and Priscilla. They arrived in Corinth because of Claudius' order to expel the Jewish people from Rome – circa 49 C.E. (Acts 18:1–2). Whether Aquilla and Priscilla were the first believers in Corinth or the founders or the leaders of a pre-existent Messianic community, it is impossible to determine and is purely speculative. Most scholars suggest that Sha'ul was the founder, as well as the leader of the Corinthian Messianic community. As a result of Sha'ul's preaching in the Synagogue, a separate congregation, consisting of Jewish people and God Fearers who formed the core group of the Messianic community, was established in the house of Titus Justus (Acts 18:7–8).

The believers met in homes. The homes that are mentioned are of Titus Justus (Acts 18:7); Cenchreae, a village in the municipality of Corinth which may have been the home of Phoebe (Rom. 16:1); and the home of Priscilla and Aquilla (Rom. 16:3–5). Another possibility is that there existed a group of believers that met at the home of Chloe (1 Cor. 1:11).

Individuals associated with the Corinthian community are mentioned in Acts 18:1–18, Romans 16:1–44, and 1 Corinthians 1:11–12. Gerd Theissen, in his article "Social Stratification in the Corinthian Community: A Contribution to the Sociology of Early Hellenistic Christianity" evaluates the social status of seventeen people that Scripture associates with the believers at Corinth.

> Of the seventeen persons (including one group) listed, nine belong to the upper classes. The result is clear. The great majority of the Corinthians known to us by name probably enjoyed high social status. We need not for that reason cast doubt on Paul's statement that 'few Corinthians belonged to the upper strata (1 Cor. 1:26). In the letters it is understandably the most important people who are most likely to be mentioned by name, who keep in touch with Paul (that is, were free to travel), and who exercise influence within the congregation … Those of the lower strata scarcely appear as individuals in the Corinthian correspondence.

The scholarly consensus is that those believers who belonged to the lower strata of society were exclusively non-Jews. This is not the case. My research as presented in the section "The History of Jewish Corinth" has drawn a different conclusion. The Jewish community of Corinth was atypical because most of its constituents were minimally paid laborers and craftsmen who were relegated to the lower strata of society.

Scholars also equate poverty with a lack of education. However, the theological complexities of the entire Corinthian correspondence seem to indicate that most of the believers at Corinth irrespective of their ethnic background had a sophisticated grasp of Scripture and Jewish practices.[39]

Eventually, some of the leaders at Corinth such as Sosthenes, Priscilla, and Aquila accompanied Sha'ul on his journeys to assist him in the spreading of the Besorah Tovah (Good News) to the Greco-Roman world (1 Cor. 1:1; 16:19).

From the source material that is available, it is apparent that Corinth boasted a significant community of Jews and that it was the most important Jewish community in Southern Greece. The Jewish

---

39. Joshua D. Garroway, *Paul's Christians as Gentile-Jews: Neither Jew nor Gentile, but Both* (Basingstoke: Palgrave Macmillan, 2012), 47.

community was a politeuma who exercised the right to govern its own internal affairs. Evidence suggests that the preponderance of Corinth's Jewish inhabitants were craftsman or manual laborers who belonged to a lower socio-economic class. The immorality of the city had a direct effect on the moral condition of all segments of Jewish society regardless of their theological persuasion. This commentary on 1 Corinthians will address these issues.

1 CORINTHIANS OUTLINE

CHAPTER ONE

I. Opening Declarations (1:1–9)

- Sha'ul establishes his authority as a *shaliach* (apostle) of Yeshua who by the will of God was sent to the believers at Corinth (1:1–2)
- Sha'ul blesses the Corinthians, thanks God for His active presence in their lives, and commends them for their faithfulness. (1:3–9)

II. Sha'ul addresses the divisions in the community and appeals for unity (1:10–17)

III. Depending on Human Wisdom Divides - Depending on Godly Wisdom Unites (1:18–2:16)

- The wisdom of God is the message of the cross (1:18)
- The message of the cross is the power of God (1:18)
- The contrast between God's wisdom and human wisdom (1:19-23)
- God's wisdom through the message of the cross unites Jews and Greeks (1:24–31)
- Sha'ul's message does not rest on human wisdom but on God's power (2:1–5)
- God's wisdom has been revealed through the power of the Ruach HaKodesh (Holy Spirit) (2:6–9)
- Believers are united by accepting the revelation of the wisdom of God which is the mind of the Messiah (2:10–16)

IV. Faithful Servants of the Messiah (3:1–4:21)

- Faithful servants are mature (3:1–3)
- Faithful servants are not divided (3:4–9)
- Faithful servants build on a common foundation, Yeshua the Messiah (3:10–17)
- Faithful servants depend on godly wisdom not human wisdom or personalities (3:18–23)
- The apostles are examples faithful servants (4:1–13)
- Faithful servants must humble themselves or suffer the consequences of arrogance (4:14–21)

V. Immorality in the Corinthian Community (5:1–6:20)

- Sha'ul condemns the Corinthian's indifference and attitudes towards sexual sins (5:1–12)
- Sha'ul condemns the Corinthians' unethical way of settling legal disputes (6:1–8)
- The consequences of immoral behavior (6:9–10)
- The blessings of being sanctified and being set apart for God (6:11)

VI. Sha'ul Responds to the Questions Posed by the Corinthian Community (7:1–14:40)

- Marriage and Divorce
- Sexual mores in marriage (7:1–9)
- Believers and divorce (7:10–16)
- Believers should be content with their God given status - married or single, circumcised or uncircumcised, slave or free (7:17–24)
- Guidance for virgins and single men (7:25–40)
- Eating Meat Sacrificed to Idols and Self-Restraint (8:1–11:1)
- Sha'ul connects the themes of a believer's freedom and self-restraint
- Eating meat sacrificed to idols or and exercising self-restraint for the sake of a weaker brother (8:1–13)

- Sha'ul has set aside his freedoms and exercised self-restraint for the sake of the Gospel (9:1–27)
- Israel's lack of self-restraint led to idolatry and immorality (10:1–13)
- Believers have the freedom to eat meat sacrificed to idols; however, they should not because in reality the sacrifices by pagans are offered to demons. This means by eating meat sacrificed, one is participating in idol worship (10:14–22)
- Freedom has its limits and is subject to those practices which glorify God (10:23–11:1)
- Various Instructions for Communal Gatherings (11:2–14:40)
- Head coverings for men (11:2–9)
- Head coverings for women (11:10–16)
- The Lord's Pesach/Passover Seder/Supper (11:17–34)
- Manifestations of the Ruach HaKodesh (12:1–11)
- The comparison of parts of a body with ministry roles and responsibilities (12:12–31)
- Godly love for one another is the overriding principle that guarantees unity in the Body of Messiah and its communal activities (12:31b–13:13)
- Godly love promotes orderly worship (14:1)
- Tongues, prophecy, and orderly worship (14:2–40)
- The Resurrection of the Dead - The Transformation of The Body of The Messiah (15:1–58)
- The resurrection of the Yeshua the Messiah (15:1–19)
- The resurrection of Yeshua is the first fruits and guarantee of the resurrection from the dead (15:20–28)
- Life is meaningless without the resurrection (15:29–34)
- The nature of the resurrection body (15:35–50)
- The process of the resurrection (15:51–58)

VII. Final Instructions and Comments (16:1–24)

- Tzedakah – the collection for the poor (16:1–3)
- Future travel plans for various leaders (16:4–18)
- Final greetings (16:19–24)

1 CORINTHIANS 1

INTRODUCTORY COMMENTS

After a brief salutation (1:1–3) and a declaration of thanksgiving for the manifestation of God's abundant grace among the Corinthians (1:4–9), Sha'ul begins to subtly initiate the unraveling of the factions' misperceptions regarding the concept of godly wisdom and the dismantling of these rival groups with the ultimate goal of restoring unity to the Corinthian community (1:17–2:16). Sha'ul accomplishes his purpose by presenting a *midrashic* homily – an exegesis concerning the contrast between human wisdom and godly wisdom (vv. 4–7[a]), a theme which he also intersperses throughout this letter. The debate pertaining to the "true" meaning of wisdom divided the faith community into factions. Each faction adhered to the viewpoint of a particular teacher such as Apollos or Kefa (v.12). The complex nature of this initial Midrash demonstrates that though many of the Corinthians possessed a lower social status, they were highly educated. W. D. Davies remarks, "What each party stood for we can only guess. But we do know that there must have been a considerable Jewish element in the Church at Corinth; the use of Rabbinic methods in the Epistle points to this."[40]

1 From: Sha'ul, called by God's will to be an emissary of the Messiah Yeshua; and from brother Sosthenes

2 To: God's Messianic community in Corinth, consisting of those who have been set apart by Yeshua the Messiah and

---

40. William D. Davies, *Paul and Rabbinic Judaism: Some Rabbinic Elements in Pauline Theology* (LONDON: SPCK, 1979), 50.

called to be God's holy people — along with everyone everywhere who calls on the name of our Lord Yeshua the Messiah, their Lord as well as ours:

3 Grace to you and *shalom* from God our Father and the Lord Yeshua the Messiah. (1:1–3)

1:1. From Sha'ul: Sha'ul is the undisputed author of 1 Corinthians. The occasion of the letter as stated in the introductory article "The Challenge Sha'ul Faced - Restoring a Congregation in Crisis," is the deterioration and subsequent crises that arose in the Corinthian community sometime after he left for Ephesus.

Called by God's will to be an emissary of the Messiah Yeshua: The letter begins as an apologia or a defense of Sha'ul's role as a *shaliach* (apostle). Sometime after he left Corinth, the Messianic community had begun to question his credentials as a shaliach (1 Cor. 9:1–2; 2 Cor. 10:10). He attempts to reaffirm his Apostolic authority as an approved leader in the Messianic Movement (Acts 9:15; 1 Tim. 2:7; 2 Tim. 1:11) by connecting his role as a shaliach with God's will. Other instances of the connection with God's will can be found in 2 Corinthians 1:1; Galatians 1:1; Ephesians 1:1; Colossians 1:1; and 2 Timothy 1:1.

Matthew 23:15 demonstrates that the Pharisees embraced the concept of being sent to a particular community as a shaliach.

> "Woe to you hypocritical Torah-teachers and P'rushim! You go about [as a shaliach] over land and sea to make one proselyte; and when you succeed, you make him twice as fit for Gei-Hinnom as you are!" (Matt. 23:15)

Hermann Vogelstein clearly states that the concept of the shaliach "must be understood from a historical point of view as having developed out of the Jewish apostolate."[41]

---

41. Hermann Volgelstein,, "The Development of the Apostolate in Judaism and Its Transformation in Christianity" https://www.jstor.org/stable/23502509,100.

In its Jewish context, a shaliach can be a person "who, whether a man or woman, was the agent or emissary of the sender: the concept of *shaliah shel' adam kemoto* ['a person's agent is as the person himself'] and thus fully representative of the sender."[42] Inherent in this definition is the idea of being chosen as a representative of a higher power such as God or a king and of having the authority to transmit the message of the one who sent him. Vogelstein says, "This office was found as early as at the time of the composition of the Books of Chronicles. Two categories of apostle could be ascertained, viz. (1) apostles of the central authorities to the various communities, and (2) apostles of the communities to the various central authorities."[43]

Ezra is an example of the prototype shaliach, as he was sent as the representative of King Artaxerxes to the Jewish community in Jerusalem (Ezra 7:14). In a similar fashion, Artaxeres sends Nehemiah to Jerusalem to authorize the rebuilding of the city of Jerusalem (Neh. 2:5).

In the *Brit Hadashah* (New Covenant), one of the clearest examples of the Jewish concept of an apostle can be found in the synoptic Gospels where Yeshua appoints or commissions his twelve *talmidim* (disciples) as *shlikhim* (apostles) (Matt. 10:1–2; cf. Mark. 3:13–19; Luke 6:12–16). According to Heinrich Schuetz, as quoted by Volgelstein, the phrase "sent out" as appears in Mark is the literal translation of the Hebrew expression, חילש השע, which in all cases means "to appoint" as a plenipotentiary (an authorized representative).

As Sha'ul had been commissioned by Yeshua (Acts 9:3–6) and his calling had been affirmed by the apostles in Jerusalem (9:26–28), the Messianic community in Corinth, whose core constituency was comprised of Jewish people and God Fearers, would have been familiar with the office of a shaliach, and should have enabled them to accept the full weight of Sha'ul's authority and message.

---

42. Levine and Brettler, *Jewish Annotated New Testament,* 112.

43. Hermann Volgelstein, "The Development of the Apostolate in Judaism and Its Transformation in Christianity," 99.

From brother Sosthenes: Sosthenes, the synagogue ruler mentioned in Acts 18:17.

1:2. To: God's Messianic community in Corinth: The Greek word for Messianic community often translated as "church" is *ekklessia* which is the Hebrew word *qahal* that can be translated as "assembly." In the Tanach, Israel is frequently called the assembly of God (Deut. 5:22[a]; Judg. 20:2; 1 Kgs. 8:14).

In the Brit Hadashah, the term *ekklēsia* or *qahal* has an added dimension. It is related to belief in Yeshua and his imminent return (1 Cor. 7:29; 15:1–58; 1 Thess. 4:13–18). Therefore, the believers at Corinth can be aptly described as the eschatological assembly of God.

Those who heard the term ekklēsia in antiquity may have understood a range of meanings, but certainly a political, civic assembly would have been evoked in an urban context (to which Paul's letters are aimed, after all: Meeks 2003). The term in the classical period had referred to the democratic assembly of the city, usually made up of free adult male citizens. At the time of Paul's writings, political assemblies in Greek cities around the Roman Empire still bore the name ekklēsiai, or in the singular, ekklēsia, and still met to engage in democratic deliberation about what was best for their cities (Miller). Were the ekklēsiai to which Paul wrote places of democratic debate and deliberative discourse, of authoritative speeches and challenges to those speeches, of the busy roil of argument, struggle, and the testing of ideas (Schüssler Fiorenza 1987; 1993)?[44]

Though one of the Hebrew equivalents for synagogue (Greek-*synagogue*) is also *qahal,* the Corinthians met in homes, not in a building known as a synagogue. The homes that are mentioned are the homes of Titus Justus (Acts 18:7), Cenchreae a village in the municipality of Corinth which may have been the home of Phoebe (Rom. 16:1), and the home of Priscilla and Aquila (Rom. 16:3–5).

---

44. www.academia.edu/7457182/Chapter_length_commentary_on_1_Corinthians_Fortress_Press, 3.

Another possibility is that there existed a group of believers that met at the home of Chloe (1 Cor. 1:11).

Consisting of those: Even though the Corinthians were divided into factions and engaged in a multitude of controversies, Sha'ul still acknowledges them as God's community.

Set apart by Yeshua the Messiah: Set apart as God set apart the children of Israel (Lev. 11:44–45; 20:8).

And called to be God's holy people: Compares the calling of the Corinthians to be holy (Lev. 23:3) where the feasts of *ADONAI* are to be set apart and called holy.[45]

Along with everyone everywhere: The Corinthians' connection with the universal family of God. This phrase echoes LXX Malachi 1:11 and Haggai 2:7 and suggests that the Corinthians are part of the fulfillment of God's plan to be worshipped among the Gentiles.[46]

1:3. Grace to you and shalom: A common salutation that appears at least a dozen times in Sha'ul's epistles. Some examples can be found in Romans 1:7; 1 Corinthians 1:3; and 1 Timothy 1:2.

Grace - (*charis* Greek / *chesed* Hebrew): Believers have received an unmerited gift that flows from God's grace (*chesed*). Chesed appears 190 times in the Tanakh and its Greek cognate charis appears 156 times in the Brit Hadashah, including four times in the letter to Titus (1:4, 2:11, 3:7, 3:15). Chesed can be understood in a variety of ways. It can be defined as giving oneself fully, with love and compassion. Yeshua's redemption of humanity is the ultimate expression of God's grace, and God's chesed is personified as a teacher that instructs a child in the way of righteousness (Titus 2:11).

---

45. John Lightfoot, in *Acts - 1 Corinthians* (Peabody: Hendrickson Publishers, 1997), 172.
46. Brian S. Rosner and Roy E. Ciampa, in *First Letter to the Corinthians* (Nottingham, UK: Apollos, 2010), 217.

God's chesed is the active presence of the *Ruach HaKodesh* (Holy Spirit), which sustains a believer (2 Cor. 13:14).

Shalom – שָׁלוֹם Used both as a greeting and farewell, *shalom* carries with it the concept of peace, prosperity, harmony, and well-being. The word *shalom* appears 236 times in the Tanakh, and its Greek cognate *eirēnē* appears 92 times in the Brit Hadashah. For followers of Yeshua, shalom is the peace, soundness, health, freedom from worry and the tranquil state of a soul assured of its salvation that comes through the healing works and forgiving words of Yeshua (Acts 10:36). Yeshua imparts to those who trust in him a shalom that surpasses our human understanding.

> **6** Don't worry about anything; on the contrary, make your requests known to God by prayer and petition, with thanksgiving. **7** Then God's shalom, passing all understanding, will keep your hearts and minds safe in union with the Messiah Yeshua. (Phil. 4:6–7; cf. John 14:27, 16:33)

Another cogent example of God's shalom is Yosef's response to Pharaoh regarding the interpretation of his troubling dreams. God would answer him with a peaceful explanation and satisfactory solution to avert the coming crisis (Gen. 41:16).

אֱלֹהִים יַעֲנֶה אֶת-שְׁלוֹם פַּרְעֹה. "Yosef answered Pharaoh, 'It isn't in me. God will give Pharaoh an answer that will set his mind at peace.'"

> **4** I thank my God always for you because of God's love and kindness given to you through the Messiah Yeshua, **5** in that you have been enriched by him in so many ways, particularly in power of speech and depth of knowledge. **6** Indeed, the testimony about the Messiah has become firmly established in you; **7** so that you are not lacking any spiritual gift and are eagerly awaiting the revealing of our Lord Yeshua the Messiah. **8** He will enable you to hold out until the end and thus be blameless on the Day of our Lord Yeshua the Messiah — **9** God

is trustworthy: it was he who called you into fellowship with his Son, Yeshua the Messiah, our Lord. (1:4–9)

1:4–7. Employing the form of a standard epistolary greeting, Sha'ul enumerates the gifts of God's love and kindness which is an expression of divine favor that have been freely given to the Corinthians.

1:7ᵇ–8. ⁷ Eagerly awaiting the revealing of our Lord Yeshua the Messiah. ⁸ He will enable you to hold out until the end and thus be blameless on the Day of our Lord Yeshua the Messiah: An allusion to the commonly held apocalyptic belief in the *Parousia* (Second Coming). Sha'ul indicates in 7:29–31 that the appointed time was soon approaching and in 15:1–13 (cp. 1 Thess. 4:13–18) that the time of the *"techiat hameteem"* or the resurrection from the dead was imminent.

> ¹⁰ Nevertheless, brothers, I call on you in the name of our Lord Yeshua the Messiah to agree, all of you, in what you say, and not to let yourselves remain split into factions but be restored to having a common mind and a common purpose. ¹¹ For some of Chloe's people have made it known to me, my brothers, that there are quarrels among you. ¹² I say this because one of you says, "I follow Sha'ul"; another says, "I follow Apollos"; another, "I follow Kefa"; while still another says, "I follow the Messiah!" ¹³ Has the Messiah been split in pieces? Was it Sha'ul who was put to death on a stake for you? Were you immersed into the name of Sha'ul? ¹⁴ I thank God that I didn't immerse any of you except Crispus and Gaius — ¹⁵ otherwise someone might say that you were indeed immersed into my name. ¹⁶ (Oh yes, I did also immerse Stephanas and his household; beyond that, I can't remember whether I immersed anyone else.) (1:10–16)

1:10. Nevertheless, brothers, I call on you in the name of our Lord Yeshua the Messiah to agree, all of you, in what you say,

and not to let yourselves remain split into factions but be restored to having a common mind and a common purpose: The appeal for unity (*achdut*). Achdut means to focus on shared common beliefs while respectfully having a good relationship with members of one's faith community who may have some beliefs that you do not share. What it means to be unified is best expressed by the Hebrew expression עם אחד בלב אחד *am echad, b'lev echad* — One People with One Heart.

1:11. Chloe and her people: Not much is known about Chloe. She was the head of her household. "Chloe's people" may mean her relatives or that they were her employees. Which faction the statement pertains to, and for what reasons it was made, are unknown and subject to interpretation.

1:12. Sha'ul: His followers were mostly Gentiles because he was the Shaliach to the Gentiles (Gal. 1:15–16).

Apollos: He was a Jew from Alexandria where the first systematic attempt to apply Greek philosophical concepts to Jewish doctrines was made by Philo Judaeus (Philo of Alexandria) in the 1st century C.E. Philo was influenced by Platonic and Stoic philosophers.[47] It is possible that the Corinthians who embraced Greek philosophy were his followers.

Apollos is described as well-versed in Scripture and was well instructed in the way of the Lord Yeshua. After receiving some theological fine-tuning from Priscilla and Aquila, he was sent to Achaia (Corinth), where he demonstrated his ability to be a powerful apologist for the Messiahship of Yeshua of Nazareth (Acts 18:24–28).

Kefa: Though he frequently ministered to non-Jews (Acts 10:1–11;18), *Kefa* (Peter) was the Shaliach to the Jewish people (Gal. 2:7–8).

---

47. www.britannica.com/topic/Judaism/Jewish-philosophy

The Messiah: Members of the community who were not affiliated with any faction and who were not predisposed to engage in any conflict. My sense is that they were content to be believers with no axe to grind.[48]

1:14. Crispus: A Jewish former official of the synagogue who had a Latin name (Acts 18:7).

Gaius: He is mentioned in Acts 19:29 and Romans 16:23. He was Sha'ul's co-worker in Ephesus. He is frequently identified with Titius Justus (Acts 18:7). There is a Gaius that is mentioned in 3 John 1:1, but it is not certain if he is the same Gaius who is mentioned in Acts 18:7; 19:29 or Romans 19:29.

> **17** For the Messiah did not send me to immerse but to proclaim the Good News — and to do it without relying on "wisdom" that consists of mere rhetoric, so as not to rob the Messiah's execution-stake of its power. **18** For the message about the execution-stake is nonsense to those in the process of being destroyed, but to us in the process of being saved it is the power of God. **19** Indeed, the *Tanakh* says,
>
> "I will destroy the wisdom of the wise
> and frustrate the intelligence of the intelligent."
>
> **20** Where does that leave the philosopher, the *Torah*-teacher, or any of today's thinkers? Hasn't God made this world's wisdom look foolish? **21** For God's wisdom ordained that the world, using its own wisdom, would not come to know him. Therefore, God decided to use the "nonsense" of what we proclaim as his means of saving those who come to trust in it. **22** Precisely because Jews ask for signs and Greeks try to find wisdom, **23** we go on proclaiming a Messiah executed on a stake as a criminal! To Jews this is an obstacle, and to Greeks it is nonsense; **24** but to those who are called, both Jews and

---

48. My comment about "simple believers" is meant to be complimentary not pejorative.

Greeks, this same Messiah is God's power and God's wisdom! **25** For God's "nonsense" is wiser than humanity's "wisdom." And God's "weakness" is stronger than humanity's "strength." **26** Just look at yourselves, brothers — look at those whom God has called! Few of you are wise by the world's standards, not many wield power or boast noble birth. **27** But God chose what the world considers nonsense in order to shame the wise; God chose what the world considers weak in order to shame the strong; **28** and God chose what the world looks down on as common or regards as nothing in order to bring to nothing what the world considers important; **29** so that no one should boast before God. **30** It is his doing that you are united with the Messiah Yeshua. He has become wisdom for us from God, and righteousness, holiness, and redemption as well! **31** Therefore — as the *Tanakh* says — "Let anyone who wants to boast, boast about *ADONAI*." (1:17–31)

1:17. Proclaim the Good News — and to do it without relying on "wisdom" that consists of mere rhetoric: The transition from addressing the issue of factionalism to an in-depth treatise or midrashic homily on God's wisdom seems awkward unless one of the major conflicts between the competing groups derives primarily from a Hellenistic[49] and/or a Greek philosophical (Duane Litfin [50] and Bruce Winter [51]) misunderstanding of true wisdom.[52]

---

49. Yongbom Lee, "Conflict over Wisdom: The Theme of 1 Corinthians 1–4 Rooted in Scripture." *Contributions to Biblical Exegesis and Theology 63*," Scholarly Publishing Collective (Duke University Press, January 1, 2012), www.scholarlypublishingcollective.org/psup/biblical-research/article/22/3/449/300287/Conflict-over-Wisdom-The-Theme-of-1-Corinthians-1.

50. Duane Litfin, *St. Paul's Theology of Proclamation: 1 Corinthians 1-4 and Greco-Roman Rhetoric* (Cambridge: Cambridge University Press, 1994).

51. Bruce William Winter, *Philo and Paul among the Sophists* (Cambridge: Cambridge University Press, 1997).

52. www.thegospelcoalition.org/themelios/review/conflict-over-wisdom-the-theme-of-1-corinthians-14-rooted-in-scripture/

According to Inkelaar, the Corinthians clung to a concept of wisdom which was at odds with Sha'ul's gospel.[53]

> At Corinth, wisdom is understood not only in terms of cosmology and theology but also in terms of sociology. The question of who has true wisdom and knowledge percolates throughout the letter. Paul extends a challenge: "Where is the one who is wise?" (1:20). In 1 Corinthians 2:6, Paul renders wisdom into something he and others can impart, and only to the "perfect" or "initiates" (*teleioi*).[54]

Ciampa and Rosner, quoting Winter, add that the terms "quarrels" and "jealousy" (1:11, 3:3) were terms for sophistic discipleship.[55]

> The language of wisdom at Corinth emerges in a context of many traditions that honored wisdom and knowledge in the ancient world, whether Jews, members of philosophical schools, or those who honored a goddess like Isis; it emerged in the context of rich philosophical debates and diverse stories about the creation of the world, including much debate over the interpretation of Plato's Timaeus. Paul and the Corinthians perhaps had different understandings of the terminology of wisdom and knowledge, of flesh, soul, and spirit…such Jewish and Christian debates about wisdom and knowledge, about flesh, soul, and spirit, happened in the context of a culture that produced images of the gods in human form, and happened in conversation with Greek philosophical texts and with the strong traditions of wisdom theology in Judaism, characterized by texts like Ben Sira and the Wisdom of Solomon, among many others.[56]

---

53. "Conflict over Wisdom: The Theme of 1 Corinthians 1–4 Rooted in Scripture," The Gospel Coalition, accessed February 8, 2023, www.thegospelcoalition.org/themelios/review/conflict-over-wisdom-the-theme-of-1-corinthians-14-rooted-in-scripture/.

54. www.academia.edu/7457182/Chapter length_commentary_on_1_Corinthians_Fortress Press_, 18.

55. Brian S. Rosner and Roy E. Ciampa, *First Letter to the Corinthians*, 69.

56. www.academia.edu/7457182/Chapter_length_commentary_on_1_Corinthians_Fortress_Press_, 16.

For Sha'ul the importance of understanding the concept of the wisdom of God was of the utmost importance. In this letter the term "wisdom" (*sophia*) appears seventeen times as opposed to appearing once in Romans and once in 2 Corinthians. The word *sophos* "wise") appears eleven times in 1 Corinthians and only four times in Romans. In this treatise on wisdom (1:10–2:16) he refers to it 11 times.

The following verses are negative portrayals of human wisdom whether their source is Judaism or Greek philosophy:

1:11"wisdom" that consists of mere rhetoric

1:19 the wisdom of the wise

1:20 the world's wisdom

1:21 the world, using its own wisdom

2:1 surpassing eloquence or wisdom

2:5 so that your trust might not rest on human wisdom

2:6 the wisdom of this world

The following verses are positive portrayals God's wisdom:

1:21 God's wisdom

1:24 Messiah is God's power and God's wisdom

1:30 He (Messiah) has become wisdom for us from God

2:7 A secret wisdom from God which has been hidden until now, but which before history began.

Judaism interpreted Deuteronomy 4:6 as equating the Torah with the wisdom of God.

"Therefore, observe them; and follow them; for then all peoples will see you as having wisdom and understanding. When they hear of all these laws, they will say, 'This great nation is surely a wise and understanding people.'"

As a result, Judaism described itself with the Hellenic term "the wisdom of its people." To those in the Greco-Roman world who admired Judaism it [Judaism] was referred to as the cult or philosophy of wisdom.[57] Eventually, the Pharisees embraced and incorporated the concept of God's Wisdom and its ramifications as well as its manifestations into their systematic theology.[58]

1:18–19. For the message about the execution-stake: Hans Conzelmann labels Sha'ul's treatise on wisdom as "The Word of the Cross as the Judgment of the Wisdom of the World."[59] Sha'ul then presents his argument in "cosmological" terms which are contrary to a contemporary Jewish and general worldview with respect to its understanding of the cross.

> Theologically Judaism viewed crucifixion in a negative light. Such an expression (crucifixion), however, has become and remains for Jews *skandalon*, "a stumbling block," i.e., "the stumbling block of the cross" (Gal. 5:11). It is such because, as Paul puts it in Galatians 3:13, Christ became a "curse" of the law, an allusion to Deuteronomy 21:23, which says that a "hanged man is accursed by God." In the Roman period of Palestine, that saying of Deuteronomy was understood to refer to crucifixion, as 4QpNah 3–4 i 4–9 and 11QTemplea 64:6–13 now make clear, when they are related to Josephus, Ant. 13.14.2 380; J.W. 1.4.5 93–98. Hence the crucified Christ could be seen as accursed, and thus a stumbling block (Fitzmeyer, *Paul and the Dead Sea Scrolls*, 607–609).[60]

---

57. Jacob Neusner, *Judaism in the Beginning of Christianity* (Philadelphia: Fortress Press, 1984), 51.
58. Particularly prominent in *Pirkei Avot, The Sayings of the Fathers*.
59. Hans Conzelmann, *et al*, 40.
60. Joseph A. Fitzmeyer, *1 Corinthians* (New York: Doubleday, 2007), 159.

For the general population, Yeshua died the death that was known in the contemporary Roman world as servile supplicium, "the slave's punishment" (Valerius Maximus, *Factorum* 7.12; cf. Hengel, *Crucifixion*, 5e1–63).[61] It was inconceivable that a divine being or Son of God could suffer and die like a criminal.[62]

The message of the cross or execution stake is not dependent on Jewish theology or Greek philosophy which, according to Sha'ul, is methodologically expressed through *en Sophia logou* "in cleverness of speaking." To the contrary, it is a manifestation of the will of God which nullifies humanity's wisdom and intelligence: a wisdom that is obscured from human comprehension.

1:19. "I will destroy the wisdom of the wise and frustrate the intelligence of the intelligent." Though the immediate verse that is quoted is Isaiah 29:14, it is a florilegium[63] whose function is to point to similar verses in Isaiah. These verses speak about the foolish wisdom of Pharoah's advisers (Isa.19:11f; 33:18). The context of Isaiah 33 is the appearance of the Messianic King (33:17), who by implication has rendered the speech of the wise, insolent, and arrogant (bold people) as garbled and incomprehensible. Abarbanel understands the king to be the Messiah, while Rashi adds that verse 17 is an eschatological reference to the divine presence which will be enjoyed by the righteous in the hereafter.[64]

1:20–21. God's wisdom is a paradox: a seemingly absurd and self-contradictory statement or proposition that when investigated or explained may prove to be well founded or true. It is counterintuitive:

---

61. Ibid., 160.

62. William Fridell Orr, *I Corinthians: A New Translation, and Introduction with a Study of the Life of Paul, Notes, and Commentary* (Garden City: Doubleday, 1976), 159.

63. Hans Conzelmann, p. 42.

64. I. W. Slotki and A. J. Rosenberg, *Isaiah: Hebrew Text & English Translation* (New York: Soncino Press, 1987), 157.

contrary to intuition or to common-sense expectation but nevertheless true. For those who depend on human wisdom, including scribes and educated philosophers (sophists), the wisdom of the cross is foolishness.

1:22–23. Jews ask for signs and Greeks try to find wisdom:

The Jews: In the LXX, the phrase "portents and signs" often occurs (Exod.7:3; Deut. 4:34; 28:46; 34:11; Ps. 135:9; Isa. 8:18) to describe the mighty acts of God on behalf of his people Israel. From this tradition came the practice of asking God for a sign (Isa. 7:11).[65]

The Scribes and the Pharisees demanded a sign to prove that Yeshua was the Messiah (Mark 8:11–13; Matt. 12:38; Luke 11:16; cf. Matt. 16:1–4; John 6:30).

> **11** The *P'rushim* came and began arguing with him; they wanted him to give them a sign from Heaven, because they were out to trap him. **12** With a sigh that came straight from his heart, he said, "Why does this generation want a sign? Yes! I tell you; no sign will be given to this generation!" **13** With that, he left them, got into the boat again and went off to the other side of the lake. (Mark 8:11–13)

In the first century C.E., the miraculous sign that the Jewish people were looking for was the reestablishment of the Kingdom of Israel — physical liberation from the yoke of Roman occupation, not a crucified Messiah.[66]

This was Yeshua's disciples' expectation: [6] When they were together, they asked him, "Lord, are you at this time going to restore self-rule to Isra'el?" (Acts 1:6) Rabbi Akiva also maintained this hope, and that is why, due to Bar Kochba's success against the

---

65. Fitzmeyer, *1 Corinthians*, 159-160.

66. Hilary Le Cornu and Joseph Shulam, *A Commentary on the Jewish Roots of Acts, Vol. 1* (Jerusalem: Netivyah Bible Instruction Ministry, 2003), 12-13.

Roman army, Akiva declared him to be Melech Ha Mashiach (132 – 136 C.E.),[67] King Messiah.

The following is the general Jewish conception of how to identify the Messiah:

> The mashiach will be a great political leader descended from King David (Jeremiah 23:5). The mashiach is often referred to as "Mashiach ben David" (Messiah, son of David). He will be well-versed in Jewish law, and observant of its commandments (Isaiah 11:2-5). He will be a charismatic leader, inspiring others to follow his example. He will be a great military leader, who will win battles for Israel. He will be a great judge, who makes righteous decisions (Jeremiah 33:15). But above all, he will be a human being, not a god, demi-god or other supernatural being.
>
> The mashiach will bring about the political and spiritual redemption of the Jewish people by bringing us back to Israel and restoring Jerusalem (Isaiah 11:11–12; Jeremiah 23:8; 30:3; Hosea 3:2–5). He Israel will establish a government in Israel that will be the center of all world government, both for Jews and gentiles (Isaiah 2:2–4; 11:10; 42:1)11:10; 42:1). He will rebuild the Temple and re-establish its worship (Jeremiah 33:18). He will restore the religious court system of Israel and establish Jewish law as the law of the land (Jeremiah 33:15)[68]

---

67. Perhaps the most famous reference to Bar Kochba in the rabbinic literature is one in which the venerated Rabbi Akiva says to his colleagues of Ben-Cosiba, *hu malcha mashicha*, "he is the king messiah," and references the biblical phrase "a star will come forth from Jacob." Another rabbi then drily replies, "Grass will be growing from your cheeks and the son of David will still not have come" (Midrash Rabba Eicha 2:2.4).

This appears to strongly indicate that, while it was by no means a consensus opinion, there was a strong and widespread belief that Bar Kochba was the promised messiah. In all likelihood, then, the revolt was not only a political or military event but also a strongly religious one, powered by the intense passions of messianic belief in the coming redemption of Israel.

Called the "Cave of Letters," it contained a cache of documents that included several letters from Bar Kochba himself, which shed unprecedented light on his personality and style of rule. In one of the unearthed letters, Bar Kochba is described as *nasi Yisrael*, "prince of Israel," indicating that the leader had or claimed to have restored the Jewish kingship, which was considered an essential accomplishment for any messianic claimant.

68. www.worldhistory.org/The_Bar-Kochba_Revolt/

The Greeks: According to Herodotus, "All Greeks are busily engaged in the pursuit of all wisdom."[69] The "Greeks" were seeking to produce logical philosophical arguments that could intellectually satisfy and support the message of the cross. Their attempt was an impossible task because they were leaning on their own understanding and not taking into consideration the wisdom that is received through the Spirit and revelation (2:6–7).

1:26–30. Just look at yourselves: A different approach to the interpretation of this section is to understand it as an allusion to God's act of creation which was *Creatio ex nihilo* (Latin for "creation out of nothing"). In other words, the crucifixion of Yeshua is God's incarnate power and wisdom. The Creator took the material of the Corinthians' "nothingness" which was society's perception of their persona, and, through his mighty power, He formed each one of them into a "New Creation."

> **17** Therefore, if anyone is united with the Messiah, he is a new creation — the old has passed; look, what has come is fresh and new! **18** And it is all from God, who through the Messiah has reconciled us to himself. (2 Cor. 5:17)

As a new creation, Yeshua has become their source of life imparting to them righteousness, sanctification, and redemption (1:30).

1:31. "Let anyone who wants to boast, boast about *ADONAI*."

To clarify the meaning of verse 31, one needs to know the context of Jeremiah 9:23.

> **22 (23)** Here is what *ADONAI* says:
>
> "The wise man should not boast of his wisdom,
> the powerful should not boast of his power,
> the wealthy should not boast of his wealth;

---

69. www.jewfaq.org/mashiach

23 (24) instead, let the boaster boast about this:
that he understands and knows me —
that I am *ADONAI*, practicing grace,
justice and righteousness in the land;
for in these things I take pleasure," says *ADONAI*.

God has said "no" to all human wisdom, power, wealth, and worldly status to salvation. [70] His recreative, redemptive power is a manifestation of His divine wisdom and grace which cannot be duplicated or concocted through human wisdom. Therefore, if one does boast, one should boast about one's personal understanding and experience of God's inimitable grace, justice, and righteousness.

Maimonides wrote, "Having acquired this knowledge (Jer. 9:2): he will then be determined to always seek loving-kindness, judgment and righteousness and thus to imitate the ways of God."[71]

Thus, the gospel faith simply repeats in a new guise the word spoken at creation (1 Cor. 1:28; cf. Rom. 4:17; 2 Cor. 4:6).[72]

---

70. Günther Bornkamm, *Paul, Paulus* (Minneapolis: Fortress Press, 1995), 161.

71. Harry Freedman and A. J. Rosenberg, *Jeremiah: Hebrew Text & English Translation* London: Soncino Press, 1985, 73.

72. *Paul, Paulus*, 161.

1 CORINTHIANS 2

INTRODUCTORY COMMENTS

Sha'ul's argument in chapter 2 is the fact that God's wisdom can only be grasped through the revelatory power of the Spirit. It is not gauged by or subject to human criteria but confounds all human criteria.[73] Sha'ul says that from a human perspective his message of the cross seems weak and ineffectual but, his message is a demonstration of the Spirit and power.

> **2:1** As for me, brothers, when I arrived among you, it was not with surpassing eloquence or wisdom that I came announcing to you the previously concealed truth about God; **2** for I had decided that while I was with you, I would forget everything except Yeshua the Messiah, and even him only as someone who had been executed on a stake as a criminal. **3** Also I myself was with you as somebody weak, nervous, and shaking all over from fear; **4** and neither the delivery nor the content of my message relied on compelling words of "wisdom" but on a demonstration of the power of the Spirit, **5** so that your trust might not rest on human wisdom but on God's power. (2:1–5)

2:1–5. As for me: Sha'ul is saying that he did not come to Corinth to boast about his persona, accomplishments, or education (all human wisdom, power, wealth, and worldly status).

2:5. Your trust: Instead, he came to boast about the redemptive power of the crucifixion of Yeshua which is the wisdom of God, and

---

73. *1 Corinthians: A Commentary on The First Epistle to the Corinthians,* 55.

his hope is that by his example the Corinthians would learn to do the same thing.

> **6** Yet there is a wisdom that we are speaking to those who are mature enough for it. But it is not the wisdom of this world or of this world's leaders, who are in the process of passing away. **7** On the contrary, we are communicating a secret wisdom from God which has been hidden until now but which, before history began, God had decreed would bring us glory. **8** Not one of this world's leaders has understood it; because if they had, they would not have executed the Lord from whom this glory flows. **9** But, as the *Tanakh* says,
>
> "No eye has seen; no ear has heard
> and no one's heart has imagined
> all the things that God has prepared
> for those who love him." (2:6–9)

2:6. To those who are mature: Sha'ul's message is for the mature. In verse 6 the word "mature" is to be understood as a dig at the Corinthians who considered themselves to be mature. The word "mature" was the haughty way the Corinthian 'spirituals' described themselves. "It corresponds to a mode of thought and speech both current in Gnosticism and common in the early church, and on their lips meant those who, by virtual of their exceptional possession of the Spirit, had gone beyond the state of mere faith and attained to deeper knowledge of divine revelation."[74]

2:7. Secret wisdom: God's wisdom is a mystery that has been deliberately concealed from the rulers of this age and predestined to be revealed on the cross. The term "mystery" denotes knowledge of God's wisdom, a comprehensive, deterministic divine scheme which guides the unfolding of history and creation, presented to the Corinthians as a revealed truth. For the Corinthians, understanding

---

74. *Paul, Paulus*, 162.

this mystery requires Sha'ul's teaching and guidance, which he provides through his letters and visits (cf.3:1–2; 4:20). There is a pedagogical dimension to Sha'ul's heavenly mysteries.

2:8. Not one…. has understood it: God's Wisdom has overturned the world system which consists of an overdependence on human wisdom and understanding. This overdependence led to the mistaken action of "crucifying the Lord of glory," which was paradoxically a part of God's plan.

2:9. No eye has seen…: Sha'ul reinforces his contention by quoting Isaiah 64:4 and further expounds upon the subject by reinforcing the idea that the physical body's senses, organs, and mind do not have the capacity to comprehend what God has in store for those who love Him. The Greek word often translated "mind" is *kardia* which means "heart." Kardia is also associated with the place of man's emotions as well as his intellectual capacity (Matt. 13:15; Mark 2:8). God's wisdom can only be apprehended by opening one's heart to the revelation of the Spirit.

> **10** It is to us, however, that God has revealed these things. How? Through the Spirit. For the Spirit probes all things, even the profoundest depths of God. **11** For who knows the inner workings of a person except the person's own spirit inside him? So too no one knows the inner workings of God except God's Spirit. **12** Now we have not received the spirit of the world but the Spirit of God, so that we might understand the things God has so freely given us. **13** These are the things we are talking about when we avoid the manner of speaking that human wisdom would dictate and instead use a manner of speaking taught by the Spirit, by which we explain things of the Spirit to people who have the Spirit. **14** Now the natural man does not receive the things from the Spirit of God — to him they are nonsense! Moreover, he is unable to grasp them because they are evaluated through the Spirit. **15** But the person

who has the Spirit can evaluate everything, while no one is in a position to evaluate him.

For who has known the mind of *ADONAI*?
Who will counsel him?

But we have the mind of the Messiah! (2:10-16)

2:10. God has revealed these things: Sha'ul then explains the role of the Ruach in transmitting (revealing) God's thoughts which enables one to understand the mind of God which he equates with having the mind of the Mashiach.

2:16. But we have the mind of the Messiah: Paul's use of LXX Isaiah 40:13 "is not only Christological, but also eschatological and apocalyptical in character. In the cross of Christ, 'the salvific plan of God,' hidden in the past is revealed in the present. The 'once hidden-now revealed' contrast is, once again, implicitly present (v. 16). For Paul, the eschatological age of revelation (v. 16) is identical to the messianic age of fulfilment (v. 16)."[75]

---

75. Jurnal Teologic, "Jurnal Teologic 18.2 (2019)," Jurnal Teologic Baptist Theological Institute of Bucharest | School of Baptist Theology, University of Bucharest, March 29, 2021, www.jurnalteologic.ro/jurnal-teologic-18-2-2019/, 140 .

1 CORINTHIANS 3

INTRODUCTORY COMMENTS

Sha'ul continues the process of unraveling and dismantling factionalism by uncovering the Corinthian's true spiritual condition. They are immature believers who do have the mind of the Mashiach, who do not live by the Spirit (*pneumatikoi*) but continue to conduct their lives according to the precepts of worldly (*sarkikos*) wisdom. By employing the word sarkikos, Sha'ul is implying that the members of the factions are being controlled or governed by their sub-human animal nature instead of by the Spirit of God as evidence by their displays of jealousy and quarreling. Sha'ul then deliberately insults the members of the factions by calling them infants.

> **3** As for me, brothers, I couldn't talk to you as spiritual people but as worldly people, as babies, so far as experience with the Messiah is concerned. **2** I gave you milk, not solid food, because you were not yet ready for it. But you aren't ready for it now either! **3** For you are still worldly! Isn't it obvious from all the jealousy and quarrelling among you that you are worldly and living merely by human standards? **4** For when one says, "I follow Sha'ul" and another, "I follow Apollos," aren't you being merely human? **5** After all, what is Apollos? What is Sha'ul? Only servants through whom you came to trust. Indeed, it was the Lord who brought you to trust through one of us or through another. (3:1–5)

3:1. As babies: Paul extensively uses the imagery of "children" in a positive sense to reflect his own apostolic relationship with his converts. In such cases the word is always *teknon* (child); however, the word used here *nēpios*, ("baby" or "mere infant") almost always has a pejorative sense, in contrast with being adult, and refers to thinking or behavior that is not fitting for a grown up. That is certainly his concern here. It is not so much that they have not made progress—that is part of the problem, they think they have—but that they are "adults" acting otherwise when it comes to the life of the Spirit, hence "mere infants."[76]

3:2. I give you milk: According to David E. Garland, "The contrast between milk (*gala*) and solid food (*brōma*) seems to be a transparent metaphor for rudimentary and advanced teaching (cf. Heb. 5:12–14). The metaphor is found in a variety of ancient sources relating to stages of education and development (cf. Philo, Husb. 2 §§8–9; Dreams 2 §§10–11; Sobr. 2–3 §§9–10; Migr. Abr. 6 §29; Conzelmann 1975: 72 n. 26; Gaventa 1996: 104–5)"[77]

3:3. Still worldly: Mature believers do not align themselves with competing factions but are committed to, as well, being united by a Spirit-engendered common vision.

> [6] I planted the seed, and Apollos watered it, but it was God who made it grow. [7] So neither the planter nor the waterer is anything, only God who makes things grow — [8] planter and waterer are the same. However, each will be rewarded according to his work. [9] For we are God's co-workers; you are God's field, God's building. [10] Using the grace God gave me, I laid a foundation, like a skilled master-builder; and another man is building on it. But let each one be careful how he builds. [11] For no one can lay any foundation other than the one already laid, which is Yeshua the Messiah. [12] Some will use

---

76. Ned Bernard Stonehouse, F. F. Bruce, and Gordon D. Fee, *The New International Commentary on the New Testament* (Grand Rapids: Eerdmans, 1951) 133-134.

77. David E. Garland, *1 Corinthians* (Grand Rapids: Baker Academic, 2008).

gold, silver, or precious stones in building on this foundation; while others will use wood, grass, or straw. **13** But each one's work will be shown for what it is; the Day will disclose it, because it will be revealed by fire — the fire will test the quality of each one's work. **14** If the work someone has built on the foundation survives, he will receive a reward; **15** if it is burned up, he will have to bear the loss: he will still escape with his life, but it will be like escaping through a fire.

16 Don't you know that you people are God's temple and that God's Spirit lives in you? **17** So if anyone destroys God's temple, God will destroy him. For God's temple is holy, and you yourselves are that temple. (3:6–17)

Sha'ul is attempting to promote unity among the factions by utilizing the related metaphors of planting a garden and building God's Temple.

> Today I have placed you over nations and kingdoms
> to uproot and to tear down,
> to destroy and to demolish,
> to build and to plant. (Jeremiah 1:10. cp. Jer. 18:9; 24:6, cf.
> Sir. 49:7; Philo, Alleg. Interp. 1.15 §48; Odes Sol. 38:16–22.[78])

Significantly, later Judaism also spoke of Solomon's Temple as a "field" (Targum Pseudo-Jonathan 27:27; Pesiqta Rabbati Piska 39).

Sha'ul depicts himself and Apollos as God's servants whose role is like of a household servant (*diakonoi*) whose master has assigned them the joint task of directing the servants of the master to plant a garden or to construct a building. These roles were often taken by high-status slaves or freepersons who had risen in the ranks of a household, promoted by their masters for more authoritative roles (Martin 1990).[79]

---

78. David E. Garland, *1 Corinthians* (Grand Rapids: Baker Academic, 2008), (Kindle Locations 2992-2993).

79. https://academia.edu/7457182/Chapter_length_commentary_on_1_Corinthians_ Fortress_Press, 19.

Sha'ul emphasizes that no group of people can successfully complete the task of planting a garden or building a building unless they cooperate with one another. God has called the Corinthians to be coworkers, not competitors.

3:6–8. I planted: In the metaphor of a garden, Sha'ul planted the seed, Apollos watered the seed, but God enabled the seed to grow. The Corinthians are collectively God's garden and his building.

3:9: God's building: In a similar fashion, by relying upon the grace (unmerited favor) of God, Sha'ul laid the essential foundation of Yeshua HaMashiach at Corinth (v. 11) with, by implication, the assistance of Apollos and Kefa.

Lanci finds the metaphor of a building in Tacitus, Historiae 4.53; Plutarch, Pericles 12; and Josephus, Ant. 8.2.9–3.9 §§58–98. M. Mitchell (1993: 99–105) also shows that the image of a building was a common metaphor in the ancient world for political stability and concord.[80]

It is evident that the metaphor of a building is analogous to the construction of Solomon's Temple. Some of the materials mentioned in verse 12 (gold, silver, precious stones, and wood) are mentioned for the building of Solomon's Temple (1 Chron. 22:14, 16; 29:2; 2 Chron. 3:6; Hag. 2:8).

3:13–15. It will be revealed by fire: On the Day of Judgment, the quality of the material and the skill of each builder will be evaluated by the refiner's fire.

> But who can endure the day when he comes?
> Who can stand when he appears?
> For he will be like a refiner's fire,
> like the soap maker's lye. (Malachi 3:2)

---

80. *1 Corinthians* (Kindle Locations 3041-3042).

A similar idea of judgment by fire appears in chapter 13 of "The Testament of Abraham" which describes Puruel, the angel who has power over fire, as testing the deeds of men by making them pass through the fires of judgment. Whether Paul knew the "Testament of Abraham," or another form of the tradition cannot be determined with certainty.[81]

3:16. You are God's Temple: God has designed the Corinthian community to be His collective, unified, eschatological temple. Each Corinthian was intended to be one of the integral components of His building.

> **18** Let no one fool himself. If someone among you thinks he is wise (by this world's standards), let him become "foolish," so that he may become really wise. **19** For the wisdom of this world is nonsense, as far as God is concerned; inasmuch as the *Tanakh* says, "He traps the wise in their own cleverness,"[a] **20** and again, "*ADONAI* knows that the thoughts of the wise are worthless."[b] **21** So let no one boast about human beings, for all things are yours — **22** whether Sha'ul or Apollos or Kefa or the world or life or death or the present or the future: they all belong to you, **23** and you belong to the Messiah, and the Messiah belongs to God. (3:18–22)

3:19. For the wisdom of this world is nonsense, as far as God is concerned: Sha'ul begins to summarize the principal points of his midrashic homily. The Corinthian factions need to jettison their concept of wisdom which was created by the present world system: a wisdom that the Lord considers to be foolish and futile. He follows the pattern of underscoring his point by appealing to Scripture (Job 5:13; Psalm 94:11).

---

81. Michael E. Stone, *Jewish Writings of the Second Temple Period: Apocrypha, Pseudepigrapha, Qumran, Sectarian Writings, Philo, Josephus, Vol. 2* (Assen, Netherlands: Van Gorcum, 1984), 63.

He continues his summation by referring to the initial Scripture that he cited at the beginning of his treatise (midrash) regarding wisdom (Isa. 29:14).

3:21. So let no one boast about human beings: The root cause of the boasting was aligning oneself with a particular "teacher" who was idolized for his superior knowledge of worldly wisdom. Self-identification with a leader by osmosis lends itself to pride and a sense of self-importance that results in boasting about who one follows and one's own wisdom.

3:22. You belong to Messiah: God's Spirit-revealed wisdom which is the redemptive act of a crucified Mashiach is the ultimate reality. To paraphrase Gordon Fee: "The person who has obtained all things without possessing this reality has nothing."[82]

In the Mashiach we do not belong to any leader or faction - we only belong to the One who has redeemed us. One's life is to be humbly devoted to serve the Messiah Yeshua in the establishment of his eschatological temple. Everyone, including the apostles, is a fellow servant and on an equal footing. Whatever one accomplishes is for him, so there is no reason to boast about one's accomplishments for the King of God. We are one in him.

Sha'ul's summation of his midrashic homily continues through 4:17.

---

82. Gordon D. Fee, *The First Epistle to the Corinthians* (Grand Rapids: William B. Eerdmans Publishing Company, 2014), 155.

1 CORINTHIANS 4

INTRODUCTORY COMMENTS

In this chapter, Sha'ul, presents himself as God's servant as well as a loving father, who must sternly address his children's ill-mannered behavior with the hope that they might repent from their arrogance (v. 18).[83]

> **1** So, you should regard us as the Messiah's servants, as trustees of God's secret truths. **2** Now the one thing that is asked of a trustee is that he be found trustworthy. (4:1–2)

4:1. Servants: Sha'ul further emphasizes the fact that even though he and Apollos are shlichim they are under-rowers or galley slaves (*hypēretēs*), those who are on the bottom deck and are subservient to their Master.

Trustees: A manager (*oikonomos*): A term that goes back to the practice of assigning to one servant the responsibility for distributing supplies, tools, and food to the workers on ancient Greek estates.[84] The choice of word *oikonomos* is an allusion to the Mashal of the Faithful Manager (Luke 12:42–44).

> **42** The Lord replied, "Who is the faithful and sensible manager whose master puts him in charge of the household staff to give them their share of food at the proper time? **43** It will go well with that servant if he is found doing his job when his master comes. **44** Yes, I tell you he will put him in charge of all he owns."

---

83. Verse 18 includes my comments on arrogance.
84. William Fridell Orr, 176.

It is evident that Sha'ul frequently alludes to the sayings of Yeshua. In his classic book *Paul and Rabbinic Judaism,* W. D. Davies states:

> We gather that in addition to any traditional material that Sha'ul used he also had the words of Yeshua to which he turned for guidance. In 1 Corinthians (along with Romans), as the lists drawn up by Resch show, Sha'ul makes most use of the words of Yeshua that reflect His ethical exhortations. Moreover, at the most personal point of all his Epistles we cannot help tracing the impact of the teaching of Yeshua.[85]

Secret truths: See comments on 2:7

> **3** And it matters very little to me how I am evaluated by you or by any human court; in fact, I don't even evaluate myself. **4** I am not aware of anything against me, but this does not make me innocent. The one who is evaluating me is the Lord. **5** So don't pronounce judgment prematurely, before the Lord comes; for he will bring to light what is now hidden in darkness; he will expose the motives of people's hearts; and then each will receive from God whatever praise he deserves. (4:3–5)

4:5. Judgment: The Lord is the Righteous Judge. An additional allusion to the words of Yeshua found in The Mashal of the Sheep and the Goats (Matt. 25:31–46). The day of Judgment is reserved for the time of the *Eschaton,* and judgment cannot be accurately assessed in the present time because it is an eschatological matter.[86]

> **6** Now in what I have said here, brothers, I have used myself and Apollos as examples to teach you not to go beyond what the *Tanakh* says, proudly taking the side of one leader against another. **7** After all, what makes you so special? What do you have that you didn't receive as a gift? And if in fact it was a gift, why do you boast as if it weren't? (4:6–7)

---

85. William D. Davies, *Paul and Rabbinic Judaism: Some Rabbinic Elements in Pauline Theology,* 141.
86. William Fridell Orr, 180.

4:6. Use myself and Apollos as examples: As paradigms of the wisdom of the cross, follow our example as hardworking, faithful servants who are planters and builders.

Not to go beyond what the *Tanakh* says: Perhaps invoked to remind the Corinthians that Paul and Apollos derive their teaching from scripture, unlike "false" apostles (2 Cor 11:13) who teach secret knowledge beyond the text (see 1 En. 104:10–11).[87]

Proudly taking: Acting puffed up, or "inflated" (4:18–19; 5:2; 8:1; 13:4), displaying an arrogance based on knowledge (see Rom. 15:4, Philo, Leg. Gai. 86; 4QCatenaa frag. 5; Sib. Or. 3.738–39).[88]

4:7. Receive as a gift: Whatever one possesses, whether material abundance or spiritual riches is a gift from the Almighty.

> Raise not to the heights your pride, you who speak with insolence and insult. For neither from sunrise nor from sunset nor from the wilderness comes glorification. For God is the Judge, He lowers one and raises another. (Ps. 75:6–8, *Artscroll*)[89]

Ibn Ezra comments, "He alone has the final word as to who will prosper and who will fail. Therefore, let no man raise his pride to the heights for he deserves no credit for his wisdom strength or riches."[90]

> **8** You are glutted already? You are rich already? You have become kings, even though we are not? Well, I wish you really were kings, so that we might share the kingship with you! **9** For I think God has been placing us emissaries on display at the tail of the parade, like men condemned to die in the public arena: we have become a spectacle before the whole universe, angels as well as men. **10** For the Messiah's sake we are fools, but united

---

87. Amy-Jill Levine and Marc Zvi Brettler, 293.

88. Ibid, 192.

89. Avrohom Chaim Feuer and Nosson Scherman, in *Tehillim: Sefer Tehilim: A New Translation with a Commentary Anthologized from Talmudic, Midrashic and Rabbinic Sources*, vol. 2 (Brooklyn, NY: Mesorah Publications, 1985), 75.

90. Ibid., 75.

with the Messiah you are wise! We are weak, but you are strong; you are honored, but we are dishonored. **11** Till this very moment we go hungry and thirsty, we are dressed in rags, we are treated roughly, we wander from place to place, **12** we exhaust ourselves working with our own hands for our living. When we are cursed, we keep on blessing; when we are persecuted, we go on putting up with it; **13** when we are slandered, we continue making our appeal. We are the world's garbage, the scum of the earth — yes, to this moment! (4:8–13).

With a succession of ironic rebukes (saying one thing and meaning another), Sha'ul utilizes hyperbole, exaggerated statements or claims not meant to be taken literally. Sha'ul continues to chide the Corinthians for their boasting by puncturing their inflated view of themselves.[91] Notice the role reversal. The Corinthians are wealthy kings (v. 8) while the *shlichim* (apostles) are far from reigning: they are public spectacles worthy of death (v. 9), garbage, the scum of the earth (v. 13).

4:8 You are rich: The Corinthians are a perfect example of how abundance, not just material abundance but even abundance of spiritual gifts, leads to loss of restraint and perspective (cf. Philo, Abr.134f.).[92]

4:12. When we are cursed, we keep on blessing: An allusion to Luke 6:27–28.

> **27** Nevertheless, to you who are listening, what I say is this: "Love your enemies! Do good to those who hate you, **28** bless those who curse you, pray for those who mistreat you."

> **14** I am not writing you this to make you feel ashamed, but, as my dear children, to confront you and get you to change. **15** For even if you have ten thousand trainers in connection with the Messiah, you do not have many fathers; for in connection with the Messiah Yeshua it was I who became your

---

91. Brian S. Rosner and Roy E. Ciampa, *First Letter to the Corinthians*, 174-182.

92. Ben Witherington, *Conflict and Community in Corinth: A Socio-Rhetorical Commentary on 1 and 2 Corinthians* (Grand Rapids: W.B. Eerdmans, 1995), 194.

father by means of the Good News. [16] Therefore I urge you to imitate me. [17] This is why I have sent you Timothy, my beloved and trustworthy child in the Lord. He will remind you of the way of life I follow in union with the Messiah Yeshua and teach everywhere in every congregation. (4:14-17)

Sha'ul compares his relationship with the Corinthians as a father and his children. He became their father by means of the Good News (v. 16).

4:15. Ten thousand trainers: There are a multitude of people who are qualified to be a pedagogue or a trainer-mentor in the Mashiach, but the pedagogue could never be their father. God has appointed Sha'ul to be their only father in the faith. The father gives his children life, whereas the pedagogue was only their instructor for a limited period.[93]

4:15. Fathers: In Judaism, teachers are frequently portrayed as father figures (B. Sanhedrin 19b); thus, when Sha'ul addresses the Corinthians as his "dear children" he is, by common practice, identifying them as his talmidim. Neudecker, in his article "Master-Disciple/Disciple-Master Relationship in Rabbinic Judaism and in the Gospels," states: "The rabbinic interpretation of biblical "father" and "son" as "master" and "disciple" is common,[94] and, according to Boyarin, "becoming a 'disciple of the sages' often meant accepting a rabbinic father in place of one's biological father."[95] The Book of Knowledge *Talmud Torah* (Sefer Mada), also known as The Laws of Torah Study, exemplifies the idea that becoming a "disciple of the sages" often meant not only accepting a rabbinic father in place of one's biological father but that the role of a rabbi could even supersede that of a father.

---

93 . David John Williams, *Paul's Metaphors: Their Context and Character* (Peabody, MA: Hendrickson Publishers, 2007), 62.

94. Reinhard Neudecker, *Master-Disciple/Disciple-Master Relationship in Rabbinic Judaism and in the Gospels*, Gregorianum, Vol. 80, No. 2 (1999), (GBPress- Gregorian Biblical), 245-261.

95. Daniel Boyarin, *The Talmud - a Personal Take: Selected Essays*. Tübingen: Mohr Siebeck, 2017. See the story of Rabbi Eliezer ben Hyrcanus in *Goldin, The Fathers According to Rabbi Nathan, 43* (chap. 6), and parallels.

> There is no greater honor than that due to a teacher, and no greater awe than that due to a teacher. Our sages declared: "Your fear of your teacher should be equivalent to your fear of Heaven."[96]

Samuel Lachs connects these statements in Talmud Torah 5:1 with Luke 14:26, which, in a similar fashion, declares that a *talmid's* rabbi is to be more highly esteemed than one's father.[97] "If anyone comes to me and does not hate his father, his mother, his wife, his children, his brothers and his sisters, yes, and his own life besides, he cannot be my *talmid.*"

4:17. Timothy....my trustworthy child: Sha'ul sends to Corinth Timothy who is his true (1Tim. 1:2) and dear (2 Tim. 1:2) son in their common faith. Timothy is an example of what it signifies to be a child who models his father's (Sha'ul) godly way of life. Timothy has become a responsible adult so Sha'ul is hopeful that once the Corinthians become acquainted with Timothy, that they will be inspired without reservation to accept him (Sha'ul) as their spiritual father.

> **18** When I didn't come to visit you, some of you became arrogant. **19** But I am coming to you soon if the Lord wills; and I will take cognizance not of the talk of these arrogant people but of their power. **20** For the Kingdom of God is not a matter of words but of power. **21** Which do you prefer — should I come to you with a stick? or with love in a spirit of gentleness? (4:18–21)

As we shall see in chapter 5, arrogance leads to pride and boasting which lead to sexual immorality and idolatry. Sha'ul is planning to rectify this problem by visiting in a loving manner, but if their arrogance continues, he will need to correct them with a rod of discipline.

---

96. *Sefer Mada.*

97. Samuel Tobias Lachs, *A Rabbinic Commentary on the New Testament: The Gospels of Matthew, Mark, and Luke* (Hoboken, NJ: KTAV Publ. House, 1987), 187.

1 Corinthians 5

Introductory Comments

Sexual impurity (*porneia*) is a subject that is frequently expounded upon in the Tanakh. In Ezekiel 6:9; 16:15–34; 23:1–49 it is associated with idolatry. Scripture often uses sexual lust or promiscuity (*zanah*) as a metaphor for idol worship. Radak agrees while Maimonides, in Igeres HaShmad 2, interprets the Hebrew word *zanah* to mean "loose morals."[98]

Since the Jewish people are God's spouse, idolatry is a form of spiritual adultery.

> *ADONAI* said to Moshe, "You are about to sleep with your ancestors. But this people will get up and offer themselves as prostitutes to the foreign gods of the land where they are going. When they are with those gods, they will abandon me and break my covenant which I have made with them. (Deut. 31:16)

Jacob Neusner highlights the place of idolatry and sexual relations in the biblical texts that deal with the question of impurity [99] while Christine Hayes points to several Pauline passages that "suggest that the impurity of unbelievers, arising from deeds of sexual immorality and idolatry in particular, defiles the holiness of believers."[100]

---

98. Moshe Eisemann, *Yechezkel the Book of Ezekiel: Sefer Yeḥezḳel: A New Translation with a Commentary Anthologized from Talmudic, Midrashic, and Rabbinic Sources* (Brooklyn, NY: Mesorah Publications, 1980), 388-389.

99. Jacob Neusner, *The Idea of Purity in Ancient Judaism: The Haskell Lectures, 1972-1973* (Eugene, OR: Wipf and Stock, 2006) 13-15.

100. Christine E. Hayes, *Gentile Impurities and Jewish Identities, Intermarriage and Conversion from the Bible to the Talmud* (New York: Oxford University Press, 2002), 93.

In Romans 1:22–25 Sha'ul connects worldly wisdom with idol worship and sexual immorality.

> **22** Claiming to be wise, they have become fools! **23** In fact, they have exchanged the glory of the immortal God for mere images, like a mortal human being, or like birds, animals, or reptiles! **24** This is why God has given them up to the vileness of their hearts' lusts, to the shameful misuse of each other's bodies. **25** They have exchanged the truth of God for falsehood, by worshipping and serving created things, rather than the Creator — praised be he forever. *Amen.*

> **1** It is actually being reported that there is sexual sin among you, and it is sexual sin of a kind that is condemned even by pagans — a man is living with his stepmother! **2** And you stay proud? Shouldn't you rather have felt some sadness that would have led you to remove from your company the man who has done this thing? (5:1–2)

5:1. A man is living with his stepmother: There was a tension between commonly accepted social practices relating to incest and the Torah. The dynamics of incestuous relationships for those who were patrons or socially prominent in Corinthian society are thoroughly detailed in John K. Chow's article "The Rich Man."[101] They were allowed certain liberties when it came to sexual sin. However, incest is explicitly forbidden in the Torah (Lev. 18:8).

Sha'ul's comment regarding incest as a sin not tolerated by the pagans is also a reference to Roman law which prohibited incest[102] or to the Sibylline Oracles.

> You do not fear the existing God who guards all things. . ..
> Alas for a race which rejoices in blood, a crafty and evil race
> of impious and false double-tongued men and immoral
> adulterous idol worshipers who plot deceit.

---

101. Edward Adams and David G. Horrell, *Christianity at Corinth: The Quest for the Pauline Church*, 198.
102. William Fridell Orr, 194.

> They will have no fidelity at all. Many widowed women will love other men (stepson) secretly for gain. and those who have husbands will not keep hold of the rope of life.
> (Sibylline Oracles 3.33–45, trans. J. J. Collins in OTP 1:362–63)[103]

The root cause of incest is arrogant pride which would lead to a premature death.[104]

5:2. Proud: Since the illicit marriage is something of a cause célèbre and its resolution is not to send the woman packing, it is likely that one or both parties are high-status individuals.[105]

> **3** For I myself, even though I am absent physically, am with you spiritually; and I have already judged the man who has done this as if I were present. **4** In the name of the Lord Yeshua, when you are assembled, with me present spiritually and the power of our Lord Yeshua among us, **5** hand over such a person to the Adversary for his old nature to be destroyed, so that his spirit may be saved in the Day of the Lord. (5:3–5)

5:3. I have already judged the man: As God's designated authority, Sha'ul has passed judgment on the sinful individual which he would formally administer at a trial in Corinth.

5:5. Hand over such a person to the Adversary: Many expositors, including Lightfoot, conclude based on Sha'ul's question as to why the Corinthians did not "remove from your company the man who has done this thing?" (v. 2), that handing a person over to the Adversary refers to excommunication. [106] In some cases, an excommunicated person such as Miriam was still considered to be a member of the community of faith (Num. 12).

---

103. Pheme Perkins, 87.
104. William Fridell Orr, 188-189.
105. Pheme Perkins, *1 Corinthians (Paideia: Commentaries on the New Testament)*, 86.
106. John Lightfoot, *Acts - 1 Corinthians* (Peabody: Hendrickson Publishers, 1997), 193.

Satan is God's prosecuting attorney (Job 1:6). According to Rashi, the role of Satan was to present in the heavenly courtroom the merit and guilt of all of God's creatures. Rabbi Dr. Victor E. Reichert adds that Satan is the "Opposer." His part is to oppose men in their pretensions to a right standing with God and to test their sincerity (Job 1–2; cp.3:1)[107]

A parallel verse is 1 Timothy 1:19^b–20:

> By rejecting conscience, some have made shipwreck of their trust; **20** among them are Hymenaeus and Alexander. I have turned them over to the Adversary, so that they will learn not to insult God.

Final judgment would be carried out on the Day of the Lord (Dan. 7:9–14; Rev. 20:11–15).

> **6** Your boasting is not good. Don't you know the saying, "It takes only a little *hametz* to leaven a whole batch of dough?" **7** Get rid of the old *hametz*, so that you can be a new batch of dough, because in reality you are unleavened. For our *Pesach* lamb, the Messiah, has been sacrificed. **8** So let us celebrate the *Seder* not with leftover *hametz*, the *hametz* of wickedness and evil, but with the *matzah* of purity and truth. (5:6–8)

5:6. Your boasting is not good...It takes only a little *hametz*: Sha'ul compares the process of removing *hametz* or leaven during Pesach with excommunicating an immoral individual. Like hametz, they are boastful people, they are full of arrogant pride which will spread to the members of the faith community, so remove them (cp. Exod. 12:15–20).

---

107. Victor E. Reichert, et. al., *Job: Hebrew Text & English Translation with an Introduction and Commentary* (Soncino Press, 1976), 2-3.

9 In my earlier letter I wrote you not to associate with people who engage in sexual immorality. **10** I didn't mean the sexually immoral people outside your community, or the greedy, or the thieves or the idol-worshippers — for then you would have to leave the world altogether! **11** No, what I wrote you was not to associate with anyone who is supposedly a brother but who also engages in sexual immorality, is greedy, worships idols, is abusive, gets drunk or steals. With such a person you shouldn't even eat! **12** For what business is it of mine to judge outsiders? Isn't it those who are part of the community that you should be judging? **13** God will judge those who are outside. Just expel the evildoer from among yourselves. (5:9–13)

5:9–11. Not to associate with people who engage in sexual immorality: Vice lists were common rhetorical devices that were employed to vehemently emphasize a point.[108] Conzelman refers to these lists as catalogues of virtues and vices that are attested to within the framework of philosophy and Hellenistic Judaism.[109] Sha'ul concludes his instructions by constructing a "vice list" from Deuteronomy.

5:13. Just expel the evildoer from among yourselves: The phrase "expel the evildoer" appears in various contexts in Deuteronomy. False prophets are evildoers that must be expelled (Deut. 13:5), as well as idol worshippers and, as mentioned above, idol worship is linked to sexual immorality (Deut.17:7). Evildoers also include false witnesses (Deut. 19:19), those that are promiscuous (Deut. 24:21), fornicators (Deut. 24:24), and kidnappers (Deut. 24:7).

The person who committed incest, as well as all the sexually impure must be expelled or they will contaminate the faith community.

---

108. Amy-Jill Levine and Marc Zvi Brettler, *The Jewish Annotated New Testament*, 295.
109. Hans Conzelmann, *et al*, 100-102.

1 CORINTHIANS 6

INTRODUCTORY COMMENTS

The theme of this chapter revolves around the subject of sexual immorality. There is a subtle link between 5:1–2 and chapter 6, in that the case of incest might have led to a legal case such as Sha'ul mentions in 6:1–11.[110]

> **1** How dare one of you with a complaint against another go to court before pagan judges and not before God's people? **2** Don't you know that God's people are going to judge the universe? If you are going to judge the universe, are you incompetent to judge these minor matters? **3** Don't you know that we will judge angels, not to mention affairs of everyday life? **4** So if you require judgments about matters of everyday life, why do you put them in front of men who have no standing in the Messianic Community? **5** I say, shame on you! Can it be that there isn't one person among you wise enough to be able to settle a dispute between brothers? **6** Instead, a brother brings a lawsuit against another brother, and that before unbelievers! (6:1–6)

6:1. You go to court before pagan judges: The man who committed incest was being tried within the parameters of biblical Jewish jurisprudence. The Torah requires the Jewish people to establish their own court system (Deut. 16:18). Acts 18:14-15 indicates that the Roman government had granted judicial autonomy to the Jewish

---

110. Joseph A. Fitzmeyer, *1 Corinthians*, 232.

community, in other words, the right to establish its own court system. Cases regarding Jewish law were to be arbitrated in these courts while misdemeanors or serious crimes were to be decided in Roman courts. However, the Roman judicial system did permit cases related to sexual matters such as adultery [111] and incest to be adjudicated. [112]

6:3. We will judge angels, not to mention affairs of everyday life: Angels are subject to the saints' judgment (Dan. 4:14; 2 Pet. 2:4; Jude 1:6–15; 1 En. 14:21–24; 15; 19; 21; 41.9; 46.7; y. Shabb. 6.10 [8d]; b. Sanh. 38b). [113] The affairs of everyday life may be an allusion to a saying of Yeshua that states that his talmidim will judge the Twelve Tribes of Israel (Matt. 19:28; Luke 22:30).

6:4–6. Why do you put them in front of men who have no standing in the Messianic Community? Apparently, wealthy Corinthian believers were bypassing the Jewish court system to settle their differences regarding sexual matters in Roman courts with the hope that because of their status they would receive more favorable treatment. In general, even though sexual offenses were capital crimes, it seems that because of societal norms the Roman courts were much more lenient regarding rendering a judgment of guilt.

It is interesting to note that when a Roman judge pronounced a legally binding verdict of "not guilty," he used the word *dikaiosis*, which literally means "declared to be righteous or justified." Employing this term meant that the accused person was acquitted and pronounced free of condemnation and punishment. [114] Sha'ul

---

111. Edward Adams and David G. Horrell, *Christianity at Corinth: The Quest for the Pauline Church*, (Westminster, John Knox Press), 204.

112. Ibid. 202.

113. Amy-Jill Levine and Marc Zvi Brettler, 295.

114. David John Williams, *Paul's Metaphors: Their Context and Character* (Grand Rapids: Baker Academic), 145-154.

employs the word *dikaiosis* to explain the concept of justification (Rom. 3:21–5:11).

Theoretically, by going before a Roman court, a believer could say that he disagreed with Sha'ul's assessment of his actions especially because, unlike Sha'ul, a Roman judge had already determined that his sexual sin was not a moral or capital crime and that he had been declared as being "righteous and justified."

> **7** Actually, if you are bringing lawsuits against each other, it is already a defeat for you. Why not rather be wronged? Why not rather be cheated? **8** Instead, you yourselves wrong and cheat; and you do it to your own brothers! **9** Don't you know that unrighteous people will have no share in the Kingdom of God? Don't delude yourselves — people who engage in sex before marriage, who worship idols, who engage in sex after marriage with someone other than their spouse, who engage in active or passive homosexuality, **10** who steal, who are greedy, who get drunk, who assail people with contemptuous language, who rob — none of them will share in the Kingdom of God. **11** Some of you used to do these things. But you have cleansed yourselves, you have been set apart for God, you have come to be counted righteous through the power of the Lord Yeshua the Messiah and the Spirit of our God. (6:7-11)

6:7–9[a]. Bringing lawsuits: Sha'ul considers filing a lawsuit against another believer for the purpose of gaining an advantage or proving a point as sinful and has dire consequences – the exclusion from having a share in the World to Come.

6:9[b]–11. Unrighteous people: He lumps the litigious Corinthians with the sexually immoral as well as with a host of other behavioral sins. This vice list is expressed in terms which are substantially equivalent to the so-called "Noachide commandments."[115]

---

115. Markus Bockmuehl, N A., *Revelation and Mystery in Ancient Judaism and Pauline Christianity* (Eugene, OR: Wipf & Stock, 2009), 155.

12 You say, "For me, everything is permitted"? Maybe, but not everything is helpful. "For me, everything is permitted"? Maybe, but as far as I am concerned, I am not going to let anything gain control over me. **13** "Food is meant for the stomach and the stomach for food"? Maybe, but God will put an end to both of them. Anyhow, the body is not meant for sexual immorality but for the Lord, and the Lord is for the body. **14** God raised up the Lord, and he will raise us up too by his power.

15 Don't you know that your bodies are parts of the Messiah? So, am I to take parts of the Messiah and make them parts of a prostitute? Heaven forbid! **16** Don't you know that a man who joins himself to a prostitute becomes physically one with her? For the *Tanakh* says, "The two will become one flesh" **17** but the person who is joined to the Lord is one spirit. **18** Run from sexual immorality! Every other sin a person commits is outside the body, but the fornicator sins against his own body. **19** Or don't you know that your body is a temple for the *Ruach HaKodesh* who lives inside you, whom you received from God? The fact is, you don't belong to yourselves; **20** for you were bought at a price. So use your bodies to glorify God. (6:12–20)

6:12. Everything is permitted: Literally all things are lawful (*exesti)* a term that is used to describe those actions permitted in the Torah (cp. Matt.12:12; Mark 3:4; Luke 6:12). The Corinthians have misconstrued their newfound liberty in Yeshua as their right to subjectively decide what is permissible. Such notions may reflect Greek philosophers or Jewish literature.[116] True freedom is keeping God's commandments.

6:13. The body is not meant for sexual immorality but for the Lord: Believers do not have the luxury or the liberty to yield to their

---

116. Joseph A. Fitzmeyer, *1 Corinthians*, 263.

bodily passions and appetites because God created the body to serve His purpose. Succumbing to such desires renders the body unfit to serve the Creator in *repairing the world* (Tikkun HaOlam). Believers have become members of the body of the Mashiach and are united with Yeshua as a man is united with his wife (Gen. 2:24). Sexual immorality fractures this unity and is analogous to idolatry.[117]

6:18–20. Run from sexual immorality: Believers need to flee from sexual sin because it defiles the body which is the holy temple of the Ruach HaKodesh (cp. 3:16–17). The temple of the Holy Spirit is analogous to the *Shekinah* (Presence) of God in the *Mishkan* (Tabernacle in the wilderness, Exod. 40:34). Believers who indulge in such vices dishonor the Lord and extinguish and nullify the power of His presence.

---

117. See my comments on chapter 5:1

1 CORINTHIANS 7

INTRODUCTORY COMMENTS

Sha'ul's instructions regarding human sexuality were prompted by a letter that he had received from the Corinthian community. Although he received many letters, having just expounded upon the sexual impurity and its ramifications, it is logical that he would opine about the proper place of intimacy in the life of a believer.

Phrases such as "I suppose that in a time of stress like the present it is good for a person to stay as he is (7:26)" and "What I am saying, brothers, is that there is not much time left: from now on a man with a wife should live as if he had none (7:29)" are driven by his apocalyptic world view that the *parousia* was imminent.[118]

In this chapter the theme of the nearness of the "End" shapes the substance of Sha'ul's pastoral advice.[119] Ben Witherington III posits that theologically Sha'ul's eschatological worldview includes the belief that the form or pattern (schema) of the world is passing away, and this would include the institution of marriage, which is a worldly phenomenon (v. 31). Sha'ul is attempting to inculcate in the Corinthians a sense of what it means to live in the eschatological age. Sha'ul believes that the followers of Yeshua are already living in that age, begun by the Messiah's death and resurrection, and so are living on borrowed time.[120]

---

118. See my comments, Introduction p. 14

119. Paula Fredriksen, *Paul: The Pagan's Apostle* (New Haven, CT: Yale University Press, 2018).

120. Ben Witherington, *Conflict and Community in Corinth: A Socio-Rhetorical Commentary on 1 and 2 Corinthians* (Grand Rapids: W.B. Eerdmans, 1995), 238.

[1] Now to deal with the questions you wrote about: "Is it good for a man to keep away from women?" [2] Well, because of the danger of sexual immorality, let each man have his own wife and each woman her own husband. [3] The husband should give his wife what she is entitled to in the marriage relationship, and the wife should do the same for her husband. [4] The wife is not in charge of her own body, but her husband is; likewise, the husband is not in charge of his own body, but his wife is. [5] Do not deprive each other, except for a limited time, by mutual agreement, and then only so as to have extra time for prayer; but afterwards, come together again. Otherwise, because of your lack of self-control, you may succumb to the Adversary's temptation. [6] I am giving you this as a suggestion, not as a command. [7] Actually, I wish everyone were like me; but each has his own gift from God, one this, another that. (7:1–7)

7:1. Is it good for a man to keep away from women? According to Daniel Boyarin "We can thus explain all of the details of 1 Corinthians 7 on the basis of the assumption that Paul maintains a two-tiered system of thought regarding sexuality: celibacy as the higher state but marriage as a fully honorable condition for the believing Christian. This is by and large identical to actually attested forms of Palestinian Judaism and not very far from Philo."[121]

Though celibacy was eschewed by Judaism because of the first positive commandment, to be fruitful and multiply,[122] Dale C. Allison claims that Paul, in 1 Corinthians 7, is indebted to Jewish "apocalyptic celibacy."[123]

---

121. Daniel Boyarin, *A Radical Jew: Paul and the Politics of Identity* (Berkeley: University of California Press, 1994), 192.

122. Genesis 1:28; cp. (*Yev.* 62b; *Shulchan Aruch Even HaEzer* 1;1)

123. Gabriele Boccaccini and Carlos A. Segovia, *Paul the Jew: Rereading the Apostle as a Figure of Second Temple Judaism* (Minneapolis: Fortress Press, 2016), 84.

Sha'ul equates celibacy, which is a gift from God that is not granted to everyone (v. 7, cp. Matt. 19:10–12), with the "Spirit," and, though permissible as a concession (v. 6), he equates marriage with the "flesh."[124]

Far from regarding celibacy as a means to the attainment of holiness, Judaism views it as an impediment to personal sanctification. This is strikingly illustrated by the rabbinic use of the term *kiddushin* (sanctification) for marriage and by the insistence that the High Priest be married (Lev. 21:13), especially at the time when he officiates in the Holy of Holies on the holiest day of the year (Yoma 1:1).[125]

7:2. Because of the danger of sexual immorality: To maintain the purity of the body of the Mashiach, which is the sanctified temple of the Ruach HaKodesh, any person who could not achieve the higher standard of celibacy should be married.

7:3–6. The husband should give his wife what she is entitled to in the marriage relationship, and the wife should do the same for her husband: Sha'ul unfolds the dynamics of the times and seasons for marital intimacy. Though a hierarchy exists, decisions regarding marital relations should be determined by mutual consent. The Mishnah teaches that a husband has an obligation to have sexual relations with his wife. How frequently he is obligated depends on his job. The idea that a husband has an obligation to periodically have relations with his wife is derived from Exodus 21:10 which states that if a man takes a second wife, he cannot diminish from her (his first wife) three things: food, clothing, or conjugal rights.

Prescribed times for the cessation of intimacy for spiritual purposes were permitted. Shammai says that a vow of celibacy

---

124. Daniel Boyarin, *A Radical Jew: Paul and the Politics of Identity*, 193.

125. https://www.jewishvirtuallibrary.org/celibacy

should be limited to two weeks while Hillel says one week. Others, such as Rabbi Elezer, say even without the permission of their wives thirty days (Mishnah Ketubah 5:6).[126]

> **8** Now to the single people and the widows I say that it is fine if they remain unmarried like me; **9** but if they can't exercise self-control, they should get married; because it is better to get married than to keep burning with sexual desire.
>
> **10** To those who are married I have a command, and it is not from me but from the Lord: a woman is not to separate herself from her husband **11** But if she does separate herself, she is to remain single or be reconciled with her husband. Also, a husband is not to leave his wife.**12** To the rest I say — I, not the Lord: if any brother has a wife who is not a believer, and she is satisfied to go on living with him, he should not leave her. **13** Also, if any woman has an unbelieving husband who is satisfied to go on living with her, she is not to leave him. **14** For the unbelieving husband has been set aside for God by the wife, and the unbelieving wife has been set aside for God by the brother — otherwise your children would be "unclean," but as it is, they are set aside for God. **15** But if the unbelieving spouse separates himself, let him be separated. In circumstances like these, the brother or sister is not enslaved — God has called you to a life of peace. **16** For how do you know, wife, whether you will save your husband? Or how do you know, husband, whether you will save your wife? (7:8–16)

7:8–9. Now to the single people and the widows: Sha'ul repeats the theme of his preference for exercising self-restraint over bodily passions, which was a philosophical discipline cultivated by Neoplatonists, Aristotelians, Stoics, Cynics, Philo, and rabbis (Philo, *On the Creation* 164; *Avot* de R. Natan 16).[127]

---

126. https://www.sefaria.org/English_Explanation_of_Mishnah_Ketubot.5.6.1

127. Amy-Jill Levine and Marc Zvi Brettler, *The Jewish Annotated New Testament*, 297.

7:10–11. To those who are married I have a command: Sha'ul received this command about divorce directly from Yeshua (Matt. 5:32–32, 19:3–9; Mark 10:1–12; Luke 16:18). This teaching is applicable to a marriage where both partners are believers.

7:12–13. If any brother has a wife who is not a believer, and she is satisfied to go on living with him, he should not leave her. ¹³ Also, if any woman has an unbelieving husband who is satisfied to go on living with her, she is not to leave him. Sha'ul interprets this Scripture as applicable to couples where only one of the partners is a believer.

7:14. The unbelieving wife/husband set aside (sanctified) for God: The reality is that no one can say with absolute certainty what this phrase means. I propose a few ways to interpret this phrase:

1. Sha'ul's contention is that the status of the believing spouse is transferred to the unbelieving spouse and subsequently to their children. He has in view the marriages of Moshe and Zipporah (Exod. 2:21–22) and of Boaz and Ruth (Ruth 4:13–17). Sha'ul's view that unbelievers do not defile believers aligns itself with rabbinic opinion that regards sexual contact with Gentiles as neutral (Sifra Pereq Zavim 1.1).[128] During Sha'ul's time, Jewish descent was patrilineal (though from the second century C.E. Jewish descent has been determined matrilineally). The complicated issue of "Who is a Jew" and how it impinges upon determining the status of a child is analogous to the situation at Corinth. This subject is thoroughly expounded upon by Shaye J. D. Cohen in his book *The Beginnings of Jewishness – Boundaries, Varieties, Uncertainties*.[129]

---

128. Ibid.

129. Cohen Shaye J D., *The Beginnings of Jewishness: Boundaries, Varieties, Uncertainties* (Berkeley: Univ. of California Press, 2009).

2. A more compelling solution or explanation is rooted in the Jewish wedding ceremony. It was solidified between the years 40 B.C.E. and 10 B.C.E.[130] Discussions regarding the proper procedures for a wedding ceremony are recorded in the Talmud (Eduyot 4:7; Kiddushin 11ᵃ,12ᵃ) as taking place between the House of Shammai and the House of Hillel circa 30 B.C.E. to 10 B.C.E.

The marriage ceremony consisted of two phases: the betrothal or *erusin* which since Talmudic times is known as *kiddushin*. Once the betrothal occurred, the couple was considered to be married. However, conjugal rights were not permitted until the second phase of the wedding ceremony had been completed. The second part of the ceremony, still known as *nissuin* took place after the bridegroom (*chatan*) would go to his father's house to prepare a place for his bride (*kallah*). Once this task was completed, he would return for his kallah. They would then complete the nissuin ceremony which would be followed by a seven-day wedding celebration. It is not clear whether it was during erusin or during nissuin that the chatan placed a ring upon on his bride's finger. (In Biblical times there was no exchange of rings.)

The wedding vow, which is still utilized today, is "Be sanctified (*mekudeshet*) to me with this ring in accordance with the law of Moses and Israel." הרי את מקודשת לי. *Hare et m'kudeshet li.*

The relevant point for interpreting 1 Corinthians 7:14 is that the wedding vow substitutes the word "made holy" or "sanctified" for the word "to be married." In other words, a marriage ceremony is a process of sanctification. Sha'ul's analogy is that by virtue of becoming one flesh, the believing spouse sanctifies the unbeliever as well as their children.

---

130. www.bavlionline.org/roman-origins-of-the-jewish-marriage-kiddushin-procedure/

The two-stage wedding procedure is attested to in Matthew 1:18–19 and alluded to in Matthew 25:1–13 and John 14:1–3.

18 Here is how the birth of Yeshua the Messiah took place. When his mother Miryam was engaged to Yosef, before they were married, she was found to be pregnant from the *Ruach HaKodesh*. **19** Her husband-to-be, Yosef, was a man who did what was right; so he made plans to break the engagement quietly, rather than put her to public shame. (Matt.1:18–19)

25:1 "The Kingdom of Heaven at that time will be like ten bridesmaids who took their lamps and went out to meet the groom. **2** Five of them were foolish and five were sensible. **3** The foolish ones took lamps with them but no oil, **4** whereas the others took flasks of oil with their lamps. **5** Now the bridegroom was late, so they all went to sleep. **6** It was the middle of the night when the cry rang out, 'The bridegroom is here! Go out to meet him!' **7** The girls all woke up and prepared their lamps for lighting. **8** The foolish ones said to the sensible ones, 'Give us some of your oil, because our lamps are going out.' **9** 'No,' they replied, 'there may not be enough for both you and us. Go to the oil dealers and buy some for yourselves.' **10** But as they were going off to buy, the bridegroom came. Those who were ready went with him to the wedding feast, and the door was shut. **11** Later, the other bridesmaids came. 'Sir! Sir!' they cried, 'Let us in!' **12** But he answered, 'Indeed! I tell you, I don't know you!' **13** So stay alert, because you know neither the day nor the hour (Matt. 25:1–13)

14:1 "Don't let yourselves be disturbed. Trust in God and trust in me. **2** In my Father's house are many places to live. If there weren't, I would have told you; because I am going there to prepare a place for you. **3** Since I am going and preparing a place for you, I will return to take you with me; so that where I am, you may be also (John 14:1–3).

7:16. How do you know … whether you will save your husband?... or your wife: "For I hate divorce, says the Lord." (Mal. 2:16) was a verse that was frequently referred to Pharisaic thought.[131] Yeshua said "Moshe allowed you to divorce your wives because your hearts are so hardened. But this is not how it was at the beginning." As a Pharisee and as a believer, the bottom line for Sha'ul is absolutely no divorce.

> [17] Only let each person live the life the Lord has assigned him and live it in the condition he was in when God called him. This is the rule I lay down in all the congregations. [18] Was someone already circumcised when he was called? Then he should not try to remove the marks of his circumcision. Was someone uncircumcised when he was called? He shouldn't undergo *b'rit-milah*. [19] Being circumcised means nothing and being uncircumcised means nothing; what does mean something is keeping God's commandments. [20] Each person should remain in the condition he was in when he was called.
>
> [21] Were you a slave when you were called? Well, don't let it bother you; although if you can gain your freedom, take advantage of the opportunity. [22] For a person who was a slave when he was called is the Lord's freedman; likewise, someone who was a free man when he was called is a slave of the Messiah. [23] You were bought at a price, so do not become slaves of other human beings. [24] Brothers, let each one remain with God in the condition in which he was called.
>
> [25] Now the question about the unmarried: I do not have a command from the Lord, but I offer an opinion as one who by the Lord's mercy is worthy to be trusted. [26] I suppose that in a time of stress like the present it is good for a person to stay as he is. [27] That means that if a man has a wife, he should not seek to be free of her; and if he is unmarried, he should not look for a wife. [28] But if you marry you do not sin, and if a girl marries, she does not sin. It is just that those who get married

---

131. Israel Abrahams, *Studies in Pharisaism and the Gospels* (Eugene, Or.: Wipf & Stock, 2004), 69.

will have the normal problems of married life, and I would rather spare you. **29** What I am saying, brothers, is that there is not much time left: from now on a man with a wife should live as if he had none — **30** and those who are sad should live as if they weren't, those who are happy as if they weren't, **31** and those who deal in worldly affairs as if not engrossed in them — because the present scheme of things in this world won't last much longer. **32** What I want is for you to be free of concern. An unmarried man concerns himself with the Lord's affairs, **33** with how to please the Lord; but the married man concerns himself with the world's affairs, with how to please his wife; **34** and he finds himself split. Likewise, the woman who is no longer married or the girl who has never been married concerns herself with the Lord's affairs, with how to be holy both physically and spiritually; but the married woman concerns herself with the world's affairs, with how to please her husband. **35** I am telling you this for your own benefit, not to put restrictions on you — I am simply concerned that you live in a proper manner and serve the Lord with undivided devotion. (7:17–35)

7:17–21. Only let each person live the life the Lord has assigned him: This section is thought to be primarily addressing sociological concerns (Nasrallah) [132] and its clear purpose is eschatological (vv. 26:29).

7:29. What I am saying, brothers, is that there is not much time left: Sha'ul passionately declares the present scheme of things in this world won't last much longer (vv.26, 29, 31). Being engrossed in matters of marital, social, or ethnic identity is a distraction which diminishes one's capacity to serve the Lord.

According to Gabriele Boccaccini, "Paul is heavily indebted to the apocalyptic ideology of his time because he had been an apocalyptic Diaspora Pharisee before his conversion. Apocalyptic is for Paul the

---

132. https://genius.com/LSMN

bearer of prophecy in new circumstances. It keeps alive the prophetic promises about a new act of God in the future that will surpass God's acts in the past and bring about a transformed creation."[133]

> **36** Now if a man thinks he is behaving dishonorably by treating his fiancée this way, and if there is strong sexual desire, so that marriage is what ought to happen; then let him do what he wants — he is not sinning: let them get married. **37** But if a man has firmly made up his mind, being under no compulsion but having complete control over his will, if he has decided within himself to keep his fiancée a virgin, he will be doing well. **38** So the man who marries his fiancée will do well, and the man who doesn't marry will do better.**39** A wife is bound to her husband as long as he lives, but if the husband dies, she is free to marry anyone she wishes, provided he is a believer in the Lord. **40** However, in my opinion, she will be happier if she remains unmarried, and in saying this I think I have God's Spirit. (7:36–40)

7:36–38. So, the man who marries his fiancée will do well, and the man who doesn't marry will do better: Sha'ul wants the Corinthians to know that even though the "time is short" marriage is not a sin, but he prefers that engaged couples refrain from marrying so that they can individually fully devote themselves to the service of ADONAI.

7:39–40. She will be happier if she remains unmarried: Widows are free to marry. However, in the light of the imminent return of Yeshua, Sha'ul discourages widows from remarrying. Instead of becoming engrossed in the daily concerns of married life, they need to prepare themselves for Mashiach's return.

---

133. Gabriele Boccaccini and Carlos A. Segovia, *Paul the Jew: Rereading the Apostle as a Figure of Second Temple Judaism*, Philadelphia: Fortress Press, 85.

1 Corinthians 8

Introductory Comments

Sha'ul takes advantage of the question regarding eating meat offered to idols to readdress the issue of self-restraint (6:12). The cultural context which underlies the question is twofold: the custom of publicly eating sacrificial meat in pagan temples and the Corinthian government's practice of distributing leftover meat that was sold in the city's *macellum* (marketplace) to the needy. The problem was that the meat that was given to the needy had been sacrificed to idols.

Meat was a luxury but knowing that the meat had been sacrificed to idols violated the conscience of some of the "weaker" members of the faith community. The term "weak" can be understood in two ways. "Weak" is a socio-economic term that refers to the poor but also, as in the context of this verse, to the inability to grasp the knowledge of spiritual truth.[134]

> **8:1** Now about food sacrificed to idols: we know that, as you say, "We all have knowledge." Yes, that is so, but "knowledge" puffs a person up with pride, whereas love builds up. **2** The person who thinks he "knows" something doesn't yet know in the way he ought to know. **3** However, if someone loves God, God knows him.

---

134. Edward Adams and David G. Horrell, *Christianity at Corinth: The Quest for the Pauline Church* (Westminster: John Knox Press), 258-259.

4 So, as for eating food sacrificed to idols, we "know" that, as you say, "An idol has no real existence in the world, and there is only one God." **5** For even if there are so-called "gods," either in heaven or on earth — as in fact there are "gods" and "lords" galore — **6** yet for us there is one God, the Father, from whom all things come and for whom we exist; and one Lord, Yeshua the Messiah, through whom were created all things and through whom we have our being. (8:1–6)

8:1–2. We all have knowledge: The vast majority (implied) of the Corinthians know that eating meat for the several reasons that Sha'ul enumerates (8:4–6) is not problematical, but the purpose of knowledge is to lovingly build each other up rather than to boost the sense of one's ego.

8:4–6. An idol has no real existence in the world, and there is only one God: An idol is a lifeless, powerless, inanimate object made from wood, stone, or a precious metal. Even the "gods' that idols represent are powerless and subject to the authority of the One who has permitted them to exist: the Creator of the universe who is the one true God, the Father of the Lord Yeshua HaMashiach. Idols and the "gods" that they represent have no power over believers.

7 But not everyone has this knowledge. Moreover, some people are still so accustomed to idols that when they eat food which has been sacrificed to them, they think of it as really affected by the idol; and their consciences, being weak, are thus defiled. **8** Now food will not improve our relationship with God — we will be neither poorer if we abstain nor richer if we eat. **9** However watch out that your mastery of the situation does not become a stumbling block to the weak. **10** You have this "knowledge"; but suppose someone with a weak conscience sees you sitting, eating a meal in the temple of an idol. Won't he be built up wrongly to eat this food which has been sacrificed to idols? **11** Thus by your "knowledge" this weak person is destroyed, this brother for whom the Messiah died; **12** and so, when you sin against the brothers by wounding their conscience when it is weak, you are sinning against the Messiah! **13** To sum up, if food will be a snare for my brother, I will never eat meat again, lest I cause my brother to sin. (8:7–13)

8:7–8. But not everyone has this knowledge: The weaker brother is not aware of the truth, so he is still under the impression that eating meat that was sacrificed to idols is spiritually detrimental.

8:9–13. However, watch out that your mastery of the situation does not become a stumbling block to the weak: For the knowledgeable consuming or not consuming of such meat is irrelevant and does not violate their conscience, but knowledge of the truth needs to be tempered by self-restraint. The right to publicly eat meat in a public area or a pagan idol's temple [135] is to be sublimated for the purpose of not destroying and wounding the faith of a weaker brother.

---

135. David John Williams, *Paul's Metaphors: Their Context and Character*, 19.

1 CORINTHIANS 9

INTRODUCTORY COMMENTS

Unlike chapter 7 (v. 1) and chapter 8 (v. 1), the exact question in this chapter is not specifically indicated. The question that Sha'ul seems to be attempting to answer is "What are my rights and responsibilities now that I am set free by the Son of God?" (John 8:36).

Sha'ul has started to undertake this issue in chapter 8. Sha'ul moves on from the Corinthians' misuse of knowledge to their misuse of the freedom they have in union with the Messiah.[136] He then points to himself as an example of what it truly means to be free in the Messiah Yeshua. The summation of his argument is that true freedom is the freedom to release one's personal rights "in the newness and power of the Ruach HaKodesh"[137] and to serve God as a slave serves his master. One of the key concepts in this chapter is that Sha'ul has voluntarily become God's slave so that he could become all things to all people to win as many people as possible (10:19-23).

The most cogent explanation of these verses can be found in Messianic Jewish Rabbi David J. Rudolph's *A Jew to the Jews: Jewish Contours of Pauline Flexibility in 1 Corinthians 9:19–23* which explores this key passage from a post-supersessionist perspective. In line with the most recent scholarship from what

---

136. David H. Stern, *Jewish New Testament Commentary: A Companion Volume to the Jewish New Testament* (Clarksville, MD: Messianic Jewish Publishers), 480.
137. Brian S. Rosner and Roy E. Ciampa, *First Letter to the Corinthians*, 398.

Zetterholm has termed "the radical new perspective" on Paul, Rudolph writes with the conviction that Paul never abandoned his ancestral faith, but rather operated within clear halachic boundaries in his efforts to win both Jew and Gentile to faith in Messiah.[138]

David Flusser claims that a saying of Hillel the Elder that appears in Tosefta Berachot 2:21 serves as a backdrop for verses 19–23. Hillel's saying is a Midrash on Ecclesiastes 3:4–5.[139]

> There is a time and a season for everything!
> a time to weep and a time to laugh,
> a time to mourn and a time to dance,
> a time to throw stones and a time to gather stones (build a building),
> a time to embrace (marital relations) and a time to refrain.
> (Eccles. 3:4–5) [140]

In other words, there is a time and a season for Sha'ul to put himself in the position of a Jew to win Jews, as well as a time and a season for Sha'ul to put himself in the position of someone outside the *Torah* to win those outside the *Torah*. According to Derech Eretz Zeira, it was a general rule that no man should act differently from the behavior of his neighbor.[141]

> **9:1** Am I not a free man? Am I not an emissary of the Messiah? Haven't I seen Yeshua our Lord? And aren't you yourselves the result of my work for the Lord? **2** Even if to others I am not an emissary, at least I am to you; for you are living proof that I am the Lord's emissary. **3** That is my defense when people put me under examination.
>
> **4** Don't we have the right to be given food and drink? **5** Don't we have the right to take along with us a believing wife, as do

---

138. "Messiah Journal," First Fruits of Zion, 76.

139. David Flusser, *Judaism and the Origins of Christianity* (Jerusalem: Magnes Press, 1988), XIV.

140. A. J. Rosenberg and A. Cohen, *The Five Megilloth; Hebrew Text, English Translation and Commentary.* (Hindhead, Surrey: Soncino Press, 1984), 124.

141. David Flusser, *Judaism and the Origins of Christianity*, XIV.

the other emissaries, also the Lord's brothers and Kefa? **6** Or are Bar-Nabba and I the only ones required to go on working for our living? **7** Did you ever hear of a soldier paying his own expenses? or of a farmer planting a vineyard without eating its grapes? Who shepherds a flock without drinking some of the milk? **8** What I am saying is not based merely on human authority, because the *Torah* says the same thing — **9** for in the *Torah* of Moshe it is written, "You are not to put a muzzle on an ox when it is treading out the grain." If God is concerned about cattle, **10** all the more does he say this for our sakes. Yes, it was written for us, meaning that he who plows and he who threshes should work expecting to get a share of the crop. **11** If we have sown spiritual seed among you, is it too much if we reap a material harvest from you? **12** If others are sharing in this right to be supported by you, don't we have a greater claim to it?

But we don't make use of this right. Rather, we put up with all kinds of things so as not to impede in any way the Good News about the Messiah. **13** Don't you know that those who work in the Temple get their food from the Temple, and those who serve at the altar get a share of the sacrifices offered there? **14** In the same way, the Lord directed that those who proclaim the Good News should get their living from the Good News.

15 But I have not made use of any of these rights. Nor am I writing now to secure them for myself, for I would rather die than be deprived of my ground for boasting! **16** For I can't boast merely because I proclaim the Good News — this I do from inner compulsion: woe is me if I don't proclaim the Good News! **17** For if I do this willingly, I have a reward; but if I do it unwillingly, I still do it, simply because I've been entrusted with a job. **18** So then, what is my reward? Just this: that in proclaiming the Good News I can make it available free of charge, without making use of the rights to which it entitles me. (9:9–18)

9:1. Am I not a free man? Three things merit his exercising his rights and freedom: He was a *shaliach*, Yeshua had appeared to him, and his work in the Lord among the Corinthians.

9:3. That is my defense: Using legal language (*apologia*- a legal defense) to spotlight his reasons for relinquishing his rights to prevent anyone (weaker brothers) from stumbling.

9:4. Food and drink: Rights relating to food and drink (cp. 8:1–13; 9:13–14).

9:5. A believing wife: Rights relating to marriage which includes sexual expression. Sha'ul chose to be celibate to serve as an example to those who were struggling with their sexuality (cp. 7:1–40).

9:6–12. Required to go on working for our living: Rights relating to fair compensation for his ministry as a *shaliach*. Since the Corinthians were craftsmen situated in the lower socio-economic strata of society,[142] Sha'ul earned his own living (Acts 18:2–3), wanting the Corinthians to understand that he knew what it meant to work by the sweat of one's brow. It is my experience that a common perception today is that ministry (far from the true reality) is an easy profession that requires minimal time and effort.

9:15–18. But I have not made use of any of these rights: For Sha'ul, exercising the legitimate rights mentioned above would be tantamount to boasting about the rewards he had received for the achievements that he had accomplished as a *shaliach*. His work as a *shaliach* did not require any compensation because his reward was preaching the *Besorah* — the Good News— free of charge.

---

142. See the Introductory article "The History of Jewish Corinth."

19 For although I am a free man, not bound to do anyone's bidding, I have made myself a slave to all in order to win as many people as possible. **20** That is, with Jews, what I did was put myself in the position of a Jew, in order to win Jews. With people in subjection to a legalistic perversion of the *Torah*, I put myself in the position of someone under such legalism, in order to win those under this legalism, even though I myself am not in subjection to a legalistic perversion of the *Torah*. **21** With those who live outside the framework of *Torah*, I put myself in the position of someone outside the *Torah* in order to win those outside the *Torah* — although I myself am not outside the framework of God's *Torah* but within the framework of *Torah* as upheld by the Messiah. **22** With the "weak" I became "weak," in order to win the "weak." With all kinds of people, I have become all kinds of things, so that in all kinds of circumstances I might save at least some of them.

23 But I do it all because of the rewards promised by the Good News, so that I may share in them along with the others who come to trust. **24** Don't you know that in a race all the runners compete, but only one wins the prize? So then, run to win! **25** Now every athlete in training submits himself to strict discipline, and he does it just to win a laurel wreath that will soon wither away. But we do it to win a crown that will last forever. **26** Accordingly, I don't run aimlessly but straight for the finish line; I don't shadow-box but try to make every punch count. **27** I treat my body hard and make it my slave so that, after proclaiming the Good News to others, I myself will not be disqualified. (9:19-27)

9:19. For although I am a free man, not bound to do anyone's bidding, I have made myself a slave to all in order to win as many people as possible.: Sha'ul calls himself a slave. The Hebrew word *eved* (*doulos* in Greek) can be understood figuratively as "slave" and, in this sense, means "a person or persons who are devoted to the well-being of others in the service of God" (Joel 2:29,

Zech. 1:6, Jer. 7:25, Ezek. 38:17, Amos 3:7). Examples where *doulos* is often translated as "slave" in the New Testament are Romans 1:1, Philippians 1:1, and Titus 1:1. Sha'ul's self-description also matches that of a slave whose cultural adaption is expected as part of his job requirements with the caveat that his adjustment to the cultural reality of the family that he is serving would be confined by the constraints of his faith in Yeshua.[143]

9:21. As upheld by the Messiah: Usually translated as Messiah's or Christ's Law, Sha'ul believed that the resurrection was the incipient act that inaugurated the Messianic age. Theologically, the Brit Hadashah interprets the book of Jeremiah as espousing the view that in the Messianic age, the Messiah would introduce a new way of understanding the Torah (Jer. 31:31–34). Yeshua affirms this when He declares:

> [17] "Don't think that I have come to abolish the *Torah* or the Prophets. I have come not to abolish but to complete. [18] Yes indeed! I tell you that until heaven and earth pass away, not so much as a *yud* or a stroke will pass from the *Torah* — not until everything that must happen has happened. [19] So whoever disobeys the least of these *mitzvot* and teaches others to do so will be called the least in the Kingdom of Heaven. But whoever obeys them and so teaches will be called great in the Kingdom of Heaven." (Matt. 5:17-19)

Davies correctly explains:

> True to this expectation Jesus had come and preached a new Torah from the mount and had yet remained loyal to the old Torah, displaying "universalism in belief and particularism in practice." In view of all this, it would not be unnatural for Paul also to believe that loyalty to the new law of Christ did not involve disloyalty to the Torah of his fathers, while at the same

---

143. Brian S. Rosner and Roy E. Ciampa, in *First Letter to the Corinthians*, 424-425.

time holding that the latter, in its full sense, had also predicted that the Gentiles should share in the glories of the Messianic Age. There was no reason Paul should not reject the view that Gentiles should be converted to Judaism before entering the Messianic Kingdom and at the same time insist that for him as a Jew the Torah was still valid. In so doing he was being true both to the universalist tradition of Judaism and at the same time showing his identification with the Israel according to the flesh: he was being true to the 'new' and the 'old' Israel.[144]

Practical considerations: Both of my parents were halachically Jewish, though they were not stringently Torah observant. Due to the influence of my maternal grandmother, who was from Belarus, our household maintained a modicum of Orthodoxy. After their passing (I was still in high school), I lived with a foster family who was similarly observant. When I became a believer, while still living with them, I continued in the traditional lifestyle to which I was accustomed.

When my wife and I lived in Israel as believers, we leaned towards Orthodoxy, some examples being not driving on the Shabbat, following the decorum of the local synagogue we attended, and keeping kosher. Since I was studying at an Orthodox Yeshivah, I wore a *kippah* and *tzitzit*, and put on *tefillin* at the appropriate times.

In 2022, we were invited to go to Lusaka, Zambia, to participate in the one-hundredth anniversary celebration of a Catholic church. I spoke at the conclusion of the mass. I first addressed the seven-hundred people who had gathered there with a few words in one of the Zambian dialects. I then gave a message utilizing liturgical phrases that were like the Mass such as "the words of Jesus Christ as found in the Gospel of Saint Matthew the Apostle." Adapting my message by using familiar terms enabled me to connect with the

---

144. William D. Davies, *Paul and Rabbinic Judaism: Some Rabbinic Elements in Pauline Theology*, 92.

parishioners. I concluded the mass by sounding the shofar. After the mass there was a meal for the invited guests. The meal was an outdoor buffet which permitted us to select the foods that we considered to be biblically permitted to consume. We sat with nuns and Catholic and Coptic priests and interacted with government officials. The tenor of the conversations gave the impression that we were best friends who had known each other for years.

In other words, in Israel (those within the framework of the Torah) and in Zambia, (those outside the framework of the Torah), without compromising the Torah of Yeshua, we became all things to all people.

9:24–27. So then, run to win! Sha'ul metaphorically compares the process of successfully fulfilling God's will to become his slave/servant by emulating an athlete in training. The Corinthians were quite familiar with terminology related to athletics because sports were an important aspect of life in the Greco-Roman world. Sha'ul reminds the faith community that just as self-discipline and controlling the body's appetites are essential for competitors to win the race or the boxing match, serving as God's slave/servant requires equal training.

1 CORINTHIANS 10

INTRODUCTORY COMMENTS

I am proposing a novel approach as the key to understanding this chapter. I interpret these verses as a *midrash* on Pesach (Passover), which includes references from Scripture, beginning with the cloud and the baptism of Moshe (10:1–2),[145] the Exodus from Egypt, along with some of the subsequent events in the wilderness (10:3–10),[146] as well as the Lord's Passover Seder (10:16–17).[147] In addition, there are references to non-biblical Second Temple sources such as *Jubilees*, written in the second century B.C.E., which devotes a long section to Passover in (cp. 49 on Exod. 12),[148] and the Mishnah, especially Pesachim 10 which includes pre-C.E 70 discussions concerning the liturgical elements that should be included in the Passover seder.

The sequence of the Seder in the first century, prior to the destruction of the Temple, may be summed up as follows: (1) Kiddush; (2) dipping of herbs; (3) the child's three (or four?) questions; (4) the father's answer; (5) the meal, concluded with the eating of the Paschal lamb, matzah, maror, and charoset; (6) the cup of wine following the after-meal grace; and (7) the chanting of Hallel. The Talmud states that Hallel was chanted after the eating of

---

145. Ex. 14:19-25; Isa. 63:11-14

146. Ex. 15:22-17:1-7; Psalms 106:7-ff

147. Matthew 26:17-30; 1Corinthians 5:6-8

148. Baruch M. Bokser, *Origins of the Seder: The Passover Rite and Early Rabbinic Judaism* (Berkley: Univ of California Press, 2020), 19.

the Paschal lamb (Pesachim 86[a]), and that prior to the introduction of the four cups, the entire Hallel was chanted after the meal.[149]

This interpretation of the seder is attributed to Rabban Gamaliel. In Pesachim 101 he is depicted as reclining at the seder (cp. John 13:23–26). It is plausible that Rabban Gamaliel is Sha'ul's teacher.[150]

For a description of Yeshua's Passover seder please see my article in the Ruminations section.

It is important to understand that prior to the 1st century C.E., *Pesach* (Passover) and *Chag HaMatzot* (Feast of Unleavened Bread) were synthesized into one holiday (cp. Ezra 6:19–22),[151] and *Shavuot* (Pentecost) was considered to be an appendage to Pesach. The distinction between Chag HaPesach and Chag HaMatzot lies in the historical arena which each holiday seeks to reflect. Chag HaPesach reenacts the events of the 14th of Nisan (the pre-exodus period) while Chag HaMatzot marks the actual departure from Egypt which concluded with the crossing of the Red Sea.[152]

> **10:1** For, brothers, I don't want you to miss the significance of what happened to our fathers. All of them were guided by the pillar of cloud, and they all passed through the sea, **2** and in connection with the cloud and with the sea they all immersed themselves into Moshe, **3** also they all ate the same food from the Spirit, **4** and they all drank the same drink from the Spirit — for they drank from a Spirit-sent Rock which followed them, and that Rock was the Messiah. **5** Yet with the majority of them God was not pleased, so their bodies were strewn across the desert.

---

149. Abraham P. Bloch, *The Biblical and Historical Background of the Jewish Holy Days* (New York: Ktav, 1978), 133.

150. However, Sefaria points out that Rabban Shimon ben Gamliel could also refer to one of the following rabbis: the son of Sha'ul's teacher Rabban Shimon b. Gamliel one of the Tannaim of the Second-Generation c.40 - c.80 CE, or Rabban Shimon b. Gamliel (II) one of the Tannaim of the Fifth-Generation c.135 - c.170 CE.

151. www.thetorah.com/article/passover-and-the-festival-of-matzot-synthesizing-two-holidays

152. Abraham P. Bloch, *The Biblical and Historical Background of the Jewish Holy Days,* 113.

6 Now these things took place as prefigurative historical events, warning us not to set our hearts on evil things as they did. **7** Don't be idolaters, as some of them were — as the *Tanakh* puts it, "The people sat down to eat and drink, then got up to indulge in revelry."[a] **8** And let us not engage in sexual immorality, as some of them did, with the consequence that 23,000 died in a single day. **9** And let us not put the Messiah to the test, as some of them did, and were destroyed by snakes. **10** And don't grumble, as some of them did, and were destroyed by the Destroying Angel.

11 These things happened to them as prefigurative historical events, and they were written down as a warning to us who are living in the *acharit-hayamim*. **12** Therefore, let anyone who thinks he is standing up be careful not to fall! **13** No temptation has seized you beyond what people normally experience, and God can be trusted not to allow you to be tempted beyond what you can bear. On the contrary, along with the temptation he will also provide the way out, so that you will be able to endure. **14** Therefore, my dear friends, run from idolatry! **15** I speak to you as sensible people; judge for yourselves what I am saying. (10:1-15)

10:1ᵃ. What happened to our Fathers: Sha'ul wants the Corinthians to understand that as the spiritual descendants of Abraham (Gal. 3:7–9), they are connected to one of the pivotal moments that is indelibly linked to Pesach, namely the crossing of the Red Sea. This event connects past and future generations. Passover is a reminder of the covenant of the Jews who came out of Egypt (Lev. 26:45; Deut. 29:24; Jer. 31:31). The Exodus, a generic term for Passover, is considered to be the traditional anniversary of the Abrahamic covenant (seder Olam chapter 5).[153]

---

153. Abraham P. Bloch, in *The Biblical and Historical Background of the Jewish Holy Days, 104.*

According to the sages, every generation of God's covenant people was present at the going out of Egypt. The theological basis can be found in Shavuot 39, 9 and Deuteronomy 29:14:

> From the phrase: "But with he who stands here with us this day" (Deut. 29:14), I have derived only that those who stood at Mount Sinai were included in this covenant. From where do I derive that the subsequent generations, and the converts who will convert **in** the future, were also included? The verse states: "And also with he who is not here with us this day"

This concept is also found in Pesachim 10^a, 5:

> Rabban Gamaliel stated: In each and every generation a person must view himself as though he personally left Egypt, as it is stated: "And you shall tell your son on that day, saying: It is because of this which the Lord did for me when I came forth out of Egypt" (Exod. 13:8). In every generation, each person must say: "This which the Lord did for me," and not: "This which the Lord did for my forefathers."

This mishnaic phrase is also included in the Haggadah.

A parallel idea is expressed in Acts 2:39: "For the promise is for you, for your children, and for those far away — as many as *Adonai* our God may call!"

Sha'ul then begins to unfold the history of the Passover, beginning with the crossing of the Yam Suph (10:1–2) and continuing with the incidents that took place in the wilderness (10:6–10) which serve as a permanent reminder and example of the Israelites sinful ways. The pattern of rehearsing the history of our people can be found in Psalms 106 and in the liturgy of the Haggadah.

10:1. Guided by the pillar of cloud: The people were under the cloud which was the manifest Presence (*Shekinah*) of God that "saved them from the hand of the enemy and redeemed them from the hand of the foe" (Psalm 106:10). Malbim explains that "saving" indicates merely a temporary rescue, whereas "redemption" is for all time.[154]

10:1c. They all passed through the sea: The Hebrew name for the Red Sea is Yam Suf יַם-סוּף (Exod. 10:9; 13:18; 15:14–22) Suf can also be understood to mean "end" or "conclusion" which can homiletically imply that the crossing of the Yam Suf represents the end of one era (Egyptian bondage) and the beginning of a new era as freed people.[155]

10:2. Immersed themselves into Moshe:

The baptism of Moshe is a spiritual baptism which took place at the Red Sea.

> **11** But then his people remembered
> the days of old, the days of Moshe:
> "Where is he who brought them up from the sea
> with the shepherds of his flock?
> Where is he who put his Holy Spirit
> right there among them,
> **12** who caused his glorious arm to go
> at Moshe's right hand?
> He divided the water ahead of them,
> to make himself an eternal name;
> **13** he led them through the deep
> like a sure-footed horse through the desert;
> **14** like cattle going down into a valley
> the Spirit of *ADONAI* had them rest.
> This is how you led your people,
> to make yourself a glorious name." (Isa. 63:11–14)

---

154. Avrohom Chaim Feuer and Nosson Scherman, in *Tehillim Sefer Tehilim: A New Translation with a Commentary Anthologized from Talmudic, Midrashic and Rabbinic Sources*, vol. 2 (Brooklyn: Mesorah Publications, 1985), 1289.

155. Cp. Wisdom of Solomon (18:2-15, 37-41), Philo (Special Laws, 2:148, Vol. 7. Pp. 396-397).

The baptism of Moshe is analogous to the baptism of Yeshua (1 Cor. 12:13):

> 13 For it was by one Spirit that we were all immersed into one body, whether Jews or Gentiles, slaves or free; and we were all given the one Spirit to drink.

Yeshua's baptism is a "baptism of the Spirit." This phrase appears six times: Matthew 3:11, Mark 1:8, Luke 3:16, John 1:33–34, Acts 1:5, and Acts 11:16. Pheme Perkins adds "baptized into Moses" corresponds to "baptized into Christ" as participants in the group that experienced God's saving acts."[156]

Sha'ul may also be alluding to the ceremonial cleansing that took place directly before Passover (John 11:55).

> By the time of Christ, ceremonial cleanliness by water had become institutionalized into a purity ritual involving full immersion in a *mikveh*, a "collection of water." Mikveh purification was required of all Jews before they could enter the Temple or participate in major festivals. Hundreds of thousands of pilgrims converged on Jerusalem for Passover and other major feasts. One hundred mikvehs, attesting to the need for water purification before entering into Temple rites, have been found by Hebrew University's Benjamin Mazar around the wall adjacent to Herod's Temple.[157]

This act of ritual purity before Passover is a spiritual immersion.

> Spiritual immersion in a *Mikveh* is equated with going back to creation and being spiritually cleansed from every impurity (Rabbi Israel Meir Lau. *Practical Judaism.* p. 381). The Christian observance of water baptism is derived from this Jewish observation in the *Mikveh*, a type of spiritual cleansing. After all of the physical and spiritual preparations were completed, the people would be ready to observe the Feast of Passover. [158]

---

156. Pheme Perkins, *1 Corinthians (Paideia: Commentaries on the New Testament)*, 123.

157. www.earlychurchhistory.org/medicine/ancient-jews-cleanlines

158. www.jewelsofjudaism.com/preparing-for-passover/

10:3–4. Food from the Spirit: Spiritual food and drink point to the matzah and the wine that are included in the rituals of the Passover seder. The matzah represents redemption which is symbolic of Yeshua's body (Matt. 26:26), while the cup of wine represents the blood of the New Covenant (Matt. 26:27–28). The ritual of the Matzah and the cup of wine is an act of remembrance (Luke 22:19) that reminds the participants that the first redeemer was Moshe, but the final Redeemer is the Mashiach Yeshua.

> R. Berekiah said in the name of R. Isaac: As the first redeemer [*i.e., Moses*] was, so shall the latter Redeemer be. What is stated of the former redeemer? And Moses took his wife and his sons, and set them upon an ass (Exod. IV, 20). Similarly will it be with the latter Redeemer, as it is stated, Lowly and riding upon an ass (Zech. IX, 9)." (Ecc. R. I:28)

Yeshua is the Shiloh (Messiah) who is to come.[159]

Spirit-sent Rock: Jewish tradition considers the rock to be Miriam's well (Talmud, Taanit 9). Sha'ul says that the Rock was Yeshua because he is the source of *mayim chaim*, living water (cp. John 37–39).

10:5–9. Yet with the majority of them God was not pleased, so their bodies were strewn across the desert: Building upon the theme of an athlete in training, Sha'ul compares the sinful behavior of the children of Israel to a lack of self-discipline (cp. 9:24–27) which resulted in their failure to cross the finish line, entering into the Promised Land.

10:13. Along with the temptation he will also provide the way out, so that you will be able to endure: Sha'ul is alluding to the Sermon on the Mount (Matt. 5:1–7, 29) and specifically the Lord's prayer (Matt. 6:9–13) that promises that ADONAI would deliver his

---

159. Meir Zlotowitz, *Bereshis: Genesis Vol. 1* (Brooklyn: Mesorah Publications, 1986). 2152-2157.

people from times of temptation. The word "temptation" (*peirasmos*) can also be understood to signify a test or trial, which also points to Abraham as a person who overcame temptation and trials by trusting in God (Rom. 4). Pirkei Avot 5:3 states: "With ten tests our father Abraham was tested, and he withstood them all—in order to make known how great was our father Abraham's love [for God]."

> **16** The "cup of blessing" over which we make the *b'rakhah* — isn't it a sharing in the bloody sacrificial death of the Messiah? The bread we break, isn't it a sharing in the body of the Messiah? **17** Because there is one loaf of bread, we who are many constitute one body since we all partake of the one loaf of bread. **18** Look at physical Isra'el: don't those who eat the sacrifices participate in the altar? **19** So, what am I saying? That food sacrificed to idols has any significance in itself? or that an idol has significance in itself? **20** No, what I am saying is that the things which pagans sacrifice, they sacrifice not to God but to demons; and I don't want you to become sharers of the demons! **21** You can't drink both a cup of the Lord and a cup of demons, you can't partake in both a meal of the Lord and a meal of demons. **22** Or are we trying to make the Lord jealous? We aren't stronger than he is, are we? (10:16–22)

10:16. The cup of blessing: Sha'ul then associates the question of meat offered to idols with the Passover seder themes that I have previously discussed in the Introductory Remarks section of this chapter (Matt. 26:27; Mark 14:23; Luke 22:20).

10:16[b]. The bread we eat: At the end of the Passover seder, a piece of matzah is broken and then every participant receives a portion from that one piece (Matt. 26:26; Mark 14:22; Luke 22:19).

10:18–22. [18] Look at physical Isra'el: don't those who eat the sacrifices participate in the altar? The Passover meal is a holy, collective meal that can be compared to the sacrifices on the altar that were eaten by the priests. The eating of the matzah and paschal sacrifice and the drinking of the cup of Messianic redemption are reminders of the New Covenant which is incompatible with meat sacrificed to demons. Sha'ul is saying that under ordinary circumstances, eating meat that is sold in the marketplace is permissible, but the reality is that eating such meat is duplicating their forefathers sinful eating of meat that they had sacrificed to idols. His reasoning is based on Deuteronomy 32:17-21.[160]

> They sacrificed to demons, non-gods,
> gods that they had never known,
> new gods that had come up lately,
> which your ancestors had not feared.
> **18** You ignored the Rock who fathered you,
> you forgot God, who gave you birth.
>
> *(iv)* **19** "*ADONAI* saw and was filled with scorn
> at his sons' and daughters' provocation.
> **20** He said, 'I will hide my face from them
> and see what will become of them;
> for they are a perverse generation,
> untrustworthy children.
> **21** They aroused my jealousy with a non-god
> and provoked me with their vanities;
> I will arouse their jealousy with a non-people
> and provoke them with a vile nation.
>
> **23** "Everything is permitted," you say? Maybe, but not everything is helpful. "Everything is permitted?" Maybe, but not everything is edifying. **24** No one should be looking out for his own interests, but for those of his fellow. **25** Eat whatever is sold in the meat market without raising questions of conscience, **26** for the earth and everything in it belong to the Lord. **27** If some unbeliever invites you to a meal, and you want to go, eat whatever is put in front of you without raising

---

160. Brian S. Rosner and Roy E. Ciampa, *First Letter to the Corinthians*, 481.

questions of conscience. **28** But if someone says to you, "This meat was offered as a sacrifice," then don't eat it, out of consideration for the person who pointed it out and also for conscience's sake — **29** however, I don't mean your conscience but that of the other person. You say, "Why should my freedom be determined by someone else's conscience? **30** If I participate with thankfulness, why am I criticized over something for which I myself bless God?" **31** Well, whatever you do, whether it's eating or drinking or anything else, do it all so as to bring glory to God. **32** Do not be an obstacle to anyone — not to Jews, not to Gentiles, and not to God's Messianic Community. **33** Just as I try to please everyone in everything I do, not looking out for my own interests but for those of the many, so that they may be saved. (10:23–33)

10:28. "This meat was offered as a sacrifice": Knowingly eating meat sacrificed to idols is considered to lead to sexual immorality (cp 8:1–13).

10:28 – 33. Don't eat it, out of consideration for the person who pointed it out: A restatement of the argument presented in chapter 9 which deals with the balance of the rights of believers and the setting aside of one's rights for the sake of a weaker brother.

1 Corinthians 11

Introductory Comments

Sha'ul continues the theme of glorifying God for the sake of the *Besorah*, the Good News, the Gospel (10:26–33). As a servant of Yeshua, his life exemplifies this principle (v. 1). Therefore, the question that was being asked could have been, "What are the guiding principles for honoring and glorifying God in worship?" Verses 2-16 address this issue and are framed within the context of Jewish and Roman traditional cultural norms as well as Scripture. Unfortunately, due to a paucity of extant corroborating literature regarding the meaning of verses 2–16, these verses are extremely difficult to interpret.

In verses 17-34, Sha'ul specifies the Corinthians' celebration of the Passover seder as an example of failing to glorify God.

11:1 try to imitate me, even as I myself try to imitate the Messiah.
2 Now I praise you because you have remembered everything, I told you and observed the traditions just the way I passed them on to you. **3** But I want you to understand that the head of every man is the Messiah, and the head of a wife is her husband, and the head of the Messiah is God. **4** Every man who prays or prophesies wearing something down over his head brings shame to his head, **5** but every woman who prays or prophesies with her head unveiled brings shame to her head — there is no difference between her and a woman who has had her head shaved. **6** For if a woman is not veiled, let her also have her hair cut short; but if it is shameful for a woman to wear her hair cut short or to have her head shaved, then let

her be veiled. **7** For a man indeed should not have his head veiled, because he is the image and glory of God, and the woman is the glory of man. **8** For man was not made from woman, but woman from man; **9** and indeed man was not created for the sake of the woman but woman for the sake of the man. **10** The reason a woman should show by veiling her head that she is under authority has to do with the angels. **11** Nevertheless, in union with the Lord neither is woman independent of man nor is man independent of woman; **12** for as the woman was made from the man, so also the man is now born through the woman. But everything is from God. **13** Decide for yourselves: is it appropriate for a woman to pray to God when she is unveiled? **14** Doesn't the nature of things itself teach you that a man who wears his hair long degrades himself? **15** But a woman who wears her hair long enhances her appearance, because her hair has been given to her as a covering. **16** However, if anyone wants to argue about it, the fact remains that we have no such custom, nor do the Messianic communities of God. (11:1–16)

11:1. Try to imitate me, even as I myself try to imitate the Messiah: Follow me as I follow the Messiah (cp. 4:16; 1 Thess. 1:6).

11:2. Observe the traditions just the way I passed them on to you: The specific traditions that Sha'ul is commending the Corinthians for observing are unknown. Perhaps he is referring to the traditions concerning Passover that are mentioned in verses 23–26 or 15:3–4.

The Hebraic concept of transmitting traditions from one generation to another is known as *mesorah*. It is the careful chain of oral transmission of Jewish religious truth and/or tradition. Theologically, Orthodox Jews believe that *Moshe* (Moses) received the Torah and each of its commandments (*mitzvot*) as well as their oral commentary from G-d. The oral traditions include not only the correct interpretation of the Torah, but also the acceptable principles for leading a godly life. Tremendous care was taken to ensure that even the smallest detail was transmitted correctly.[161] This foundational belief is clearly delineated in the first mishnah in Pirkei Avot.

> Moshe Rabbeinu received the Torah from Har Sinai and transmitted it to Yehoshua, and Yehoshua to the Elders, and the Elders to the Prophets, and the Prophets transmitted it to the Men of the Great Assembly.

Several verses in the Brit Hadashah indicate that Sha'ul affirmed the practice of *mesorah*, meaning he transmitted to his talmidim that which was revealed to him by the Lord, exclusive of the oral Traditions of the Elders.

Regarding sound teaching:

> But thank God that although you used to be slaves of sin, you gave wholehearted obedience to the teaching that was handed down to you, which provides a pattern. (Rom. 6:17)[162]

Regarding the Good News:

> **3** For among the first things I passed on to you was what I also received, namely this: the Messiah died for our sins, in accordance with what the *Tanakh* says; **4** and he was buried; and he was raised on the third day, in accordance with what the *Tanakh* says (1 Cor. 15:3–4).

Sha'ul's implementation of the principle of *mesorah* in his letters represents his training as a Pharisee.

11:3–4. The head of a wife is her husband: It is clear from verses 7–16 that the paradigm regarding head coverings is the relationship between a husband and wife. The definition as to what constitutes prophecy is explained in chapter 14.

---

161. For a more detailed explanation regarding the concept of Mesorah please read "Mesorah: The Chain of Tradition," Torah.org, May 17, 2019, https://torah.org/learning/basics-primer-torah-mesorah.

162. Copyright © 2011 by Common English Bible (CEB)

11:5–6. But every woman who prays or prophesies with her head unveiled: It is a well attested fact in Judaism that the requirement for a married women is to wear a head covering (Num. 5:18).[163] This custom was not extended to unmarried females.

Perkins[164] and Ciampas and Rosner[165] present ample details concerning head coverings. To summarize their positions:

Adopting a certain hairstyle would imply a person's religious or sexual preferences. Male civil authorities or pagan priests wore head coverings when they were offering sacrifices to idols; long hair was the prevailing style for effeminate men or homosexuals.

For believers, a woman's head covering glorified God and was a symbol of piety, modesty, and her devotion to the God of Israel. Prophesying with unbound and disheveled hair could be regarded as appearing too similar to the ritual practices of the Dionysiac or Isis cult.[166] Roman society considered a shaved head to be a sign of shame. Temple priestesses, prostitutes, lesbians, and adulterers shaved their heads. An uncovered head might also suggest that a woman was withdrawing from her marriage with the implication that she was available. On the other hand, if she was coiffed with an elaborate hairstyle, it may be that she identified herself with the upper classes. In Corinth, class distinction was a significant problem that is expounded upon in verse 18.

11:7–12. For a man indeed should not have his head veiled, because he is the image and glory of God: Based on an exegesis of (Gen. 1:26–27, 2:20–25) Sha'ul considers head coverings as a reflection of the order of creation. The chain of authority in the Kingdom of God is that God who is the Ruler of the universe is the head of the Messiah; the Messiah, the Logos, who is the creator of

---

163. Amy-Jill Levine and Marc Zvi Brettler, *The Jewish Annotated New Testament*, 305.

164. Pheme Perkins, 136-139.

165. Brian S. Rosner and Roy E. Ciampa. *First Letter to the Corinthians*, 511-522.

166. Edward Adams and David G. Horrell, *Christianity at Corinth: The Quest for the Pauline Church*, 306.

all things (John 1:3) is the head of every man/husband; the head of every woman/wife who was created from Adam is her husband. A man does not cover his head because his head covering is the Messiah Yeshua. Whether the instructions concerning men's head coverings extend to a *kippah* is debatable.[167]

11:10. The reason a woman should show by veiling her head that she is under authority has to do with the angels: The exact reference to angels is speculative. Sha'ul may have been alluding to prevailing beliefs such as the following:

1. At Qumran, angels were perceived to be present at assemblies of believers and were liable to be offended by lapses of due order.[168]
2. Or, to avoid the lust of angels participating in and assisting worship (Ps. 138.1 LXX; lustful angels, like the "watchers," are mentioned in 1 En. 6–11; T. Naph. 3:5; Tg. Ps.-J. to Gen. 6:2).[169]

Later beliefs included that of:

- Guardian angels that watch over the seven churches mentioned in the book of The Revelation (Rev.1:4)

- From the writings of Tertullian. This vibrant North African writer is famous for his pithy statement that "you [women] are the devil's gateway" (*On the Apparel of Women* 1.1), an argument shortly expanded with the idea that female ornamentation was an invention of fallen angels in a nice reprise of the possible allusion to Genesis 6 in 1 Corinthians 11:10. In the end, he supports his argumentation by referring to a vision of a woman in his community, to whom an angel appeared, rapping on her bare neck and sarcastically suggesting that she expose more of her body (17:6).[170]

---

167. The custom of men wearing a head covering or kippah is post Talmudic.

168. C. K. Barrett, *The First Epistle to the Corinthians* (Peabody, MA: Hendrickson, 1968), 254.

169. Amy-Jill Levine and Marc Zvi Brettler, *The Jewish Annotated New Testament*, 304.

170. www:genius.com/LSMN

11:13–16. Decide for yourselves: Theological truth based on teleological[171] arguments can be found in Scripture. Sha'ul utilizes teleological arguments in verses 14–15 as well as in Acts 14:15–17 and Romans 1:20. Head coverings for women is the authoritative *mesorah*, or handed down tradition, of all messianic congregations.

> **17** But in giving you this next instruction I do not praise you, because when you meet together it does more harm than good! **18** For, in the first place, I hear that when you gather together as a congregation you divide up into cliques; and to a degree I believe it **19** (granted that there must be some divisions among you in order to show who are the ones in the right). **20** Thus, when you gather together, it is not to eat a meal of the Lord; **21** because as you eat your meal, each one goes ahead on his own; so that one stays hungry while another is already drunk! **22** Don't you have homes to eat and drink in? Or are you trying to show your contempt for God's Messianic community and embarrass those who are poor? What am I supposed to say to you? Am I supposed to praise you? Well, for this I don't praise you!
>
> **23** For what I received from the Lord is just what I passed on to you — that the Lord Yeshua, on the night he was betrayed, took bread; **24** and after he had made the *b'rakhah* he broke it and said, "This is my body, which is for you. Do this as a memorial to me"; **25** likewise also the cup after the meal, saying, "This cup is the New Covenant effected by my blood; do this, as often as you drink it, as a memorial to me." **26** For as often as you eat this bread and drink the cup, you proclaim the death of the Lord, until he comes.

---

171. The "teleological argument," better known as the "argument from design," is the claim that the appearance of "design" in nature—such as the complexity, order, purposefulness, and functionality of living organisms—can only be explained by the existence of a "designer" (typically of the supernatural variety).

27 Therefore, whoever eats the Lord's bread or drinks the Lord's cup in an unworthy manner will be guilty of desecrating the body and blood of the Lord! **28** So let a person examine himself first, and then he may eat of the bread and drink from the cup; **29** for a person who eats and **drinks** without recognizing the body eats and drinks judgment upon himself. **30** This is why many among you are weak and sick, and some have died! **31** If we would examine ourselves, we would not come under judgment. **32** But when we are judged by the Lord, we are being disciplined, so that we will not be condemned along with the world.

33 So then, my brothers, when you gather together to eat, wait for one another. **34** If someone is hungry, he should eat at home, so that when you meet together it will not result in judgment. As for the other matters, I will instruct you about them when I come. (11:17–34)

11:17. But in giving you this next instruction I do not praise you: Sha'ul addresses the failure to glorify God at the Passover seder. The traditions of Passover have been extensively explained in my comments on chapter 10.

1:18–22. You divide up into cliques: The divisions were based on social and economic status and it is a problem that is endemic to all cultures. The wealthier Corinthians had an abundant amount of food and drink to the point of becoming inebriated. At the same time, they neglected to fulfil their God-given obligation to provide food for the poor (cp. Isa. 58:7) so that the less fortunate could celebrate the seder with dignity and a full stomach. From time immemorial, it has always been a priority for Jewish communities to provide the economically distressed with the necessities to celebrate the seder.

The liturgy of the seder speaks to this issue and we continue this each Passover as we start our seder with "Let all who are hungry come and eat. Let all who are needy come and celebrate this seder with us." In general, poor families could not afford a lamb to slaughter while some households were too small to warrant an entire animal. Because it was incumbent upon the community to accommodate these situations, they turned to their neighbor, their friends, and even those they did not know for help.

> "Then he and his neighbor who is near his house shall take according to the number of people, everyone according to what he eats." Realizing that certain death is the opposite of sharing the wealth in times of need, our ancestors made sure that everyone was able to take care of themselves and their families.[172]

The *Tanach* prohibits humiliating the poor and hungry. The mitzvot of *Peah* (corners) and *Leket* (gleanings) reinforces this principle (Lev. 19:9–10) which is depicted in the book of Ruth (Ruth 21–23).

> [9] "When you harvest the ripe crops produced in your land, don't harvest all the way to corners of your field, and don't gather the ears of grain left by the harvesters. [10] Likewise, don't gather the grapes left on the vine or fallen on the ground after harvest; leave them for the poor and the foreigner; I am *ADONAI* your God."

11:23. I passed on to you: In respect to the bread and the wine, Sha'ul passed on Passover traditions to the Corinthians (the concept of mesorah) that he directly received from the Lord. David Flusser explains that as a Pharisee, Sha'ul was accustomed to first drink the cup which was followed by eating the matzah. The Essenes in a fashion like the followers of Yeshua partook of the matzah followed by the cup of wine.[173]

---

172. https://www.sefaria.org/sheets/113839?lang=bi Sharing the Paschal Lamb by AJWS StaffAJWS Staff

173. David Flusser, *Judaism and the Origins of Christianity*, 202-206.

Points to ponder: Robert Eisenman in his book *The Dead Sea Scrolls and the First Christians* arrives at the conclusion that the Teacher of Righteousness at Qumran was James, the brother of Yeshua. He claims that many of the rituals practiced by believers were identical to those that were practiced at Qumran and that sections of the Brit Hadashah are replete with Qumranisms.[174] For Orthodox Jewish scholars like Heinrich Graetz, Yeshua could be identified as an Essene, whose purpose was not to create a new religion but rather to reform Judaism.[175]

11:26. For as often as you eat this bread and drink the cup, you proclaim the death of the Lord, until he comes: Another aspect of the Seder is that it expresses an eschatological hope in the future and final Messianic redemption.[176]

11:28–34. So let a person examine himself first: A failure to examine one's conduct and motives regarding their participation during the seder leads to sickness or death.

---

174. Robert H. Eisenman, *The Dead Sea Scrolls and the First Christians: Essays and Translations* (Nashville, 2013), Chapter 9.

175. www.simonjjoseph.com

176. David Flusser, *Judaism and the Origins of Christianity,* 206.

1 CORINTHIANS 12

INTRODUCTORY COMMENTS

Since Shavuot is considered to be the concluding phase of Passover (Pesikta 30:163)[177], Sha'ul in this chapter, strategically answers the question that was posed to him concerning spiritual manifestations, literally "spirituals" (*pneumatikon*). Shavout was the Biblical feast on which God chose to pour out His Ruach on all His servants (Acts 2:1ff). It was an eschatological event that was predicted in Scripture (Joel 2:28–32; Matt. 3:1–5) and fulfilled Moshe's wish that God would bestow His Ruach on all people (Num. 11:29).

The words from Joel "blood, fire and thick smoke" that is quoted in Acts 2:17–21 are apocalyptic portents[178] and is a phrase that also appears in the Passover Haggadah. Rabbi Joseph Elias in his commentary on the Haggadah states: "This verse, quoted from Joel, speaks of the Messianic redemption rather than of the Exodus."[179]

In what sense does Shavuot complement Passover? It completes the celebration of the Exodus by rejoicing in the great bounty which the land, blessed by the Almighty, had given.[180] Rashi interprets

---

177. Abraham P. Bloch, *The Biblical and Historical Background of the Jewish Holy Days*,

178. A. Cohen, *The Twelve Prophets: Hebrew Text & English Translation with Introductions and Commentary* (London: Soncino Press, 1985), 73.

179. Nosson Scherman, Avie Gold, and Sheah Brander, *Hagadah Shel Pesaḥ Transliterated Linear Haggadah* (Brooklyn: Mesorah, 2004), 127.

180. Abraham P. Bloch, *The Biblical and Historical Background of the Jewish Holy Days*.

Isaiah 11 as indicating that in the Last Days, the Messiah will appear and gather the Jewish people from the four corners of the earth and return them to the promised land 11:6-11.[181] Yeshua states that this will take place at the time of his return (Mathew 24; Mark 13; Luke 21). The Messiah will be anointed with manifestations of the Spirit (11:1, 61:1-3) which are alluded to in verses 4-11.

The manifestations of the Spirit are then compared to the parts of a body (v.v. 12-13). Parallel discussions can be found in the Qumran writing.[182]

> **12:1** But, brothers, I do not want you to go on being ignorant about the things of the Spirit. **2** You know that when you were pagans, no matter how you felt you were being led, you were being led astray to idols, which can't speak at all. **3** Therefore, I want to make it clear to you that no one speaking by the Spirit of God ever says, "Yeshua is cursed!" and no one can say, "Yeshua is Lord," except by the *Ruach HaKodesh.* (12:1-3)

12:1. The things of the Spirit: The Corinthians had an incomplete knowledge concerning the manifestations of the Spirit. Sha'ul's answer indicates that their question was not just limited to manifestations during worship but the application of the things of the Spirit for ministry and everyday life.

Even though the word "gifts" (*charismaton*) does not appear in verse 12:1, most versions of the Bible translate *pneumatikon* as "spiritual gifts." Gifts are a subcategory of manifestations (10:4).

12:3. "Yeshua is Lord": One point of confusion was that spiritual gifts such as ecstatic utterances also manifested themselves during worship that took place in pagan temples. These moments of ecstasy

---

181. I. W. Slotki and A. J. Rosenberg, *Isaiah: Hebrew Text & English Translation* (New York: Soncino Press, 1987), 56.

182. David Flusser, *Judaism and the Origins of Christianity*, 54-60.

occurred when a person was demon possessed. A parallel example is Elijah's confrontation with the prophets of Baal when they danced around a pagan altar while calling on their god (1 Kings 18:18ff). Sha'ul reassures them that a person under the control of a demon spirit could only curse Yeshua and never say "Yeshua is Lord." Only those people who have been cleansed and filled with the Spirit of God can proclaim "Yeshua is Lord!"

> **4** Now there are different kinds of gifts, but the same Spirit gives them. **5** Also there are different ways of serving, but it is the same Lord being served. **6** And there are different modes of working, but it is the same God working them all in everyone. **7** Moreover, to each person is given the particular manifestation of the Spirit that will be for the common good. **8** To one, through the Spirit, is given a word of wisdom; to another, a word of knowledge, in accordance with the same Spirit; **9** to another, faith, by the same Spirit; and to another, gifts of healing, by the one Spirit; **10** to another, the working of miracles; to another, prophecy; to another, the ability to judge between spirits; to another, the ability to speak in different kinds of tongues; and to yet another, the ability to interpret tongues. **11** One and the same Spirit is at work in all these things, distributing to each person as he chooses. (12:4-11)

12:4–11. Now there are different kinds of gifts: Sha'ul then introduces the concept of the diversity of spiritual manifestations that God has provided for the body of the Messiah. These "gifts" have been given for the mutual benefit of each member of the faith community and to affirm the reality of the Good News (cp. Mark 16:15–18). It is important to note that the *pneumatikon* that are mentioned were not intended to be all inclusive. Additional "spirituals" are listed in Romans 12:6–8.

The manifestations are divided into three subcategories which, according to Gordon Fee, unintentionally suggest that the diversity of gifts have their roots in the triune God. [183] Grace gifts (*charismaton* 12:4) are inspired utterances such as words of wisdom, words of knowledge, prophecy and tongues which are bestowed by the Holy Spirit. (The significance of the grace gifts of prophecy and tongues will be explained in my comments on chapter 14.). The ability to serve people (*diakonion* 12:5; cp.12:28) is evidenced by those such as deacons, apostles, and teachers and comes from the Lord (*Kurios*), "Lord" being the equivalent for the Lord Yeshua. Modes of working (*diaireseis energematon* 12:6) include manifestations of power such as faith, healing, and miracles (cp. Acts 10:38).

> **12** For just as the body is one but has many parts; and all the parts of the body, though many, constitute one body; so it is with the Messiah. **13** For it was by one Spirit that we were all immersed into one body, whether Jews or Gentiles, slaves or free; and we were all given the one Spirit to drink.
>
> **14** For indeed the body is not one part but many. **15** If the foot says, "I'm not a hand, so I'm not part of the body," that doesn't make it stop being part of the body. **16** And if the ear says, "I'm not an eye, so I'm not part of the body," that doesn't make it stop being part of the body. **17** If the whole body were an eye, how could it hear? If it were all hearing, how could it smell? **18** But as it is, God arranged each of the parts in the body exactly as he wanted them. **19** Now if they were all just one part, where would the body be? **20** But as it is, there are indeed many parts, yet just one body. **21** So the eye cannot say to the hand, "I don't need you"; or the head to the feet, "I don't need you." **22** On the contrary, the parts of the body that seem to be less important turn out to be all the more necessary;

---

183. Gordon D. Fee, *The First Epistle to the Corinthians*, 647.

23 and upon body parts which we consider less dignified we bestow greater dignity; and the parts that aren't attractive are the ones we make as attractive as we can, **24** while our attractive parts have no need for such treatment. Indeed, God has put the body together in such a way that he gives greater dignity to the parts that lack it, **25** So that there will be no disagreements within the body, but rather all the parts will be equally concerned for all the others. **26** Thus if one part suffers, all the parts suffer with it; and if one part is honored, all the parts share its happiness. (12:12–26)

12:12–26. For just as the body is one but has many parts; and all the parts of the body, though many, constitute one body; so it is with the Messiah: This analogy underscores an important underlying spiritual truth that the diverse parts of the body of believers are unified by becoming one with the Messiah (v. 27). The diverse parts of the body of the Messiah can only function as an integrated interdependent system (cp. Rom. 12:4–5). Some commentators think that the emphasis on unity also evokes the motif of the Shema: just as the "Lord is One," the body is one.

27 Now you together constitute the body of the Messiah, and individually you are parts of it. **28** And God has placed in the Messianic Community first, emissaries; second, prophets; third, teachers; then those who work miracles; then those with gifts of healing; those with ability to help; those skilled in administration; and those who speak in various tongues. **29** Not all are emissaries, are they? Not all are prophets, are they? or teachers? or miracle-workers? **30** Not all have gifts of healing, not all speak in tongues, not all interpret, do they? **31** Eagerly seek the better gifts. But now I will show you the best way of all. (12:27–31)

12:28–30. And God has placed in the Messianic Community: The healthy and beneficial expressions of manifestations are dependent upon God's appointed servants whom he gave to equip the saints for the purpose of maintaining unity.

> **11** And [His gifts to the (body of believers) were varied and] He Himself appointed some as apostles [special messengers, representatives], some as prophets [who speak a new message from God to the people], some as evangelists [who spread the Good News of salvation], and some as pastors and teachers [to shepherd and guide and instruct], **12** [and He did this] to fully equip *and* perfect the saints (God's people) for works of service, to build up the (universal) body of (the Messiah); **13** until we all reach oneness in the faith and in the knowledge of the Son of God, [growing spiritually] to become a mature believer, reaching to the measure of the fullness of (the Messiah) [manifesting His spiritual completeness and exercising our spiritual gifts in unity]. (Eph. 4:11–13)

12:31. But now I will show you the best way of all: In the next chapter Sha'ul informs the Corinthians that the guiding principle that empowers each manifestation is unconditional love.

1 CORINTHIANS 13

INTRODUCTORY COMMENTS

The concluding theme of chapter 12 (v. 31) that only sincere expressions of godly love can unify the body of believers is seamlessly carried over into this chapter. The Corinthians were not manifesting the gifts of the spirit, especially tongues and prophecy in a loving manner.[184]

To address this problem, Sha'ul builds upon Hillel's well known statement concerning God's love to illustrate his point.

> A non-Jew came before Shammai and said, "I will convert if you can teach me the entire Torah while I stand on one foot." Shammai pushed the non-Jews aside with the ruler that was in his hand. The non-Jew came before Hillel and Hillel converted him saying, "What is hateful to you, do not do to your neighbor, that is the entire Torah, the rest is just commentary, now go and study." (Shabbat 31:6)

Hillel's comments are an exegesis of Leviticus 19:17–18:

> **17**You shall not hate your brother in your heart; you shall rebuke your fellow, and do not bear a sin because of him. **18**You shall not take revenge, and you shall not bear grudge against the members of your people, you shall love your companion as yourself: I am God.

> **13:1** I may speak in the tongues of men, even angels; but if I lack love, I have become merely blaring brass or a cymbal clanging.

---

184. Sha'ul expounds upon this problem in the following chapter.

2 I may have the gift of prophecy,
I may fathom all mysteries, know all things,
have all faith — enough to move mountains;
but if I lack love, I am nothing.
3 I may give away everything that I own,
I may even hand over my body to be burned;
but if I lack love, I gain nothing.
4 Love is patient and kind, not jealous, not boastful,
5 not proud, rude, or selfish, not easily angered,
and it keeps no record of wrongs.
6 Love does not gloat over other people's sins
but takes its delight in the truth.
7 Love always bears up, always trusts,
always hopes, always endures.
8 Love never ends; but prophecies will pass,
tongues will cease, knowledge will pass.
9 For our knowledge is partial, and our prophecy partial;
10 but when the perfect comes, the partial will pass.
11 When I was a child, I spoke like a child,
thought like a child, argued like a child;
now that I have become a man,
I have finished with childish ways.
12 For now we see obscurely in a mirror,
but then it will be face to face.
Now I know partly; then I will know fully,
just as God has fully known me.
13 But for now, three things last —
trust, hope, love;
and the greatest of these is love.

13:1. Love: David Stern furnishes an excellent definition for the word love:

> The word in Greek for "love" is "agape." defined in the New Testament (by passages such as this chapter, John 3:16, 17:23–26 and 1 John 2:5–4:21) as giving of and from oneself: love expresses itself in acts of benevolence, kindness and

mercy in which heart, mind and will are united because they are motivated and empowered by God. Such love goes beyond what one can generate of oneself, because it has its origin in God. When such love is experienced by one person from another, the experience is of God's love channeled through that other.[185]

Yeshua, in Matthew 7:21–23, addresses the consequences of those who only manifest the gifts of the Spirit devoid of sincere expressions of *gemilut chassidim* – acts of lovingkindness (cp. Matt. 25:31–46).

> **21** "Not everyone who says to me, 'Lord, Lord!' will enter the Kingdom of Heaven, only those who do what my Father in heaven wants. **22** On that Day, many will say to me, 'Lord, Lord! Didn't we prophesy in your name? Didn't we expel demons in your name? Didn't we perform many miracles in your name?' **23** Then I will tell them to their faces, 'I never knew you! Get away from me, you workers of lawlessness!'

13:2. Gift of prophecy: Sha'ul understood prophetic ministry to be essential to the building up of the body of the Messiah. Fee asserts that for Sha'ul, prophecy consisted of "spontaneous, Spirit-inspired, intelligible messages, orally delivered in the gathered assembly, intended for the edification or encouragement of the people."[186]

There is also a pastoral dimension to the gift of prophecy, in that, as Thiselton states,

> "[it] combines pastoral insight into the needs of persons, communities, and situations with the ability to address these with a God-given utterance or longer discourse (whether unprompted or prepared with judgment, decision, and rational

---

185. David H. Stern, in *Jewish New Testament Commentary: A Companion Volume to the Jewish New Testament*, 481.

186. Brian S. Rosner and Roy E. Ciampa, in *First Letter to the Corinthians*, 581.

reflection) leading to challenge or comfort, judgment, or consolation, but ultimately building up the addressees." [187]

13:8. Tongues will cease: The gift and place of tongues is further discussed in 14:2.

13:13. But for now, three things last — trust, hope, love; and the greatest of these is love: Believers must pursue the way of love because love never fails. Only love can heal the multiple sources of division within the Corinthian body of believers.
Sha'ul writes:

> **6** When we are united with the Messiah Yeshua, neither being circumcised nor being uncircumcised matters; what matters is trusting faithfulness expressing itself through love. (Galatians 5:6)

---

187. Ibid.

1 Corinthians 14

Introductory Comments

One of the subtle underlying themes of chapter 13 was to prepare the Corinthians for his treatise concerning the proper role of prophecy and tongues. The exercise of these gifts had descended into chaos and instead of building up the members of the body, these utterances were confusing and dividing the faith community.

Pursue love!

> **14:1** However, keep on eagerly seeking the things of the Spirit; and especially seek to be able to prophesy. **2** For someone speaking in a tongue is not speaking to people but to God, because no one can understand, since he is uttering mysteries in the power of the Spirit. **3** But someone prophesying is speaking to people, edifying, encouraging, and comforting them. **4** A person speaking in a tongue does edify himself, but a person prophesying edifies the congregation. (14:1–4)

14:1. Pursue love: The orderly and beneficial manifestation of spiritual gifts is dependent upon a heart that is filled with godly love and whose characteristics are described in chapter 13. Pride, not godly love, was the root cause of all the mania and confusion that was occurring at Corinth.

14:1[b]. Prophesy: In the "Last Days" prophetic words regardless of gender, social status or age will be proclaimed by God's people (Joel 2:28–32; Matt. 3:1–5; Acts 2:17–21). Words of prophecy are a springboard for salvation. Please refer to my previous comments on the nature of prophecy that are included on 13:2.

14:2. Speaking in a tongue: All the evidence of chapter 14 is consistent with the understanding of tongues as discourse directed toward God. Paul explicitly says that those who speak in tongues "do not speak to other people but to God.

The exact definition of "tongues" remains ambiguous and elusive. Parallels to tongues are attested to at Qumran,[188] in the Testament of Job,[189] Pythian divinization, and Dionysiac enthusiasm."[190] Dale Martin has argued that the ability to speak through spiritual power and not through the use of the mind (such as in ecstatic speech) would have been considered a high-status activity, lending itself to be abused as a sign of spiritual superiority.[191]

> **5** I wish you would all speak in tongues, but even more I wish you would all prophesy. The person who prophesies is greater than the person who speaks in tongues, unless someone gives an interpretation, so that the congregation can be edified.
>
> **6** Brothers, suppose I come to you now speaking in tongues. How can I be of benefit to you unless I bring you some revelation, knowledge, prophecy, or teaching? **7** Even with lifeless musical instruments, such as a flute or a harp, how will anyone recognize the melody if one note can't be distinguished from another? **8** And if the bugle gives an unclear sound, who will get ready for battle? **9** It's the same with you: how will anyone know what you are saying unless you use your tongue to produce intelligible speech? You will be talking to the air! **10** There are undoubtedly all kinds of sounds in the world, and none is altogether meaningless; **11** but if I don't know what a person's sounds mean, I will be a foreigner to the speaker and the speaker will be a foreigner to me. **12** Likewise with you:

---

188. David Flusser, *Judaism and the Origins of Christianity*, 59.

189. www.thecripplegate.com/the-tongues-of-angels/

190. Hans Conzelmann *et al*, 234.

191. Brian S. Rosner and Roy E. Ciampa, 585.

since you eagerly seek the things of the Spirit, seek especially what will help in edifying the congregation.

13 Therefore someone who speaks in a tongue should pray for the power to interpret. **14** For if I pray in a tongue, my spirit does pray, but my mind is unproductive. **15** So, what about it? I will pray with my spirit, but I will also pray with my mind; I will sing with my spirit, but I will also sing with my mind. **16** Otherwise, if you are giving thanks with your spirit, how will someone who has not yet received much instruction be able to say, *"Amen,"* when you have finished giving thanks, since he doesn't know what you are saying? **17** For undoubtedly you are giving thanks very nicely, but the other person is not being edified. **18** I thank God that I speak in tongues more than all of you, **19** but in a congregation meeting I would rather say five words with my mind in order to instruct others than ten thousand words in a tongue! (14:5-19)

14:5–19. The point of verses 5–19 is that speaking in a tongue doesn't edify the congregation if tongues are not accompanied by interpretation, which implies that tongues together with the interpretation of tongues are equal to the gift of prophecy.

14:13. Someone who speaks in a tongue should pray for the power to interpret: The gift of the interpretation of tongues is to translate or to interpret the words that have been uttered into the language of those present.

20 Brothers don't be children in your thinking. In evil, be like infants; but in your thinking, be grown-up. **21** In the *Torah* it is written,

"By other tongues,
by the lips of foreigners
I will speak to this people.
But even then, they will not listen to me,"
says *ADONAI.*

22 Thus tongues are a sign not for believers but for unbelievers, while prophecy is not for unbelievers but for believers. **23** So if the whole congregation comes together with everybody speaking in tongues, and uninstructed people or unbelievers come in, won't they say you're crazy? **24** But if you all prophesy, and some unbeliever or uninstructed person enters, he is convicted of sin by all, he is brought under judgment by all, **25** and the secrets of his heart are laid bare; so, he falls on his face and worships God, saying, "God is really here among you!" (14:20–25)

14:21. In the Torah it is written: As usual, Sha'ul appeals to Scripture (Isa. 28:11–12) to correct this problem. The extremely complicated circuitous nature of his reasoning affirms the Corinthians' sophisticated level of scholarship that enabled them to grasp the essence of his argument.

14:20–25. Thus, tongues are a sign not for believers but for unbelievers, while prophecy is not for unbelievers but for believers. C. K. Barrett unfolds the reasoning that underlies Sha'ul's argument.

> "It was probably the phrase 'men of other tongues' that caught Paul's eye and suggested the application of Isaiah 28:11-12 to his discussion of 'tongues.' It is this, rather than the historical setting of the prophecy, in which Isaiah threatens his people, who have failed to listen to his words, with the foreign speech of Assyrian invaders, that is in Paul's mind. His point is simply that (according to the Lord himself) when he speaks to men by means of strange tongues they will not listen-that is, they will not hear in obedience and faith. Tongues therefore are (as Paul has said throughout the chapter) ineffective as a means by which persons other than the speaker may be built up. It follows from this (i.e., from the fact that God has foretold that the wonder of strange tongues will not be attended to) that tongues serve as sign not for the believing, but for the unbelieving. In what sense? Presumably, as a sign of judgment, as in, for example, a

nearby passage in Isaiah (xx. 3), in which the naked and barefooted prophet is a sign of impending doom, of military overthrow and social servitude. When they are not met with faith (cf. Heb. iv. 2), tongues serve to harden and thus to condemn the unbeliever (cf. verses 23 f.)."[192]

26 What is our conclusion, brothers? Whenever you come together, let everyone be ready with a psalm or a teaching or a revelation, or ready to use his gift of tongues or give an interpretation; but let everything be for edification. **27** If the gift of tongues is exercised, let it be by two or at most three, and each in turn; and let someone interpret. **28** And if there is no one present who can interpret, let the people who speak in tongues keep silent when the congregation meets — they can speak to themselves and to God. **29** Let two or three prophets speak, while the others weigh what **is** said. **30** And if something is revealed to a prophet who is sitting down, let the first one be silent. **31** For you can all prophesy one by one, with the result that all will learn something and all will be encouraged. **32** Also, the prophets' spirits are under the prophets' control; **33** for God is not a God of unruliness but of *shalom*. (14:26–33)

14:32. The prophets' spirits are under the prophets' control:

An important aspect of godly love is self-restraint which is conducive to the peaceful, beneficial, and orderly dissemination of spiritual giftings.

33b As in all the congregations of God's people, **34** let the wives remain silent when the congregation meets; they are certainly not permitted to speak out. Rather, let them remain subordinate, as also the *Torah* says; **35** and if there is something they want to know, let them ask their own husbands at home; for it is shameful for a woman to speak out in a congregational meeting.

---

192. C. K. Barrett, *The First Epistle to the Corinthians*, 322-323.

> **36** Did the word of God originate with you? Or are you the only people it has reached? **37** If anyone thinks he is a prophet or is endowed with the Spirit, let him acknowledge that what I am writing to you is a command of the Lord. **38** But if someone doesn't recognize this, then let him remain unrecognized. (14:33^{b}–38)

14:34–35. Let the wives remain silent when the congregation meets: Sha'ul adds that women are contributing to the disorder during congregational meetings. Since women are permitted to publicly prophesy (11:5), the issue is woman engaging in conversations with their husbands during a service.

Sha'ul's reference to the synagogue custom of men and women sitting in separate sections separated by a dividing wall (*mechitzah*) as is the custom of Orthodox Judaism is unsubstantiated.

Rabbi Sylvia Rothschild in her compelling essay "Chayei Sarah: how Sarah's legacy got lost," arrives at the same conclusion. She includes evidence to substantiate her claim from a variety of sources including the Brit Hadashah (Acts 1:13–14; Gal. 3:28).[193]

> "These [male disciples] all continued with one accord in prayer and supplication, with the women, and Mary the mother of Jesus, and his brothers." (Acts 1:13–14)

In her essay, she further says that according to Professor Shmuel Safrai of the Hebrew University:

> It is clear "from numerous sources" that women attended synagogue in antiquity, but that "there were no women's galleries or any other known form of sex separation in synagogues." He acknowledges that there might have been some internal division of sexes (for example women seated to

---

193. https://rabbisylviarothschild.com/tag/mechitza/#_edn8

the side or to the back), but if there were, "there are no contemporaneous sources to describe them."[194]

Let them remain subordinate: Sha'ul's reference to the Torah is pertaining to the chain of authority that God established at creation (Gen. 2:21–25, 3:16). Please see my comments 11:7–12.

14:37. What I am writing you is a command of the Lord: Knowing that the Corinthians would have an extremely difficult time regarding his instructions, Sha'ul bluntly tells them that what he is saying is not his opinion but a direct command from the Lord. This command does not appear in the B'rit Hadashah but as John explains:

> But there are also many other things Yeshua did; and if they were all to be recorded, I don't think the whole world could contain the books that would have to be written! (John 21:25)

It is likely that Sha'ul received this command as a revelation or from one of the compendiums of sayings of Yeshua[195] which were like the sayings of the Rabbis in the Mishnah.

> **39** So, my brothers, eagerly seek to prophesy; and do not forbid speaking in tongues; **40** but let all things be done in a proper and orderly way. (14:39–40)

14:39–40. Even though prophecy is preferred, tongues are not forbidden. The bottom line is that godly love should be the motivating factor for the expression of spiritual gifts, not pride. Godly love engenders order, edification, and shalom!

---

194. "Was There a Woman's Gallery in the Synagogue of Antiquity? - Tarbiz," The Bornblum Eretz Israel Synagogues Website, May 14, 2019, https://synagogues.kinneret.ac.il/bibliography/was-there-a-womans-gallery-in-the-synagogue-of-antiquity-tarbiz/.

195. William D. Davies, *Paul and Rabbinic Judaism: Some Rabbinic Elements in Pauline Theology*, 141.

1 CORINTHIANS 15

INTRODUCTORY COMMENTS

Sha'ul's detailed explanation regarding the resurrection of the dead reflects an apocalyptic belief that was associated with Pharisaic messianism. Pharisaic messianism can be defined as:

> A hope for membership in an already existent heavenly kingdom to be brought from heaven by a suddenly appearing messiah: for general judgment in which the righteous should be acquitted and the wicked condemned; for resurrection of the body and a life everlasting for the righteous; for an endless age in which God and happiness should be supreme and enjoyed forever by those whom he had justified.[196]

It is interesting to note that at the beginning of this letter he emphasizes the crucifixion (1:17–2:16) and concludes with the resurrection which is the cornerstone and foundation of the Good News (15:1ff).

> **15:1** Now, brothers, I must remind you of the Good News which I proclaimed to you, and which you received, and on which you have taken your stand, **2** and by which you are being saved — provided you keep holding fast to the message I proclaimed to you. For if you don't, your trust will have been in vain. **3** For among the first things I passed on to you was what I also received, namely this: the Messiah died for our sins, in accordance with what the *Tanakh* says; **4** and he was

---

196. www.jstor.org/stable/3137007.189.

buried; and he was raised on the third day, in accordance with what the *Tanakh* says; 5 and he was seen by Kefa, then by the Twelve; 6 and afterwards he was seen by more than five hundred brothers at one time, the majority of whom are still alive, though some have died. 7 Later he was seen by Ya'akov, then by all the emissaries; 8 and last of all he was seen by me, even though I was born at the wrong time.9 For I am the least of all the emissaries, unfit to be called an emissary, because I persecuted the Messianic Community of God. 10 But by God's grace I am what I am, and his grace towards me was not in vain; on the contrary, I have worked harder than all of them, although it was not I but the grace of God with me. 11 Anyhow, whether I or they, this is what we proclaim, and this is what you believed. (15:1–11)

15:1. I must remind you of the Good News which I proclaimed to you: Sha'ul is answering the following question: "As it relates to the Good News, what is the significance of the resurrection?"

15:3–4. For among the first things I passed on to you was what I also received: Sha'ul once again refers to the authoritative chain of transmission (*mesorah*) which he received as a direct revelation from Yeshua (11:23). The revelation he received is confirmed in the Tanach. Yeshua is the suffering servant who is depicted in Isaiah 53.[197] The sacrifice of the Messiah was vicarious (Isa. 53:4–6,8–10). He was buried (Isa. 53:9) and resurrected (Isa. 53:11–12). And, like the prophet Jonah being in the belly of a great fish, the Mashiach remained in the grave for three days and three nights (Matt. 12:40).

The concept of a suffering Messiah is well attested to in Jewish literature. In a similar manner to John 19:37 and Revelation 1:7, the sages understood Zechariah 12:10 — the one who was pierced — as applying to a suffering Messiah, namely Messiah son of Joseph

---

197. Samuel Rolles Driver, *The "Suffering Servant" of Isaiah According to the Jewish Interpreters* (New York, N.Y: Hermon Press, 1969).

(Sukkah 52). The belief in the suffering Messiah son of Joseph who is followed by the conquering Messiah son of David already existed during the time of Judas Maccabaeus (167–160 B.C.E.). The popular apocalyptic Book of Enoch (90:37–38) which speaks of the Messiah son of David and the Messiah son of Joseph was well known during the time of the Maccabees.[198]

15:5–7. And he was seen: One proof of the resurrection was the testimonies of people who claimed to have seen and interacted with the resurrected Yeshua. The following question is often posed to prove the resurrection. "Would a person die for a lie, which he knows is a lie, but that would not profit him anything?"

Chuck Colson, former special counsel to President Nixon, gives a personal example of why the eyewitness accounts of Yeshua's resurrection are fact, not fiction.

> When the Watergate scandal broke, he and 11 other men— some of the toughest and most powerful in the world—met secretly, came up with a story, and swore to maintain it. But these powerful men broke. Quickly. Colson said, "I know the resurrection is a fact, and Watergate proved it to me. How? Because 12 men testified, they had seen Jesus raised from the dead, then they proclaimed that truth for 40 years, never once denying it. Everyone was beaten, tortured, stoned, and put in prison. They would not have endured that if it weren't true. Watergate embroiled 12 of the most powerful men in the world—and they couldn't keep a lie for three weeks. You're telling me 12 apostles could keep a lie for 40 years? Absolutely impossible."[199]

15:8. I was born at the wrong time: This phrase is one of Sha'ul's most heart wrenching statements. "Born at the wrong time"

---

198. David Flusser, *Judaism and the Origins of Christianity*, 424.

199. www.jdgreear.com/will-people-die-for-lie/

compares his life to that of a child who was intended to be aborted but survived and lived. Through the hand of the living God, he has escaped the death intended for him and now the life that he leads is by faith in the Son of God who gave his life for him (Gal. 2:20). This realization is the foundation for his zeal to proclaim the Good News.

> **12** But if it has been proclaimed that the Messiah has been raised from the dead, how is it that some of you are saying there is no such thing as a resurrection of the dead? **13** If there is no resurrection of the dead, then the Messiah has not been raised; **14** and if the Messiah has not been raised, then what we have proclaimed is in vain; also your trust is in vain; **15** furthermore, we are shown up as false witnesses for God in having testified that God raised up the Messiah, whom he did not raise if it is true that the dead are not raised. **16** For if the dead are not raised, then the Messiah has not been raised either; **17** and if the Messiah has not been raised, your trust is useless, and you are still in your sins. **18** Also, if this is the case, those who died in union with the Messiah are lost. **19** If it is only for this life that we have put our hope in the Messiah, we are more pitiable than anyone. (15:12–19)

15:12. How is it that some of you are saying there is no such thing as a resurrection of the dead: It is difficult to ascertain which elements at Corinth rejected the reality of the resurrection. Their backgrounds were Sadduceeic or forms of Hellenistic philosophy.

15:19. We are more pitiable than anyone: The message of the Besorah (Good News) is the crucifixion of the Messiah (1:23; 2:1–2), and the hope of the resurrection is the cornerstone of its message. If the resurrection of Yeshua is a delusion, then believers are, out of all the inhabitants of the earth, the most miserable and to be pitied above everyone else.

> **20** But the fact is that the Messiah *has* been raised from the dead, the firstfruits of those who have died. **21** For since death

came through a man, also the resurrection of the dead has come through a man. [22] For just as in connection with Adam all die, so in connection with the Messiah all will be made alive. [23] But each in his own order: the Messiah is the firstfruits; then those who belong to the Messiah, at the time of his coming; [24] then the culmination, when he hands over the Kingdom to God the Father, after having put an end to every rulership, yes, to every authority and power. [25] For he has to rule until he puts all his enemies under his feet. [26] The last enemy to be done away with will be death, [27] for "He put everything in subjection under his feet."[a] But when it says that "everything" has been subjected, obviously the word does not include God, who is himself the one subjecting everything to the Messiah. [28] Now when everything has been subjected to the Son, then he will subject himself to God, who subjected everything to him; so that God may be everything in everyone. (15:20–28)

15:20. Firstfruits: The translation of this term as "firstfruits" can be misunderstood as it is then frequently confused with *Bikkurim* – the firstfruits offering that is associated with Shavuot (Deut. 26:1–11). The more accurate translation is "the first barley harvest" עֹמֶר רֵאשִׁית קְצִירְכֶם (*omer reisheit kehtzirchem*), which is a ritual that is associated with Passover.[200] Judaism does not consider this "First Barley Harvest Offering" to be a separate Feast (Lev. 23:9–15) but incorporates it as a specific activity as part of Passover.

There was a difference of opinion as to when the *omer* was to be presented.

> Leviticus 23 says that the omer should be sacrificed "on the morrow after Shabbat." But it turns out that the interpretation of this passage was a matter of acrimonious disagreement between the rabbis and the members of the sect known as

---

200. Menachem Moshe Oppen, *The Korban Mincha: A Pictorial Guide to the Korban Mincha* (Lakewood, NJ: CIS Publishers, 1988), 40.

Boethusians. Like the Sadducees, the Boethusians rejected the authority of the rabbis and offered their own interpretations of the Torah, especially on matters of the calendar and Temple rituals.

In this case, they believed that Leviticus should be read literally, so that the omer would be brought on the day after the first Shabbat after the first day of Passover. The rabbis, on the other hand, understood the words "the morrow after Shabbat" to refer not to an ordinary Shabbat—what the rabbis call a "Shabbat of Creation," commemorating God's resting on the seventh day—but simply as a "day of rest," which can also refer to a festival. In this case, they say, it refers to the first day of Passover. This means that the omer is always offered on the same calendar date—the 16th of Nisan, the second day of Passover—and so Shavuot is always on the same date, 50 days later, which is the sixth of Sivan."[201]

Yeshua rose from the dead on the First Day of the Week following the first Shabbat after the first day of Passover. (Matt. 28:1–10; Mark 16:1–8; Luke 24:1–11; John 20:1–30). Since he is called the "First Harvest" of the resurrection, it is reasonable to assume that his disciples had embraced the Sadducees' interpretation.

The offering of the omer was a sacrifice that was known as the *Korban Omer*. In addition to the regular Passover offering, a lamb was offered together with an *omer* of barley taken from the first harvest of the land of Israel. Unique among offerings in the Temple, the Omer offering was brought with great fanfare.[202]

On the day before the festival of Passover, the agents of the court would go out [to the field] and tie [the barley] into bundles while it was still attached to the ground so that it would be easy to reap. On the evening after [the first day of]

---

201. www.tabletmag.com/sections/belief/articles/daf-yomi-256-flour-power-omer
202. Rambam, *Hilchot Temidin U'Musafin 7*

Passover, all the inhabitants of all the neighboring villages would gather so that it would be reaped with much flourish. They would have three men reap three *se'ah* of barley in three baskets with three sickles... After reaping, they would bring the barley to the Temple courtyard, where they beat, winnowed, and roasted the kernels over the fire in a cylinder. The kernels were then spread out in the Temple courtyard and the wind wafted through it. The barley was then brought to a mill and ground to produce three *se'ah* 4 (approximately 6.5 gal.), and after it had been sifted with 13 sifters, an *issaron* 5 (one-tenth) was removed.

This *issaron* of fine barley flour was taken and mixed with oil, and a handful of frankincense was placed upon it. It was waved in the eastern portion of the Temple courtyard in all four directions—up, down, right, and left. It was then brought close to the tip of the southwest corner of the altar like the other meal offerings. A handful of the meal was taken and offered on the altar's pyre. The remainder was eaten by the priests like the remainder of all other meal offerings." [203]

The 16th of Nisan begins a fifty-day period of the counting of the omer, which culminates with the offering of the two loaves (*shtei halechem*) which took place on Shavuot. This counting between these two offerings is known as the *Sefirat Ha-omer* or the counting of the omer (Lev. 23:15). The actual feast that should be translated as "Firstfruits" (*Bikkurim*) is associated with Shavuot (Deut. 26:1–11; Exod. 23:16).

The connection of the *Korban Omer* or "sacrifice of the omer of barley" with the sacrifice of Yeshua is clear. The resurrection is compared to the death of a seed that was planted in the ground which

---

203. www.chabad.org/library/article_cdo/aid/4354506/jewish/What-Was-the-Omer-Offering-Korban-Haomer.htm

springs forth from the earth (John 12:24). The seed could be wheat or some other grain (15:35–36).

> **24** Yes, indeed! I tell you that unless a grain of wheat that falls to the ground dies, it stays just a grain; but if it dies, it produces a big harvest.

> **36** Look, fool! When you put a seed into the ground, it doesn't come back to life unless it dies. **37** What you put in the ground doesn't have the shape that it will have, but it's a bare grain of wheat or some other seed.[204]

15:22. Adam: Please see my comments on 15:42–49

15:23. The Messiah is the firstfruits; then those who belong to the Messiah, at the time of his coming: Yeshua's death and resurrection is the first harvest which points to the certainty of a future greater harvest namely, the resurrection of all those who believe in him.

15:24. The culmination: This is a reference to Daniel 12:1–3 which heralds the advent of the Messianic era.[205]

> **12:1** "When that time comes, Mikha'el, the great prince who champions your people, will stand up; and there will be a time of distress unparalleled between the time they became a nation and that moment. At that time, your people will be delivered, everyone whose name is found written in the book. **2** Many of those sleeping in the dust of the earth will awaken, some to everlasting life and some to everlasting shame and abhorrence. **3** But those who can discern will shine like the brightness of heaven's dome, and those who turn many to righteousness like the stars forever and ever.

---

204. Common English Bible (CEB), 2011.

205. Judah J. Slotki, Ephraim Oratz, and Shalom Shahar, *Daniel; Ezra; Nehemiah: Hebrew Text & English Translation* (London: Soncino Press, 1994), 101.

15:27. The last enemy: Death was considered an enemy that could never be defeated. Sha'ul then midrashically applies various Scriptures (Ps. 8:7; 15:32; Isa. 22:13, 25:8; 56:12; Hos. 13:14) that indicate that Yeshua's death and resurrection have conquered the previously thought to be the unconquerable foe, death. God has placed all things including death under Yeshua's feet.

> **29** Were it otherwise, what would the people accomplish who are immersed on behalf of the dead? If the dead are not actually raised, why are people immersed for them? **30** For that matter, we ourselves — why do we keep facing danger hour by hour? **31** Brothers, by the right to be proud which the Messiah Yeshua our Lord gives me, I solemnly tell you that I die every day. **32** If my fighting with "wild beasts" in Ephesus was done merely on a human basis, what do I gain by it? If dead people are not raised, we might as well live by the saying, "Let's eat and drink, for tomorrow we die!"[b] **33 Don't be fooled. "Bad company ruins good character." 34 Come to your senses! Live righteously and stop sinning! There are some people who lack knowledge of God — I say this to your shame.**

15:29. Immersed on behalf of the dead: The custom that this phrase is alluding to is of unknown origin. It is probably referring to the preparation of a body prior to burial which included a ceremonial washing. This mitzvah was and is still carried out under the auspices of the *Chevra Kadishah.* [206]

> **35** But someone will ask, "In what manner are the dead raised? What sort of body do they have?" **36** Stupid! When you sow a seed, it doesn't come alive unless it first dies. **37** Also, what you sow is not the body that will be, but a bare seed of, say, wheat or something else; **38** but God gives it the body he intended for it; and to each kind of seed, he gives its own body. **39** Not all living matter is the same living matter; on the

---

206. Sacred Society, *Moed Katan,* 27b.

contrary, there is one kind for human beings, another kind of living matter for animals, another for birds and another for fish. **40** Further, there are heavenly bodies and earthly bodies; but the beauty of heavenly bodies is one thing, while the beauty of earthly bodies is something else. **41** The sun has one kind of beauty, the moon another, the stars yet another; indeed, each star has its own individual kind of beauty. **42** So it is with the resurrection of the dead. When the body is "sown," it decays; when it is raised, it cannot decay. **43** When sown, it is without dignity; when raised, it will be beautiful. When sown, it is weak; when raised, it will be strong. **44** When sown, it is an ordinary human body; when raised, it will be a body controlled by the Spirit. If there is an ordinary human body, there is also a body controlled by the Spirit. **45** In fact, the *Tanakh* says so: Adam, the first man, became a living human being; but the last "Adam" has become a life-giving Spirit. **46** Note, however, that the body from the Spirit did not come first, but the ordinary human one; the one from the Spirit comes afterwards. **47** The first man is from the earth, made of dust; the second man is from heaven. **48** People born of dust are like the man of dust, and people born from heaven are like the man from heaven; **49** and just as we have borne the image of the man of dust, so also, we will bear the image of the man from heaven. (15:35–49)

15:36–38. Seed: Every year, thousands of Greeks took part in the mystery rites at Eleusis which were based on the story of Demeter's search for Kore. The rituals had to do with "death" and "rebirth" which were interwoven with the theme of the hope of human immortality. Sha'ul was familiar with this story and its associated rituals. [207] Since the Corinthians were also familiar with the celebration at Eleusis, it makes sense that Sha'ul would utilize the metaphor of the seed to explain Yeshua's death and resurrection.

---

207. David John Williams, *Paul's Metaphors: Their Context and Character*, 39-40.

15:42. So it is with the resurrection: The body that is sown in the ground is raised to life by the Ruach HaKodesh. Sha'ul explained the same idea to the Roman believers:

> 11 And if the Spirit of the One who raised Yeshua from the dead is living in you, then the One who raised the Messiah Yeshua from the dead will also give life to your mortal bodies through his Spirit living in you. (Rom. 8:11)

15:45–49. The first man Adam: A complicated theology is centered around the first man Adam who is known by the Kabbalists as *Adam Kadmon*. Sha'ul simplifies this concept in the following manner: All humankind shares in the life and death of the human body of the first man Adam. The body dies because of Adam's sin (Rom. 5:12). [208] However, if they confess Yeshua as Lord, all humankind can share in the eternal, resurrected, and transformed eternal body of the Messiah Yeshua who is the second man Adam.[209]

> 50 Let me say this, brothers: flesh and blood cannot share in the Kingdom of God, nor can something that decays share in what does not decay. 51 Look, I will tell you a secret — not all of us will die! But we will all be changed! 52 It will take but a moment, the blink of an eye, at the final *shofar*. For the *shofar* will sound, and the dead will be raised to live forever, and we too will be changed. 53 For this material which can decay must be clothed with imperishability, this which is mortal must be clothed with immortality. 54 When what decays puts on

---

208. Adam's sin introduced mortality (see Gen 3.19), a widespread interpretation (Wis 2.24; 1 En. 69.11; L.A.E. 44.1; Apoc. Mos. 14.2; L.A.B. 13.8; Gen. Rab. 8.11; 16.6; Sifra 27a). Made alive, resurrected, (Dan 12.2; 2 Macc7.9ff.; T. Sim. 6.7; T. Jud. 25.1, 4; T. Zeb. 10.2; T. Benj. 10.7; 1 En. 51.1–2, Pss. Sol. 2.31; 3.12; m. Sanh. 10.1; b. Sanh. 90b–91a; Maimonides, *Commentary on the Mishnah*, Sanhedrin 10.1). Amy-Jill Levine and Marc Zvi Brettler, *The Jewish Annotated New Testament*, 311.

209. For the history of the development of the concept of the first man and second man Adam please refer to *Paul and Rabbinic Judaism* by W. D. Davies, pages 35-57.

imperishability and what is mortal puts on immortality, then this passage in the *Tanakh* will be fulfilled:

"Death is swallowed up in victory.

55 "Death, where is your victory?
Death, where is your sting?"

56 The sting of death is sin; and sin draws its power from the *Torah*; 57 but thanks be to God, who gives us the victory through our Lord Yeshua the Messiah!

58 So, my dear brothers, stand firm and immovable, always doing the Lord's work as vigorously as you can, knowing that united with the Lord your efforts are not in vain. (15:50-58)

15:51. But we will all be changed! Please see my comments on 15:20; 36–38.

15:52–56 Final Shofar: The eternal victory over the enemy death will be announced by the final sounding of the Shofar. (Isa. 27:13; Zech. 9:14; Matt. 24:31; 1 Thess. 4:16; Rev. 8:2)

The phrase "on that day" (*bah yom hahu*) (Isa. 27:13) is a technical term for "the last days."

13 On that day a great *shofar* will sound.
Those lost in the land of Ashur will come,
also those scattered through the land of Egypt;
and they will worship ADONAI
on the holy mountain in Yerushalayim.

Similarly, in 1 Thessalonians 4:13–18, Sha'ul paraphrases the words of Yeshua to restore the Thessalonians' hope in the resurrection.

13 Now, brothers, we want you to know the truth about those who have died; otherwise, you might become sad the way other people 14 do who have nothing to hope for. For since we believe that Yeshua died and rose again, we also believe that in the same way God, through Yeshua, will take with him those who have died. 15 When we say this, we base it on the Lord's

own word: we who remain alive when the Lord comes will certainly not take precedence over those who have died. **16** For the Lord himself will come down from heaven with a rousing cry, with a call from one of the ruling angels, and with God's *shofar*; those who died united with the Messiah will be the first to rise; **17** then we who are left still alive will be caught up with them in the clouds to meet the Lord in the air; and thus we will always be with the Lord. **18** So encourage each other with these words.

1 CORINTHIANS 16

INTRODUCTORY COMMENTS

Sha'ul concludes his letter by addressing a question about the collection for the believers in Jerusalem (16:1–4) and he then mentions his tentative travel plans. He will remain in Ephesus, go to Jerusalem for Shavuot and then come to Corinth (16:5–9). Next, he provides some updates with respect to some of his ministry companions who are known to the Corinthians (16:10–19). Sha'ul ends his letter with a final greeting and blessing (16:21–24).

> **16:1** Now, in regard to the collection being made for God's people: you are to do the same as I directed the congregations in Galatia to do. **2** Every week, on *Motza'ei-Shabbat*, each of you should set some money aside, according to his resources, and save it up; so that when I come I won't have to do fundraising. **3** And when I arrive, I will give letters of introduction to the people you have approved, and I will send them to carry your gift to Yerushalayim. **4** If it seems appropriate that I go too, they will go along with me. (16:1–4)

16:1. The collection: The collection was intended for the needy believers in Jerusalem (15:3).

16:2. *Motza'ei-Shabbat*: David Stern, the author of the *Complete Jewish Bible*, explains the reason he chose the phrase *Motza'ei-Shabbat* instead the "first day of the week" in this passage:

> Every week, on *Motza'ei-Shabbat*. The Hebrew expression means, literally, "departure of the Sabbath." It signifies Saturday night. It translates the Greek phrase which means

"every one of a week," that is, every first day of the week. The question is: does this refer to Saturday night or to Sunday?

In favor of the idea that "every one of a week" means Sunday are these points:

(1) Gentiles did not keep Shabbat.

(2) By the Roman system of timekeeping days began at midnight.

(3) There is good documentation that the Gentile churches have observed Sunday as a day of worship since very early times. Specifically, Ignatius writes in the early second century of Sunday as "the Lord's Day," commemorating the day Yeshua rose from the grave. This we know to have been Sunday from Matthew 28:1 and Luke 24:1; Mark 16:2 pinpoints it as "just after sunrise" on the first day of the week, that is, Sunday morning. (But Revelation 1:10 is speaking of the eschatological Day of Judgment, not Sunday.)

In favor of the idea that "every one of a week" means Saturday night are these points:

(1) The use of "one" rather than "first" shows that Sha'ul was thinking in Hebrew, not Greek (see the Hebrew of Genesis 1:5).

(2) In the Jewish calendar, days commence at sundown, so that the "first day of the week" refers to any time between sunset Saturday and sunset Sunday.

(3) In the early days of the Messianic Community, Jewish believers continued to observe Shabbat as a day of rest and met for Messianic worship in the evening after it was over.

(4) There were Jews, prominent ones, in the Corinthian congregation, so that Sha'ul would not have dealt with it as a Gentile congregation.

(5) The only other use of this Greek phrase in connection with Sha'ul speaks of an evening event where he preached so

> long that Eutychus went to sleep and fell off the window
> ledge; this was probably Saturday night (see Acts 20:7).
>
> (6) Sunday could not have been regularly celebrated by the
> early Jewish believers as Shabbat or as a *yom tov*
> ("festival," literally, "good day") because, since Judaism
> prohibits handling money on such days, Sha'ul would
> never have suggested taking up a collection then to a
> congregation with Jews in it.

I believe the reasons for Saturday night outweigh those for Sunday and accordingly translate the Greek phrase by "Moiza 'ei-Shabbat."

While the New Testament does not abrogate Shabbat as the holy day of rest for Jews stipulated in the Fourth Commandment, it also contains no command concerning a proper day for Messianic worship. At the founding of the Messianic Community the believers met together every day (Acts 2:46). In conclusion, what makes sense to me is that a Messianic Jewish congregation can choose any day (or days) of the week for Messianic worship, but worship elements specific to Shabbat should be included only on Shabbat (Friday sundown to Saturday sundown).[210]

> **5** I will visit you after I have gone through Macedonia, for I am
> intending to pass through Macedonia, **6** and I may stay with
> you or even spend the winter, so that you may help me
> continue my travels wherever I may go. **7** For I don't want to
> see you now, when I am only passing through; because I am
> hoping to spend some time with you if the Lord allows it. **8** But
> I will remain in Ephesus until *Shavu'ot,* **9** because a great and
> important door has opened for my work, and there are many
> people opposing me. (16:5–9)

---

210. David H. Stern, *Jewish New Testament Commentary: A Companion Volume to the Jewish New Testament*, 490-491.

16:8. *Shavu'ot*: Shavuot, also known as Pentecost, is one of the three "pilgrimage" feasts.

> Three times a year all your men are to appear in the presence of ADONAI your God in the place which he will choose — at the festival of matzah, at the festival of Shavu'ot and at the festival of Sukkot. They are not to show up before ADONAI empty-handed. (Deut. 16:16)

The mention of Shavout was a subtle reminder of both Yeshua's resurrection and the outpouring of the Ruach HaKodesh.

10 If Timothy comes, see that he has nothing to be afraid of while he is with you; for he is doing the Lord's work, just as I am. **11** So let no one treat him with disrespect. Help him on his way in peace, so that he will return to me, for the brothers and I are expecting him.

12 As for brother Apollos, I strongly urged him to go and visit you along with the other brothers; and although it was not at all his desire to come at this time, he will come when he has the opportunity.

13 Stay alert, stand firm in the faith, behave like men, grow strong. **14** Let everything you do be done in love.

15 Now, brothers, you know that the household of Stephanas were the first people in Achaia to put their trust in the Messiah, and they have devoted themselves to serving God's people. **16** I urge you to submit yourselves to people like these and to everyone who works and toils with them. **17** I am glad that Stephanas and Fortunatus and Achaicus are here, because they have helped make up for your not being here. **18** They have refreshed my spirit, just as they have yours. I want you to show appreciation for people like these.

19 The congregations in the province of Asia send greetings to you. Aquila and Priscilla greet you in union with the Lord, as does the congregation that meets in their house. **20** All the brothers send you, their greetings. Greet one another with a holy kiss. (16:10–20)

16:10–18. If Timothy comes: Beginning with Timothy, Sha'ul mentions the believers from Corinth who had joined him to aid him with his ministry at Ephesus. Timothy (Acts 18:5; 1 Cor. 4:17); Apollos (Acts 18:24; 1 Cor. 3:4); Stephanus (1 Cor. 1:16); Fortunatus (he only appears in verse 17; cf. Lightfoot on Clement of Rome, 1 Cor. 59(65 [ET]); Achaicus (he only appears in verse 17—Achaia is a strip of land between the gulf of Corinth in the north and Elis and Arcadia in the south); and Aquila and Pricilla (Acts 18:2;18).

> **21** Now, I Sha'ul, greet you in my own handwriting.
> **22** If anyone does not love the Lord, a curse on him! Marana, ta! [Our Lord, come!]
> **23** May the grace of the Lord Yeshua be with you.
> **24** My love is with you all, in union with the Messiah Yeshua. (16:21–24)

16:21. I Sha'ul, greet you in my own handwriting: Sha'ul's letters were normally dictated and written by an amanuensis who was, in this case, presumed to be Sosthenes (1:1). The fact that Sha'ul signed his own letter was his way of personalizing his concerns for his beloved Corinthians (16:24).

16:22. Marana, ta! [Our Lord, come!]: The *Theological Dictionary of the New Testament* gives several interpretations as to the significance of the Aramaic expression *Maranta*. It could mean "the Lord came," "the Lord is present," or, more than likely, "Lord come." "Lord come" is an expression of the waiting and longing of the faith community for the Lord's coming again in glory.[211] When Yeshua returns, all believers will become united in the eschatological body of

---

211. Gerhard Kittel and Geoffrey W. Bromiley, *Theological Dictionary of the New Testament, Volume 4* (Grand Rapids: Eerdmans, 1977), 466, 563.

the Mashiach. He will establish his Kingdom and as a result all factions, theological differences, misunderstandings, and whatever else divides believers will disappear.

16:23. May the grace of the Lord Yeshua be with you: Sha'ul encapsulates his letter with greetings of grace (1:3 and 16:23). Grace is the ultimate expression of God's love for humankind as demonstrated by the sacrifice of Yeshua. If the Corinthians would take into consideration that "by God's grace, without earning it, all are granted the status of being considered righteous before him, through the act redeeming us from our enslavement to sin that was accomplished by the Messiah Yeshua (Rom. 3:24)" then all the differences between them would be of no consequence, and, like the Lord, they would cast their neighbors' sins into the sea of forgetfulness (Mic. 7:19). For additional on God's grace please see my comments on 1:13.

THE HISTORICAL RELIABILITY OF THE BOOK OF ACTS

Any commentary on the Book of 1 Corinthians must grapple with the wide range of scholarly opinions regarding the reliability of the historicity of the Book of Acts because it gives an account of Sha'ul's ministry in Corinth (Acts 18:1–18).

W. Ward Gasque states:

> The serious student of the New Testament does not progress extremely far in his research before he becomes aware of the wide variety of opinions which exist in the world of New Testament scholarship. What to one scholar represents 'the assured results of modern criticism' is regarded by another as 'a most unlikely and, indeed, untenable hypothesis of speculative scholarship.' There are several reasons for these differences of opinion—e.g., differences in theological and philosophical presuppositions among the critics, the fragmentary and select nature of the historical data, and the use of differing historical methodologies. Some of the differences of opinion and approach (though by no means all) stem from the fact that scholars find themselves representing traditions of scholarship which have quite diverse historical roots.[212]

Some scholars give limited credence to the historical reliability of the Book of Acts. Academics, such as Haenchen and Munck, concede that The Book of Acts does contain some accurate historical

---

212. W. Ward Gasque, The Historical Value of the Book of Acts: The Perspective of British Scholarship, *Theologische Zeitschrift 28* (1972), 177-196.

data. Haenchen is aware that some details in Acts formerly deemed inaccurate have been vindicated by more recent discoveries.[213]

Johannes Munck, overall, has more respect for Acts as a historical source than has Haenchen; but he also thinks that it is unreliable as our primary source of information about Paul. (Munck; AB, LXVI-LXX and passim.) He, as well as expositors, such as William F. Orr and James Walther, accept the position that information about Paul should be garnered from his epistles, treating them as the original sources of information and Acts as a secondary source.[214]

Regarding the date of the composition of 1 Corinthians, Hans Conzelman writes that "the real facts can be derived from the epistles of Paul and the narrative of Acts."[215]

Greg Boyd in his article, "Is the Book of Acts Reliable?" states that one can be confident in the historical reliability of The Book of Acts. To support his contention, he points to the writings of Eduard Meyer, who is the greatest classical historian in the twentieth century. Meyer maintained that Luke should be regarded as one of the greatest historians of classical antiquity based on the evidence. Hengel notes that Meyer's conviction "will seem mad to some 'historical-critical' commentators—if only because they are so unfamiliar with ancient history writing and its problems."[216]

The problem is that liberal scholars cannot conceive that historical reliability and theological perspectives can be compatible. This problematical opinion is clearly stated in *The Jewish Annotated New Testament*. "Whatever historical information may be present in Acts, the selection of events, their ordering, the content of the speeches, and many of the details were determined by the theological and literary interests of the author."[217]

---

213. William Fridell Orr, *I Corinthians: A New Translation, and Introduction with a Study of the Life of Paul, Notes*, 49.

214. Ibid, 65.

215. Hans Conzelmann, *et al, 1 Corinthians: A Commentary on The First Epistle to the Corinthians*, 10.

216. E. Meyer, *Ursprung und Anfange des Christentums*, I (Berlin: Stuggart, 1921), 2ff.

217. *Jewish Annotated New Testament*

Yeshua's Last Passover Seder

One of the most moving events in Yeshua's life was the last meal that he shared with his Talmidim prior to his becoming the Pesach sacrifice. It is ironic that although this meal is called a seder - which means "order," the exact order of that evening's events is not definitively laid out in Scripture. Each of the four Gospels only presents a partial view of the seder. Based on the details found in Mattityahu (Matthew), Mark, Luke, and Yochanan (John), as well as current Jewish scholarship, I have reconstructed the probable order of Yeshua's Pesach seder.

Please remember that even though Yeshua's seder shares similarities with the Pesach seder that we observe today, differences exist with the order, scope, and sequence of a first century seder, especially a seder that was conducted prior to the destruction of the Beit HaMigdash (Temple) in 70 C.E.

The table at which Yeshua and his *talmidim* reclined was known as a *triclinium* - a low three-sided table with the fourth side of the table left open, presumably to allow service to the table. Jews reclined throughout much of the seder, a tradition that is mentioned in the Mishnah. The common explanation is that reclining was a sign of freedom in ancient days.

The seating arrangements were a specific order. Facing the triclinium from the open side and then looking to the left side of the table, Yochanan would have been reclining on the first seat followed by Yeshua reclining on the second seat. On the third seat and to the left of Yeshua was Y'hudah (Judah) from K'riot (Iscariot). Y'hudah's seat - the third seat - was known as the seat of honor. (John 13:23)

Yeshua began the seder with **Kaddish**, the sanctification of the meal by the blessing over the first cup of wine. There were only two cups used in first century seders prior to the destruction of the Temple in 70 C.E. (Luke 22:17–1).

After everyone washed their hands, **U'rchatz** (implied), Yeshua added to the order of the seder by washing his *talmidim's* feet (John 13:1-17).

Yeshua continued with **Korech**. He dipped the matzah into the *maror* (bitter herbs) and gave it to Y'hudah. It is possible that the act of dipping included the making of a matzah sandwich of maror and charoset (John 13:26). *Charoset* (also spelled *haroset* or *charoses*, in Hebrew: חֲרוֹסֶת) is a sweet, dark-colored paste made of fruits and nuts eaten at the Passover seder. Its color and texture are meant to recall mortar (or mud used to make adobe bricks) which the Israelites used when they were enslaved in ancient Egypt as mentioned in Tractate Pesahim (page 116a) of the Talmud. The word "charoset" comes from the Hebrew word *cheres* — חרס — "clay."[218]

Yeshua then preceded to explain the meaning of Pesach as it related to his death and resurrection. His explanation is the equivalent of the **Maggid** or the telling of the Pesach story. Some of the topics covered were "Love one another," "I Am the Way," "I will send you the Comforter," and "I am the True Vine" (John 13:34; 14:6; 14:15–21; 15:1).

Buried in the text are the **Four Questions**, though scholarship claims that there were only three questions at that time. Yochanan records an extensive interchange of questions and answers between Yeshua and his *talmidim*. Yeshua explains to his talmidim *Mah nishtanah halaylah hazeh mikol halaylot?* "Why *is* this night different from all other nights?" In Yochanan 13:33, Yeshua calls

---

218. https://en.wikipedia.org/wiki/Charoset.

his talmidim "my children," which I believe is an implicit reference to the "Four (or Three) Questions" typically asked by the children at the seder. (John 13:31–17:33).

They then ate the Pesach meal which is known as **Shulchan Orech**.

At the end of the meal, Yeshua broke the matzah and gave a piece to each of his *talmidim*. This section of the seder is known as **Tzafun** (Luke 22:19). Yeshua then blessed the second cup of wine and tied the significance of the second cup to the Brit Hadashah, New Covenant, calling it the cup of the New Covenant which was prophesied by Jeremiah (Luke 22:20; Jer. 31:31–37).

Yeshua and his talmidim concluded their seder by singing the **Hallel** – Tehillim (Psalms 113–118; Matt. 26:30).

I hope that this brief article has clarified the Order as well as the scope and sequence of Yeshua's Last Pesach seder on earth.

BIBLIOGRAPHY

1 CORINTHIANS

A. Bockmuehl. *Revelation and Mystery in Ancient Judaism and Pauline Christianity*. Eugene, OR: Wipf & Stock, 2009.

Abrahams, Israel. *Studies in Pharisaism and the Gospels*. Eugene, OR: Wipf & Stock, 2004.

Adams, Edward and David G. Horrell. *Christianity at Corinth: The Quest for the Pauline Church*. Louisville, KY: Westminster, John Knox Press, 2013.

Askowith, Dora. *The Toleration and Persecution of the Jews in the Roman Empire*. New York: Andersite, 1915.

Barrett, C. K. *The First Epistle to the Corinthians*. Peabody, MA: Hendrickson, 1968.

Bloch, Abraham P. *The Biblical and Historical Background of the Jewish Holy Days*. New York: KTAV, 1978.

Boccaccini, Gabriele and Carlos A. Segovia. *Paul the Jew: Rereading the Apostle as a Figure of Second Temple Judaism*. Minneapolis: Fortress Press, 2016.

Bokser, Baruch M. *Origins of the Seder: The Passover Rite and Early Rabbinic Judaism*. Berkeley: University of California Press, 2021.

Bornkamm, Günther. *Paul, Paulus*. Minneapolis: Fortress Press, 1995.

Boyarin, Daniel. *A Radical Jew: Paul and the Politics of Identity*. Berkeley: University of California Press, 1994.

Boyd, Greg. "Is The Book of Acts Reliable?" ReKnew. December 20, 2018. https://reknew.org/2018/12/is-the-book-of-acts-reliable/.

Conzelmann, Hans, *et al. 1 Corinthians: A Commentary on The First Epistle to the Corinthians*. Philadelphia: Fortress Press, 1975.

Cohen Shaye J. *The Beginnings of Jewishness: Boundaries, Varieties, Uncertainties*. Berkeley: Univ. of California Press, 2009.

Cook, John Granger. *Roman Attitudes Toward the Christians: From Claudius to Hadrian*. Tübingen: Mohr Siebeck, 2010.

Davies, William D. *Paul and Rabbinic Judaism: Some Rabbinic Elements in Pauline Theology*. London: SPCK, 1979.

Driver, Samuel Rolles. *The "Suffering Servant" of Isaiah According to the Jewish Interpreters*. New York: Hermon Press, 1969.

Eisenman, Robert H. *The Dead Sea Scrolls and the First Christians: Essays and Translations*. Nashville, 2013.

Fee, Gordon D. *The First Epistle to the Corinthians*. Grand Rapids: William B. Eerdmans Publishing Company, 2014.

Fitzmeyer, Joseph A. *1 Corinthians*. New York: Doubleday, 2007.

Flusser, David. *Judaism and the Origins of Christianity*. Jerusalem: Magnes Press, 1988.

Fredriksen, Paula. *Paul: The Pagan's Apostle*. New Haven: Yale University Press, 2018.

Freedman, Harry and A. J. Rosenberg. *Jeremiah: Hebrew Text & English Translation*. London: Soncino Press, 1985.

Garland, David E. *1 Corinthians*. Grand Rapids: Baker Academic, 2008.

Garroway, Joshua D. *Paul's Christians as Gentile-Jews: Neither Jew nor Gentile, but Both*. Basingstoke: Palgrave Macmillan, 2012.

Hayes, Christine E. *Gentile Impurities and Jewish Identities: Intermarriage and Conversion from the Bible to the Talmud*. New York: Oxford University Press, 2002.

Judge, Edwin Arthur and James R. Harrison. *The First Christians in the Roman World: Augustan and New Testament Essays*. Tübingen: Mohr Siebeck, 2008.

Keener, Craig S. *Acts. An Exegetical Commentary, Volume 3*. Grand Rapids: Baker Academic, 2014.

Kitov, Ēliyyāhû. *The Book of Our Heritage*. Jerusalem: Feldheim, 1997.

Lachs, Samuel Tobias. *A Rabbinic Commentary on The New Testament: The Gospels of Matthew, Mark, and Luke*. Hoboken: KTAV, 1987.

Levine, Amy-Jill and Marc Zvi Brettler. *The Jewish Annotated New Testament*. Oxford: Oxford Univ Press, 2017.

Lightfoot, John. *Acts—1 Corinthians*. Peabody, MA: Hendrickson Publishers, 1997.

Litfin, Duane. *St. Paul's Theology of Proclamation: 1 Corinthians 1-4 and Greco-Roman Rhetoric*. Cambridge: Cambridge University Press, 1994.

Murphy-O'Connor, J., James H. Charlesworth and Pierre Benoit. *Paul and the Dead Sea Scrolls*. New York: Crossroad, 1990.

Neusner, Jacob and Bruce Chilton. *In Quest of the Historical Pharisees*. Waco, TX: Baylor University Press, 2007.

——— *Judaism in the Beginning of Christianity*. Philadelphia: Fortress Press, 1984.

———*The Idea of Purity in Ancient Judaism: The Haskell Lectures, 1972-1973*. Eugene, OR: Wipf and Stock, 2006.

Oppen, Menachem Moshe. *The Korban Mincha: A Pictorial Guide to the Korbān Mincha*. Lakewood, NJ: CAIS Publishers, 1988.

Perkins, Pheme. *1 Corinthians, Paideia: Commentaries on the New Testament*. Grand Rapids: Baker Book House, 2012.

Rosner, Brian S., and Roy E. Ciampa. *First Letter to the Corinthians*. Nottingham, UK: Apollos, 2010.

Rudolph, David. "The Circumcised Apostle: Paul and Jewish Identity in 1 Corinthians 9:19-23." Academia.edu, June 4, 2017. https://www.academia.edu/33325804/The_Circumcised_Apostle_Paul_and_Jewish_Identity_in_1_Corinthians_9_19_23.

Shulam, Joseph, and Hillary LeCornu. *A Commentary on the Jewish Roots of Acts,* Jerusalem: Netivyah Bible Instruction Ministry, 2003.

Stern, David H. *Complete Jewish Bible: An English Version of The Tanakh (Old Testament) and B'rit Hadashah (New Testament).* Clarksville, MD: Messianic Jewish Publishers, 2017.

————*Jewish New Testament Commentary: A Companion Volume to the Jewish New Testament.* Clarksville, MD: Messianic Jewish Publishers, 1999.

Stone, Michael E. *Jewish Writings of the Second Temple Period: Apocrypha, Pseudepigrapha, Qumran, Sectarian Writings, Philo, Josephus.* Vol. 2. Assen, Netherlands: Van Gorcum, 1984.

The Bornblum Eretz Israel Synagogues Website. "Was There a Woman's Gallery in the Synagogue of Antiquity?" May 14, 2019. https://synagogues.kinneret.A.il/bibliography/was-there-a-womans-gallery-in-the-synagogue-of-antiquity-tarbiz/.

Williams, David John. *Paul's Metaphors: Their Context and Character.* Peabody, MA: Hendrickson Publishers, 2007.

Winter, Bruce William. *Philo and Paul among the Sophists.* Cambridge: Cambridge University Press, 1997.

Witherington, Ben. *Conflict and Community in Corinth: A Socio-Rhetorical Commentary on 1 and 2 Corinthians.* Grand Rapids: W. B. Eerdmans, 1995.

Wright, N. T. *Paul: In Fresh Perspective.* Minneapolis: Fortress Press, 2009.

Yee, Tet-Lim N. *Jews, Gentiles, and Ethnic Reconciliation: Paul's Jewish Identity and Ephesians.* Cambridge: Cambridge University Press, 2008.

2 Corinthians

Countering Messianic Madness

Dr. Jeffrey Seif

Acknowledgements

When one feels indebted to so many, finding words of acknowledgement and selecting names to acknowledge becomes difficult. I'll most certainly forget some important people and, among those remembered, words won't do justice.

Dr. Barri Seif, my best friend and life partner, traveled down this road with me. Because there's so much about me that would not exist if she didn't exist, it's hard to find words.

A long-deceased mentor at Moody Bible Institute, Dr. Louis Goldberg, modeled how to be true to the biblical witness, on one hand, and express its truths in ways that comported to Jewish sensibilities.

My former doctoral advisor at Southern Methodist University, the late Dr. Billy Abraham, was a guiding light in my academic career. Encouragement from my present doctoral advisor at Cambridge University, Dr. Matt Bland, puts wind in my sails that wouldn't otherwise be blowing. Though my studies at Cambridge are not in theology, the incessant press for creative thinking and evidence-pursuit leave lasting impressions.

I am very thankful for my very good friend, Rabbi Barry Rubin, who pulled me aside and encouraged me to undertake the task, to be part of the New Testament commentary series he is publishing. Were it not for his repeated efforts, this volume would have never come to term.

A Bible college and seminary professor of thirty years, myself, I am also thankful to all the students who have patiently suffered under my tutelage.

I, of course, am thankful for the LORD. Absent a touch from Israel's Messiah years ago, I would not have a heart and mind for such a project.

Lastly, I am thankful for my students and my readers. It is your concern for biblical study that has always kept me going. I thank you all.

Dr. Jeffrey Seif
August, 2023

PREFACE

In his classic *Pentateuch & Haftorahs*, Dr. J. H. Hertz, the former Chief Rabbi of the British Empire, said his goal was to write an accessible, one-volume "People's Commentary." Another British scholar, the Anglican scholar Dr. N. T. Wright, more-recently penned an easy-to-read commentary on 1 and 2 Corinthians, published under the title *Paul for Everyone*. In both cases, the premium was on opening the Bible to individuals who were not part of the professional theologian's guild. Similarly, my principal purpose here is to unpack 2 Corinthians—along with 1 Corinthians—and make the Messianic Jewish rabbi who penned them, Paul/Sha'ul, more accessible to "everyone."

Some things he said in the Corinthian correspondence are hard to understand. What did Rabbi Sha'ul/Paul mean when he said: "Hand over such a person to the Adversary [i.e., Devil] for destruction" (1 Cor. 5:5), and "Let the wives remain silent... they are not permitted to speak" (1 Cor. 14:34)? Did he forbid women to speak, and condone handing men over to the devil? What is one to make of these and other hard-to-fathom statements? Herein, we will explore these, and other, difficult sayings in 1 Corinthians, and endeavor to better understand the Rabbi from Tarsus based on how he followed up on those issues in 2 Corinthians. Dr. Yosef Koelner's commentary on 1 Corinthians serves as an excellent addition. Because this volume reaches back to 1 Corinthians, it provides an introduction to both letters.

Individuals who desire to know more of the Bible, and more about the personal God of which it speaks, benefit from theological inquiry. The personal interest that propels you to place a short volume like this in your hand will hopefully pay dividends. Not wanting to just talk about the Bible, in this volume 2 Corinthians—with its backreferencing to 1 Corinthians—is cited from cover to cover. Though various versions of the text were consulted and referenced, Dr. David Stern's renditions, as published in his well-known *Complete Jewish Bible*, are employed throughout. In addition to leaning on Dr. Stern's classic Messianic Jewish version, we also worked with and from his *Jewish New Testament Commentary*. It, similarly, is liberally cited throughout, as is the *Complete Jewish Study Bible* that employs his text.

Beyond Dr. Stern's direct influences, I opted to lean on a new resource from Oxford University Press: *The Jewish Annotated New Testament (JANT)*. The *JANT* opted to use the Revised Standard Version for its principal biblical text. Edited by Professor Amy-Jill Levine and Professor Marc Zvi Brettler, the insightful volume was packed with worthy commentary from these Jewish Studies professors, all of whom were interested in looking at the New Testament through Jewish eyes. From the *JANT*, I made use of helpful contributions from Jewish Studies scholars: Professor Shira Lander and Professor Allen Avery-Beck. Unlike the aforementioned Oxford group, Dr. Stern and I are Messianic Jewish commentators. My wife Barri, herself a Messianic Jewish scholar, helped as well. Our purpose here is to shed light on a major New Testament document, and the circumstances behind their writing.

I had the privilege of formally studying the Corinthian correspondences with Professor Victor Paul Furnish, when a graduate student at Southern Methodist University. His detailed commentary *II Corinthians: A New Translation with Introduction and Commentary* (Doubleday) is a standard in the industry. That work, coupled with insights gleaned by studying under him, have left an indelible impression on my understanding of the literature and on my style of presenting it. Professor Gordon D. Fee's commentary *The First Epistle to the Corinthians* (Eerdmans) was similarly a considerable influence and is enlisted herein. Combined, both contain 1500 pages of technical text. As is the case with much academic writing, the high quality and high quantity make the work product above the reach of the average reader. I, by contrast, endeavored to write an introductory, Messianic Jewish commentary introducing the Corinthian correspondences—2 Corinthians principally, though not exclusively. I wanted one that was serious, scholarly, and reachable—particularly for individuals who are *not* professional religious workers.

WHY DID SHA'UL/PAUL WRITE 1 AND 2 CORINTHIANS IN THE FIRST PLACE?

As you'll see, sometime after Rabbi Sha'ul pioneered and left the fledgling community he'd fathered in Corinth, contentious people emerged, exerted influence and advocated perspectives different than his own. A wealthy patroness who was loyal to Sha'ul named Chloe wrote a letter and sent it to him through dispatches. That handwritten letter, along with the verbal report of the messengers who delivered it, gave Rabbi Sha'ul a window into toxic developments in Corinth. 1 Corinthians was Sha'ul's initial response, and 2 Corinthians was his follow-up to it. Through an examination of both, readers get a window into Sha'ul's oft-times precarious world and how he dealt with people and circumstances in it. Here, through a more decidedly Jewish examination of both, you will hopefully see Sha'ul as a Messianic rabbi at work in his first century context. Special attention will be given to understanding the exigent circumstances that prompted his writings in the first century of the Christian era, along with the ebb and flow of his responses. Principles will be extracted to help us manage affairs in the twenty-first century, all the while. The better part of the book is written in the past tense, however, to facilitate modern readers' understanding they are going back two-thousand years in time, and to another place in time. The purpose for this is to help readers understand that ancient world—and then apply the understanding to the modern one.

Sha'ul had received an alarming letter from a loyal patron in Corinth, who apprised him of divisive and deteriorating situations in the community. In vv. 11-12 he reported: "Some of Chloe's people have made it known to me, my brothers, that there are quarrels among you. I say this because one of you says, 'I follow Sha'ul'; another says, 'I follow Apollos'; another, 'I follow Kefa'; while still another says, 'I follow the Messiah!'" When Sha'ul wrote, he couldn't even be sure they'd receive his correction. He was reassured here, evidenced in this follow-up letter.

In 1 Corinthians, as elsewhere, he noted he was being undermined by factions. The last faction noted explicitly, the "I follow the Messiah" group, was noted implicitly over and over again later on in this letter and the next. Suffice it to say here at the outset, this group harked then—as now—to those who claim to be super-spiritual and who, hearing the Lord's voice of God as they claim to do, and claiming to respond to that voice and that voice only, they are inclined to disregard mere mortals whom they adjudge to be but faulty human authorities. David Stern sees the expression "I follow the Messiah" as their means to "justify heeding no one," save their inner voice (David H. Stern, *Jewish New Testament Commentary* (Clarksville, MD: Jewish New Testament Publications, 1992), 442.

They believe they have heard from the Spirit, and that's the end of the matter. It simply doesn't matter what anyone says: they have heard from God!

This same disregard for legitimate authorities, in the name of having heard from a higher one, is endemic today. The "I belong to Kefa (Peter)" faction arguably harkened to detractors more inclined to identify with Kefa/Peter and his Messianic Jewish ministry to the Jews, and less inclined to identify with Sha'ul, who was judged to be more moderated in his approach toward traditional Jewish faith and practices—minded as he was to make broad room for new-coming Gentile affiliates. (See Galatians 2:8, and fn. 2:2-10, in *Complete Jewish Study Bible*, p. 1670.)

Much as some today place a premium on rigid adherence to traditional Jewish faith and practices in believing-in-Yeshua contexts, similarly, yesterday, many believers identified so strongly with being Jewish—albeit Jewish believers in Yeshua—that Sha'ul's more relaxed approach toward imposing traditional religious Jewish adherence on Gentiles invoked their ire. The "I belong to Apollos" group arguably denoted yet another faction.

Sha'ul's associate Luke introduced Apollos, as an appendage to his counting of the Corinthian mission. After describing all that God accomplished through Sha'ul in Corinth, in Acts 18:1-22, he brought forth Apollos in the narrative in v. 24. He was introduced as faring from Alexandria, Egypt, no small place. With its renowned library, at the time Alexandria was the intellectual headquarters of the known world. Luke said Apollos was "eloquent," had superior "knowledge," in v. 24, and in v. 25 that he had been "informed about the Way," had "great fervor," and "spoke accurately" and "boldly" in v. 26. In v. 28 it is said he spoke "powerfully" and "conclusively refuted others," irrefutably demonstrating by the Tanakh that Yeshua is the Messiah." In Acts 18:26, Luke further noted that Apollos was tutored in Ephesus by Priscilla and Aquila, while Sha'ul was travelling eastward. Apparently, they crisscrossed and changed places. The well-read and loquacious Apollos took up temporary residence in Corinth and made quite an impression with his breadth, depth and oratory skills.

2 CORINTHIANS 1

Reflecting on the Corinthian correspondence, Professor Victor Paul Furnish noted: "Paul [was engaged] in spirited and sometimes anguished dialogue with the congregation in Corinth."[1] That such was the case, easily observable, and will be noted herein. When Paul/Sha'ul wrote the Corinthians previously, he, at the time, wasn't sure whether his fractured and wayward recipients were minded to hear him, never mind comply with his directives. Because he is considered the decisive authority for what it means to follow Yeshua/Jesus today, because of the unrivaled and voluminous impact he has on New Testament literature. It can be hard for modern readers to comprehend that, in his day, he was not universally taken seriously, was often undermined, and in some believers' minds, was not construed as a legitimate apostle. Though not a little distressed when the battered apostle wrote previously, in 2 Corinthians, Rabbi Sha'ul was on much better footing and was arguably much less chagrined, for reasons that will be considered below.

Sha'ul opened 2 Corinthians with a standard Greco-Roman salutation, in verse 1, stating: "From Sha'ul, by God's will an emissary of the Messiah Yeshua, and brother Timothy. To God's Messianic community in Corinth, along with all God's people throughout Achaia." Though rabbis used the fraternal term "brother," it was used infrequently.[2] More predisposed to use familial language, Sha'ul furthered in verses 2–4 with a religious-oriented, well-wishing gesture: "Grace to you and *shalom* from

---

1. Victor Paul Furnish, *II Corinthians: A New Translation with Introduction and Commentary* (New York: Doubleday, 1984), p. 3.

2. Alan J. Avery-Beck in "The Second Letter of Paul to the Corinthians," in Amy Jill-Levine and Marc Zvi Brettler, Eds., *The Annotated Jewish New Testament*, p. 316.

God our Father and the Lord Yeshua the Messiah. Praised be God, Father of our Lord Yeshua the Messiah, compassionate Father, God of all encouragement and comfort; who encourages us in all our trials, so that we can encourage others in whatever trials they may be undergoing with the encouragement we ourselves have received from God." For good reasons, as we shall see, his friendly tone is markedly different here—*because the situation had dramatically changed with his recipients since the writing of the earlier document.*

Sha'ul had spoken of and boasted in his personal trials and powerlessness[3] in his previous letter (cf., 1 Cor. 15:32)[4] and went on to speak of his trials' resolution, and their part in it, later in 2 Corinthians 7:5–16. Strengthened and encouraged as he was at the time when writing 2 Corinthians, he was able to inspire the recipients: "For just as the Messiah's sufferings overflow into us," said he in verse 5, "so through the Messiah, our encouragement (παράκλησις, or "comfort") also overflows." Upbeat as he now was, in verse 7 he said: "our hope for you remains staunch," evidence of a newfound confidence—a firm belief which wasn't there when he wrote the first canonical letter.

---

3. David Stern opined: "Jews have a Scriptural reason not to hold the powerless in contempt" (Stern, David H. *Jewish New Testament Commentary*, p. 442.) As evidence thereof, he alighted upon Deuteronomy 7:7-8, where the Scripture said:

ADONAI didn't set his heart on you or choose you because you numbered more than any other people — on the contrary, you were the fewest of all peoples. Rather, it was because ADONAI loved you, and because he wanted to keep the oath which he had sworn to your ancestors, that ADONAI brought you out with a strong hand and redeemed you from a life of slavery under the hand of Pharaoh king of Egypt. God works for and through the weak.

4. Triumph comes in and through suffering. In 1 Cor. 1:21-25, for example, the cross or execution Stake is central. In vv. 21-25 he said: *Therefore, God decided to use the 'nonsense' of what we proclaim as his means of saving those who come to trust in it. Precisely because Jews ask for signs and Greeks try to find wisdom, we go on proclaiming a Messiah executed on a stake as a criminal! To Jews this is an obstacle, and to Greeks it is nonsense; but to those who are called, both Jews and Greeks, this same Messiah is God's power—in suffering—and God's wisdom! For God's 'nonsense' is wiser than humanity's wisdom. And God's weakness is stronger than humanity's strength.*

Many of Judaism's rabbis speak of *"av ha-rachamim,"* i.e., "God of mercies," and Sha'ul did, likewise. Relative to the afflictions he experienced, still, which were themselves no insignificant trifle, he said in verses 8–10: "For, brothers, we want you to know about the trials (θλίψεως, or affliction) we have undergone in the province of Asia... [were] far beyond what we could bear [and] that we even despaired of living through it. In our hearts we felt we were under [the] sentence of death. However, this was to get us to rely not on ourselves but on God, who raises the dead! He rescued (ἐρρύσατο also "has delivered") us from such deadly peril, and he will rescue us again! The one in whom we have placed our hope will indeed continue to rescue us."

Alan Avery-Beck observed that Sha'ul's reliance on providence and not on self, as noted above, comports with an early Aramaic prayer in the *Zohar,* entitled *"VeYakhel."* When the Torah Scrolls were removed from the Ark during Sabbath services, the faithful would chant: "Not on mortals do I rely... but on the God of the universe." Furthermore, he saw a connection between Sha'ul's looking toward the resurrection, and the second benediction of the Amidah when, according to the *Mishna,* Jews give voice to it (cf. *m. Sot.* 9:15; *m. Sanh.* 10:1).[5] Speaking of "giving voice," for the author, the agency of the *Ruach HaKodesh* (Holy Spirit) brings power that wouldn't otherwise be there. "I myself was with you as somebody weak, nervous and shaking all over from fear," was his word to them in 1 Cor. 2:3. Unlike the showy and savvy wordsmiths bent on undermining him, he stressed that he didn't rely on "compelling words of "wisdom," in v. 4, "but on a demonstration of the power of the Spirit." His message was confirmed by the signs that attended it (see 2 Cor. 12:12) and commended by the sincerity

---

5. Alan J. Avery-Beck, p. 317.

with which he delivered it. (Sha'ul's associate Luke ended his official record of Yeshua's teaching and actions with a comment in Luke 24:49 that Yeshua's talmidim/disciples needed to wait to be "equipped with power from above" before being dispatched to carry the world transforming message (cf. Mk. 16:20). In his second volume, called Acts, the aforementioned Lucan text is reiterated in 1:8 and then fulfilled in 2:1ff. Though Sha'ul wasn't part of the community at the time, he, nevertheless, was filled with the same miracle working Spirit, as per 2 Corinthians 12:12.

Sha'ul finished in verse 11: "And you must add your help by praying for us; for the more people there are praying, the more people there will be to give thanks when their prayer for us is answered." Prayer chains are common in modern culture. Social media provides a means to swiftly make others aware of needs and solicit help in petitioning God's throne for those needs. Without taking anything away from soliciting all the help we can from others, one is hard-pressed to think that a merciful God in Heaven is more moved by popular people who can muster a thousand friends than he is by a lesser-known person who can only muster but ten. In 2 Corinthians 1:11, the value of popular awareness is less in the fact that many are praying, much as it is the "more people there will be to give thanks when their prayer for us is answered." This point is worth keeping in mind.

Many trials or afflictions are *often* problems of their own making. The miseries can often be attributed to deficiencies in one's own immaturity, character, and judgment. In 1 Cor 3:1, he noted they were immature "babes" in v. 2 and "worldly" in v. 3—with their immaturity further evidenced through childish "jealousy and quarrelling." The "fleshly" existence, contrasted with the spiritual state, was deemed the lowest state of being. This lackluster existence was employed as a descriptive understanding of the Jewish state of being by early Christians. Rabbi Sha'ul, of course, had no such meaning in mind. For him, giving pride of place to favored teachers was perceived as a sign of worldly childishness. Not so here, however. "We take pride in this: that our conscience assures us that in our dealings with the world, and especially with you, we have conducted ourselves with frankness and godly pureness (ἁγιότητι καὶ εἰλικρινείᾳ, or "holiness and sincerity") of motive—not by worldly wisdom, but by God-given grace," was his word in verse 12. Returning to a point made earlier, Sha'ul wrote, knowing his motives and movements were being called into question—unfairly so. Happily, that was much less the case now. Still, he said in verse 13[a]: "There are no hidden meanings in our letters other than what you can read and understand." He emphatically stated he operates with no hidden agendas, and in verses 13–14, he hoped that fact will be appreciated: "My hope is that you will understand fully, as indeed you have already understood us in part; so that on the Day of our Lord Yeshua you can be as proud of us as we are of you."

Sha'ul had planned to visit them earlier but opted not to. Later in this letter he defended himself against those who questioned why he didn't deliver on those intentions—thinking him to be disingenuous. He took up the issue in verses 15–17, saying: "I had planned to come and see you, so that you might have the benefit of a second visit. I wanted to visit you on my way to Macedonia, [and] visit you again on my way back from Macedonia, and then have you send me on my way to Y'hudah." The plan in verses 15–17 was an apparent change from the plan noted in 1 Corinthians 16:5–7, where he said he planned to spend the winter. He, however, dropped the trip noted in verses 15–17 and opted for the one noted in 1 Corinthians 16.[6]

---

6. See Acts 20:1-3.

Later, in 1 Corinthians 16:23–24 and in 2 Corinthians 2:1–4, he explained his reasoning. The change in itinerary, however, enabled his critics to raise an issue and question his trustworthiness and sincerity. In verses 17–18 he noted he's not prone to vacillate: "Did I make these plans lightly? Or do I make plans the way a worldly man does, ready to say, 'Yes, yes and 'No, no, in the same breath? As surely as God is trustworthy, we don't say 'Yes' when we mean 'No.'" With Sha'ul, we would all do well to maintain congruity between our words and our deeds. We do well to make our commitments without having to embellish them with oaths that we will follow through.[7] That said, having an appreciation for the fact that things can and do come up—necessitating occasional change and flexibility—should prompt us to be flexible and gracious.

In verse 19 Sha'ul said: "For the Son of God (Θεοῦ γὰρ Υἰὸς), the Messiah Yeshua, who was proclaimed among you through us— that is, through me and Silas and Timothy—was not a yes-and-no man; on the contrary, with him it is always 'Yes!'" Worth note is that the reference to Yeshua as the "Son of God" in verse 19 is not an apostolic, or a Christian invention, given that it is not without equivalents in ancient Jewish literature. Israel is noted as "God's son" in Exodus 4:22; Jeremiah 31:20; and Hosea 11:1. David is similarly referenced as such in 2 Samuel 7:14; Psalm 2:7; and 89:26–27. Noteworthy ruler-leaders, after David, are also referred to as such in the Dead Sea Scrolls (cf. e.g., *4Q246*; *Aram. Apoc.* 50.9– 51:1), much as its applied to the "just" in *Sir.* 4.10; *Wis.* 2.17–18; and *Jub.* 1.24–25.[8] Sha'ul's usage of the appellation "Son of God" in passing, without unpacking the term, presupposed that his hearers were familiar with it. That said, understanding Christology is less his

---

7. See Matt. 5:33-37. His point is further developed in vv. 19-22.
8. Alan J. Avery-Beck, p. 317.

point, as is the fact that God and his Son, can be counted as being faithful and true.

Sha'ul affirmed he is, similarly, true to his word. Things do come up, however, and best intentions notwithstanding, he hoped his friends would be flexible without casting aspersions on his character. In verses 23–24, he said, in his own defense: "I call God to witness—He knows what my life is like—that the reason I held back from coming to Corinth was out of consideration for you! We are not trying to dictate how you must live out your trust in the Messiah, for in your trust you are standing firm. Rather, we are working[9] with you for your own happiness." The "reason" he "held" back will be elucidated in the following chapter.

---

9. The metaphor of a "co-worker" in faith does not appear in early Judaism. Alan J. Avery-Beck, p. 318.

2 CORINTHIANS 2

While consideration of people's feelings is a good thing, with ministry demands, not to mention life in general, sometimes we confront people without too much regard for their feelings, at least for a moment. When Sha'ul said in verse 1 "I made up my mind that I would not pay you another painful visit" (λύπη, or "in grief") he evidenced his inclination toward consideration of feelings, on the one hand, while showing his willingness to, in fact, disregard and make a "painful visit," on the other, if needed. Relative to the discomfort he said he caused, in verses 2–4, he said he did it for their good: "For if I cause you pain (λυπῶ)... I wrote as I did—so that when I came, I would not have to be pained by those who ought to be making me happy... I wrote to you with a greatly distressed (θλίψεως, or "afflicted") and anguished (συνοχῆς) heart, and with many tears, not to cause you pain, but to get you to realize how very much I love you." Dreading the words "I am offended," many people take pains to be as non-offensive as possible. Sometimes we must be, however, as noted herein.

Scholars are uncertain exactly when Sha'ul made the aforementioned "painful visit." There is uncertainty among scholars, as well, about the pained person noted in verses 5–11. Sha'ul referenced "someone [who] has been a cause of pain" in verse 5, and informed that the "punishment (ἐπιτιμία) [that] has already [been] imposed" upon the person is "sufficient" in verse 6. With the purpose of the discipline having run its course at the time of this writing, in verse 7 he exhorted they "forgive (χαρίσασθαι) him [and] comfort (παρακαλέσαι) him. Otherwise, such a person might be swallowed up in overwhelming depression." Given that extensive discipline can have deleterious consequences, in verse 8 he said: "I urge you to show that you really do love (ἀγάπην) him," and followed in verse 10 saying: "Anyone you forgive (χαρίζεσθε), I forgive too."

Sometimes a necessary prescribed treatment, Sha'ul believed discipline has its place in the medicine bag of the Great Physician. Mindful that bringing up egregious sins, rendering negative judgments upon malefactors, imposing temporary banishments and the like are hard pills to swallow. He cautioned against forever pressing judgment and thought it good to extend grace when the discipline runs its course and produced its desired outcome. He believed in forgiveness and noted the refusal thereof creates its own problems. He warned they "not be taken advantage of by the Adversary," by withholding it, and that "we are quite aware of his schemes," in that regard.

The question of what and to whom he is referring warrants consideration. There is one example in the previous canonical record of someone being caught in a specific egregious sin and banished. In 1 Corinthians 5:1ff a man was found wanting for having an illicit sexual affair with his stepmother. When Sha'ul heard of it, though absent at the time, he marshaled his resources, used his influence, and summarily ordered that the fellow be ostracized from the community. Given the match, there's a cogent argument that what Sha'ul was talking about in this matter is a follow up to the incident reported in 1 Corinthians 5:1ff. Therein he'd previously noted "…it is actually being reported" by messengers who had delivered a message to Sha'ul and given a verbal report with it—a reference to the correspondence to which he was responding when he wrote 1 Corinthians—there is a heinous, undisciplined sin at play in Corinth. Beyond the divisiveness noted previously, he informed in verse 1 "there is sexual sin (πορνεία) among you, and it is sexual sin of a kind that is condemned even by pagans—a man is living with his stepmother!" Bombastic! The term "father's wife" is taken from the LXX. See Leviticus 18:7–8 where it is forbidden. See also Gordon Fee, *The First Epistle to the Corinthians* (Grand Rapids: Eerdmans, 1991, p. 200.)

Licentiousness was rife in Greco-Roman culture, with the result that people were desensitized to it—especially in Corinth. "Mistresses we keep for the sake of pleasure; concubines for the daily care of the body, but wives to bear us legitimate children" was said to be the order of the day. (See Demos., or 59. 122 [Loeb. VI, 445, 447 slightly modified]).

In its day, the seaport city of Corinth—situated between the Aegean and Adriatic Seas—was known to be something of a "Sin City." This was so much the case that to simply refer to a girl as a "Corinthian" besmirched her moral character and telegraphed that she was particularly liberal in doling out sexual favors. Sha'ul's saying, "It's reported that you're doing something that even the pagans condemn" is no light matter, given the tolerance the Corinthians were known to have toward sexual improprieties.

In the case at hand, the report given Sha'ul was that a young man was sleeping with his stepmother—something that comported with nobody's sensibilities. It was common for young girls to marry shortly after puberty and to much older men. On the assumption that such was the case here, and that a man could have a son through a previous marriage who was in close proximity age-wise to a new wife, in the older husband's absence it is not beyond the pale of reason to see how a stepmother and stepson could take a liking to each other—as they could well be of comparable age. Though understandable, it was still eschewed—even by the standards of the lusty Corinthians. Roman law itself, which was not known for moral scruples, condemned this activity (cf., e.g., *Gaius, Inst.* 1.63) as did Jewish law (cf., e.g., Lev. 18:7–8; Pseudo-Phocylides, *Sent.* 179; *11Q19* 66.12 and Philo, *Spec. Laws* 3.20–28). (Shira Lander, p. 294;

see also Amos 2:7 for "father and son sleeping with the same girl"; cf. also Josephus in *Ant.* 3.274; *m. Sanh.* 7.4; b. *Sanh.* 54[a] and *T. Reub.*, passim (Gordon Fee, p. 200.)

Sha'ul often parroted traditional Jewish perspectives on sexual and marriage-related issues. In 1 Cor. 6:9-10, for example, he expressed:

> Don't delude yourselves, people who engage in sex before marriage, who worship idols, who engage in sex after marriage with someone other than their spouse, who engage in active or passive homosexuality, who steal, who are greedy, who get drunk, who assail people with contemptuous language, who rob—none of them will share (κληρονομήσουσιν, "will inherit") in the Kingdom of God (βασιλείαν Θεοῦ).

As was the case here, Sha'ul often used vice lists and virtue lists when making his points. In 1 Corinthians 6 he'd alighted upon sexual improprieties, e.g., fornication (Greek *pornoi*), adultery and homosexuality, specifically male prostitutes (Greek *malakoi*), sodomites (Greek *aresnokoitai*—a term combining "male" and "bed,") as with crimes against persons (e.g., theft, robbery, and slander). Lander thinks "sodomite" is a bad translation, that the word has nothing to do with Sodom in the Bible (Gen. 19) and that the word "Sodomite" doesn't appear in the Hebrew Bible. Writing in another spirit altogether, Sha'ul, as noted, is pressing traditional Jewish mores and, as such, would not be prone to abide modern approaches to lessening those standards (Shira Lander, p. 295). That Sha'ul had a majority Gentile community in view, principally, though not exclusively, is attested in v. 11 when he said: "Some of you used to do these things." The Greeks didn't have a moral code like the Hebrews. Homosexuality and sex outside of marriage were tolerated, not eschewed.

The Rabbi from Tarsus came to town and, in conjunction with Gentiles turning to Israel's Messiah through his ministry, made them more keenly aware of Israel's Scripture, and the implication of its moral code upon their personal faith and practices. Individuals turned to God and away from their former lifestyles. He went on to say in the verse: "But you have cleansed yourselves, you have been set apart for God, you have come to be counted righteous through the power of the Lord Yeshua the Messiah and the Spirit of our God." In v. 12 he parroted a saying in circulation among them: "You say, 'For me, everything is permitted?'" (David Stern notes: "The words 'You say' are not in the Greek text but are added [by me] to show that this was not a central principle of Sha'ul's." See *Jewish New Testament Commentary*, p. 451.)

He retorted: "Maybe, but not everything is helpful." Epictetus in *Diatr.* 41.1, and Dio Chrys. in *Or.* 3.10 say much the same, evidence of the saying's import in Hellenistic culture (Shira Lander, p. 296). Perhaps for rhetorical purposes here, Sha'ul noted it and followed with: "For me, everything is permitted? Maybe, but as far as I am concerned, I am not going to let anything gain control over me." He continued in vv. 13-14 "...the body is not meant for sexual immorality but for the Lord, and the Lord is for the body. God raised up the Lord, and he will raise us up too by his power." Much as he previously noted the body—in effect a Temple of the Holy Spirit—should not be defiled by divisiveness, here, too, he alighted upon its defilements through sexual impropriety, perhaps a capstone comment to the initiating case of a man sleeping with his stepmother. Though this was the precipitating incident in this letter, in 5:1, it was but a first of a few sex-related issues he needed to address. Again, as noted previously, his needing to attend to such matters from afar testifies to the lack of real and functioning leadership in-house. To be sure, people were leading out with feigned displays of religious enthusiasms but these, as the letter's author is keen on noted, tended to serve the interests of those profiting from it all and not the Corinthians themselves—who were being exploited.

Fee, as noted above, opined the tolerance for the sin, and the reluctance to deal with it, may well be due to sexual improprieties "prevalence in culture, and the difficulty... with its Gentile converts breaking with their former ways, which they did not consider immoral." (Gordon Fee, p. 200.)[10] Sexual impropriety was part of Corinthian culture. A once-famous temple devoted to the celebration of Aphrodite (known to the Romans also as Venus) was located adjacent to the city of Corinth. It was situated high on a towering hill, and the better part of the city's residents lived in its very shadow. An ancient historian, Strabo, once surmised there were in the vicinity of 1,000 active temple prostitutes who worked in and around the shrine. Some think the number to be over inflated. Whether his account was exaggerated or not, Corinth existed in the shadow of the temple of love, and its so doing

---

10. The expression being "part of the body of Christ" is ubiquitous in Evangelical culture. It's not unique to it, however. Sha'ul's employment of the term here—as elsewhere—was not unique and not without precedent. The "body" equaling "Israel" has parallels in the Hebrew Bible (cf., e.g., Isa. 10:18), much as, in Hellenistic culture, the state, itself, was construed as a body with the emperor as its head. The point here is that Corinthian believers were not acting like part of a *holy* body. They may not have been particularly holy in the past, but now they have transitioned—at least in theory, if not in practice. Non-Jews resident therein became enlightened and exposed to the Hebrew Scriptures, refracted through an understanding that Jesus was Jewish Messiah. To strengthen his point, the author cited a text from the Hebrew Bible, which, by the time of his writing, they would have construed as authoritative: "For the *Tanakh* says, 'The two will become one flesh'" (v. 16b). Couples being somehow "one body" is a concept held inviolate in biblical literature, with breaches of the morality code not taken lightly in Israel's covenant with its Maker. The Greeks—and then the Romans—were not tethered to such notions, save for Augustus' code which eschewed debauched practices and sought to reign in unbridled passions. Advertisements beckoning individuals to go to the temple of Aphrodite and associate with prostitutes were placed throughout the city of Corinth. Rather than run to the pagan shrine, Sha'ul said "Run from sexual immorality!" in v. 18, arguing "... the fornicator sins against his own body." He rounded off his point by returning to one made previously: "Don't you know that your body is a temple for the *Ruach HaKodesh* who lives inside you, whom you received from God?" (v. 19a) "The fact is," said he in vv. 19b-20, " you don't belong to yourselves; for you were bought at a price. So use your bodies to glorify God."

contributed to the city's reputation for debauchery. Rabbi Sha'ul was emphatic, stressing to them in vv. 15-16a: "Don't you know that your bodies are parts of the Messiah? So, am I to take parts of the Messiah and make them parts of a prostitute? Heaven forbid! Don't you know that a man who joins himself to a prostitute becomes physically one with her?"

Asceticism was a problem too. In 1 Cor. 7: 4-5 he noted "The wife is not in charge of her own body, but her husband is; likewise, the husband is not in charge of his own body, but his wife is. Therefore, do not deprive each other, except for a limited time, by mutual agreement, and then only so as to have extra time for prayer; but afterwards, come together again. Otherwise, because of your lack of self-control, you may succumb to the Adversary's temptation." In this regard, Lander is helpful: "Jewish tradition mandates a certain frequency of sexual intercourse" [and] also discusses limited period of voluntary abstinence" (see m. *Ketub.* 5.6; *t. Ned.* 5.6). (See Shira Lander, p. 297.) There the problem of denying Jewish standards in the interest of assimilating into Greco-Roman culture. Sha'ul, for example, had previously spoken of some "trying to remove (μὴ ἐπισπάσθω, 'not circumcised') the marks of circumcision" (1 Cor. 7:18). This was more than just a figure of speech. In *Antiquities of the Jews* 12:5:1, the ancient historian Flavius Josephus informed how some assimilated Jews underwent surgeries to remove the marks of circumcision. (For more on this, see *Jewish New Testament Commentary*, p. 454 and Shira Lander, p. 298.)[11] In verses 3–5, Sha'ul stepped into the prevailing Corinthian moral confusion and

---

11. Foreskin reconstruction was called *epispasm.* Interestingly, there are many Jews today—from both the Jewish mainstream and the Jewish believing in Jesus sub-stream—who are minded to distance themselves from association with Hebrew culture. They don't entertain surgery, however. Assimilation presents in various shapes, sizes and colors. Jewish believers involved in Messianic Judaism today, by contradistinction, want to retain affiliation with Jewish culture rather than assimilate into the broader culture. Sha'ul remained within the Jewish fold.

leadership void and offered a fix—one that likely seemed a bit too harsh for some: "For I myself, even though I am absent physically, am with you spiritually; and I have already judged the man who has done this as if I were present. In the name of the Lord Yeshua, when you are assembled, with me present spiritually and the power of our Lord Yeshua among us, hand over (παραδοῦναι, "deliver over") such a person to the Adversary for his old nature to be destroyed (ὄλεθρον), so that his spirit may be saved in the Day of the Lord." He called for ex-communication—something he was revisiting in 2 Corinthians, having learned of the person's subsequent repentance in response to it.

The saying "hand the person to the Adversary [i.e., Satan] for his old nature [i.e., flesh] to be destroyed" is worthy of some reflection, particularly because it seems so uncharacteristic of New Covenant faith and virtue, not to mention that it seems to fly in the face of his previous exhortation to not pass judgment before the time. Fee states, and incorrectly in this writer's opinion, "apart from similar usage in 1 Timothy 1:20, the language to 'hand over to Satan' is found nowhere else as an act of expulsion from a religious community." (Gordon Fee, p. 208) It might be better said "nowhere else in the New Testament". The language was employed when the "scapegoat" in Leviticus 16 was led away from the Hebrew community, plunged off a precipice and thrown off a cliff with the words "to Satan" you go. In that case, in classical rabbinic perspective, the animal was seen as an embodiment of sexual indiscretion and sent off to the sins' originator: Satan. Harking to "excommunication," at least for the time being, it is likely Sha'ul had the old Hebraic dictum in mind. Gordon Fee grants this saying: "this man is to be put back in the world" (Gordon Fee, p. 209.) where, absent repentance, he would come to ruin, i.e., [thus, in effect] destroyed. Additionally, Fee is helpful: "He is not [literally] being 'turned over to Satan for [literal] destruction' an idea that is quite foreign to both Paul and the rest of the [New Testament] but is being excluded from the Christian community with its life in the Spirit." "Handed over the Satan" is best construed as an archaic, Hebraic expression for ex-communication (Gordon Fee, p. 213). Fee says later: "Paul's concern throughout does not seem to be that the church as individual members dissociate from the incestuous man, but that he be excluded from the community as it gathers for worship and instruction" (Gordon Fee, p. 226).[12] There was a church tradition of interpreting the text literally, with the result that credence was given to torture for religious purposes. We do well to disavow the notion and appreciate that Sha'ul was using a now-archaic expression for excommunication. *He was not encouraging they literally destroy someone and/or hand someone over to Satan, much as he was saying, given the nature of the offense, the young man needs to be put out and debarred from communion*—at least for the time being. Since he didn't see fit to live with God's people properly, let him go live with the devil's people!

We don't know all the circumstances behind the sexual indiscretion, only that it happened. We know, as well, that the community hadn't dealt with it. Their reluctance may be attributed to the malefactors being in the household of someone with some means; individuals of lesser means in the faith community could well fear repercussions should they face the issue head on and get involved. The fact that Sha'ul had to attend to the breach was, for him, an illustration of another problem in Corinth. Sha'ul's ordering the banishment might have prompted some to say he was too harsh, initially, or, with time having passed, that he'd been harsher now by

---

12. David Stern deals with this circumstance in some detail in his *Jewish New Testament Commentary*, p. 447. Therein, he correctly notes the excommunication wasn't permanent and was meant to be restorative in nature. That was his point. The other, in v. 6a, was about their "boasting" which "is not good." Again: it turned out that a community that thought it had strong leadership really had none. If they had it, per his argument, issues like this wouldn't go unchecked in their midst.

not considering there was a change for the better in the fellow and giving him a pathway to return. Mindful of Satan's tricks and God's grace, Sha'ul was more than happy to help them welcome a sinner home, which is what he was doing here. We do well to not miss the point that reconciliation is at the very heart of the Gospel.

The point is clearly made about opening a door for the repentant sinner and returning to his itinerary now in 2 Corinthians 2:12, Sha'ul pivoted and spoke of a "door [that] had been opened for me by the Lord." Because the opportunities of a lifetime must be seized within the lifetime of the opportunities, flexibility in travel is always good— as noted previously. Figuring the complexities of travel in the ancient Mediterranean world—whether it be by arduous overland routes or precarious sea passage through the Mediterranean, Asian or Adriatic Seas—it seemed best to not be too insistent on a fixed schedule. Sha'ul spoke of his travel for a reason. He noted in verse 13 he was so desirous of seeing Titus (who had gone to Corinth), and that he left Troas and went on to Macedonia, also known as Greece. "I could not rest, because I failed to find my brother Titus.[13] So I left the people there and went on to Macedonia." He was inching toward them and wanted to go on record that he really did care for them—and, tacitly perhaps, for the person whom he had temporarily banished.

In a better mood now, he tweaked the use of a previously employed analogy in verses 14–16. In 1 Corinthians 4:9–13, he used the image of a triumphal parade, during which time he put himself and the other emissaries at the tail end of it. At the end of triumphal parades in Greco-Roman culture, the vanquished were typically put on display in the march. The unfortunate prisoners of war were forever exposed to the incessant abuse of the crowd. In 1 Corinthians 4:9 he developed a word picture, noting specifically how we were "display[ed] at the tail of the parade, like men condemned to die

---

13. More on Titus' unification with Sha'ul will be seen and developed in 2 Cor. 7.

(ἐπιθανατίους, "appointed to death") in the public arena." Later, in 2 Corinthians 2:14, by contrast, he employed an image from the front of the parade—where the proud victors strutted like peacocks: "But thanks be to God, who in the Messiah constantly leads us in a triumphal procession (θριαμβεύοντι, "leading in triumph")." With that image in view, in verses 14–16 he spoke to the senses and affirmed his ministry—hardships and all—saying: "[T]hrough us [God] spreads everywhere the fragrance of what it means to know him! For to God, we are the aroma of the Messiah, both among those being saved and among those being lost; to the latter, we are the smell of death leading only to more death; but to the former, we are the sweet smell of life leading to more life."

After noting that different people interpret him and his circumstances differently, he made a point in verse 17 that, irrespective of what some may say: "[W]e are not like a lot of folks who go about huckstering (καπηλεύοντες, "peddling") God's message for a fee; on the contrary, we speak out of a sincere heart (εἰλικρινείας, "sincerity"), as people sent by God, standing in God's presence." We do well to take a second look at the text: "[W]e are not like a lot of folks who go about huckstering God's message for a fee." The charge that he was profiting illicitly is a recurrent theme in the Corinthian correspondences and is an issue his detractors were using to stir up discontent. Profit itself, and having an entrepreneurial spirit, is not judged to be a terrible thing. Judaism, however, forbids individuals from profiting from the knowledge of Torah. Avery-Beck points to *y. B. Metz.* 2.5 [8] where Samuel bar Sursetai risks beheading rather than acting unscrupulously and benefiting from what the Law demands[14] Sha'ul could be understood as saying as much here.

---

14. Alan J. Avery-Beck, p. 319.

Given the recurrence of suspicion, and Sha'ul's offering of defensive statements in this letter, exposure to some of the background to it may be helpful. Respectful as we are of the Rabbi from Tarsus two-thousand years removed from the document—and rightly so—the notion that the now-famous emissary/apostle was disingenuous and "in it for the money" does not comport with our sensibilities at all. It seems preposterous—and indeed it is. In his own day, however, as noted above, it is helpful to realize that he was not universally construed as a religious authority on what it means to walk in the footsteps of the Messiah. The fact that he did not know Yeshua personally, never heard a single parable roll off his lips, and never drank any water he had turned to wine, was not lost to the ancients. He not only was not exposed to Yeshua/Jesus initially as the others, but he was dedicated to destroying them in the beginning. After having a profound experience with Yeshua on a road to Damascus—a story recounted three times by his biographer in the *Acts of the Apostles*—Sha'ul invested little-to-no effort acquainting himself with the original disciples in Judea but spent the better part of his time in Arabia. Luke recorded that when word of a revival in Antioch, Syria eventually broke, a disciple from Judea set off to go help there, and he picked up Sha'ul (who was then in Tarsus, in eastern Turkey) as a helper in Antioch. After a year in Syria, he and Sha'ul were dispatched from Antioch and sent forth to the Gentiles in Asia Minor/Turkey and beyond.

The locus of religious authority was vested in the Judean disciples and Sha'ul's minimal contact with them (and Yeshua) worked against him in the eyes of others. Though Sha'ul is rightfully and universally construed as a decisive authority on what it means to be a Yeshua believer today, in his own day, some questioned whether he had the right to even be considered an emissary. Even though he was one, on an honorary basis, he wasn't seen by many as on par with the rest given his lean exposure to the Lord himself and to the others who knew and walked with him.

Even though the above may appear tangential, against this historical backdrop, one can better understand why Sha'ul is often heard in his writings wrestling with others determined to undermine his authority as an emissary/apostle and discredit his teaching. The fact that thirteen documents in the New Testament corpus bear his seal attests to his having eventually won the argument. The long arm of his pen reached beyond his grave and, through his writings, left more of a mark on New Covenant consciousness than all the other writers combined. The posthumous popularity Sha'ul enjoys through his writings now, hinders readers from appreciating the situation, circumstances, message and meaning of the letters he wrote then— when he was fighting for a hearing among believers minded to discrediting him.

2 CORINTHIANS 3

Representing himself as being thrown on his heels and in a self-protecting posture for rhetorical purposes, Sha'ul began in 3:1 with one of a string of defensive statements: "Are we starting to recommend (εἰλικρινείας) ourselves again?" He is being sarcastic. His opening salvo had less to do with what he understood himself to be doing, but it was a back-handed reference to what those who disregarded him, while building atop the platform he'd constructed were doing. In 1 Cor. 3:10, he noted "I laid a foundation, like a skilled master-builder; and another man is building on it. But let each one be careful how he builds." The Greek *sophos architecton*, i.e., literally "wise builder," is rendered "skilled master builder" here. It was similarly employed by Philo and was a common metaphor in Sha'ul's day. (Philo, *Dreams* 2.8. See Shira Lander, p. 292.).

He followed with another rhetorical question, but made a point with it: "Or do we, like some, need letters of recommendation either to you or from you?" The anticipated answer is "no," of course. Sha'ul's various canonical letters contained just shy of fifty commendations, wherein he beckoned his hearers to receive so and so based on their doing such and such. Sha'ul's point here was that he needed no such introduction to them, nor any commendation for his work. Why not? He lived in Corinth for a year and a half, and they existed as a community because he fathered the congregation into existence.[15] As a result, he could boldly assert in verses 2–3: "You yourselves are our letter of recommendation, written on our hearts, known, and read by

---

15. This confidence was expressed previously. In 1 Cor. 4:10 he exhorted: "let each one be careful how he builds.".

everyone. You make it clear that you are a letter from the Messiah placed in our care, written not with ink but by the Spirit (Πνεύματι, "with [the] Spirit") of the living God, not on stone tablets but on human hearts (καρδίαις σαρκίναις, "hearts [of] human")."

Not all could say as much. He could, however, and he continued in verses 4–6 explaining why:

> Such is the confidence we have through the Messiah toward God. It is not that we are competent in ourselves to count anything as having come from us; on the contrary, our competence is from God. He has even made us competent to be workers serving a New Covenant, the essence of which is not a written text but the Spirit. For the written text brings death, but the Spirit gives life.

In verse 6 he said: "He [i.e., God] has made us competent to be workers serving a New Covenant." After boasting, that they personally know what he was all about as a man and as an authentic emissary, so as not to overstate his own importance. He then humbly alighted upon the truth that he was what he was because God was who he was and was doing what he was doing: in this case inaugurating a brand-new dispensation through Yeshua and Sha'ul's ministry.

God was up to something new in the world. "Now if that which worked death, by means of a written text engraved on stone tablets," in verses 7–8, "came with glory—such glory that the people of Isra'el could not stand to look at Moshe's face because of its brightness, even though that brightness was already fading away—won't the working of the Spirit be accompanied by even greater glory?" Sha'ul understood that God was up to something new in the world and made a point that the new dispensation he had been commissioned to advocate for, i.e., the New Covenant, was itself presaged in the Old Covenant.

Most commentators are predisposed to argue that the first economy was somehow totally eclipsed by the new. A Messianic Jewish theology, by contrast, is more inclined to understand Sha'ul to have said that the First Covenant attested to the coming of a Second Covenant, and that both serve each other's purposes. David Stern stresses the point that Sha'ul isn't speaking disparagingly of the Torah/Law. He notes that the word *nomos*, i.e., "law," is not used here or anywhere in 2 Corinthians. There is a reference to that which was inscribed on stone, true, but those moral commandments do not, in and of themselves, commend an understanding of the entire Hebrew Bible. See *Jewish New Testament Commentary*, p. 497, for a fuller treatment of the matter.

In verse 9 he said: "For if there was glory in what worked to declare people guilty, how much more must the glory abound in what works to declare people innocent!" So great is the New Covenant, according to its primary advocate, Sha'ul, "by comparison with this greater glory, what was made glorious before has no glory now. For if there was glory in what faded away, how much more glory must there be in what lasts" (vv. 10–11).

He looked back to the Hebrew Bible in verses 12–13: "Therefore, with a hope like this, we are very open—unlike Moshe, who put a veil over his face, so that the people of Isra'el would not see the fading brightness come to an end." It's coming to an "end" should be understood within the context of his argument: an end as the primary means by which humanity is reconciled to its maker—not a cessation and abrogation. Sha'ul, himself, still respected the Torah's light and lived under its shade (i.e., within the parameters of its requirements); he, however, was disinclined to insist that women and men of non-Jewish extract needed to do likewise—a point stressed by Messianic Jews today, save for a few on the movement's fringes. The New Covenant—to which the Old Covenant pointed to in Jeremiah 31:30–33 (vv. 31–34 in some translations)—provided the greater means for world redemption, was hinted at in the First Testament. David Stern, *Jewish New Testament Commentary*, p. 498.

Sha'ul saw a rabbinic *mashal,* a parable, here: "What is more," he said in verse 14, "their [i.e., many of his non-believing Jewish associates] minds were made stone-like; for to this day the same veil (κάλυμμα) remains over them when they read the Old Covenant; it has not been unveiled, because only by the Messiah is the veil taken away." Individuals do well to be particularly gracious to Jewish non-believers, given that it takes a miracle, i.e., God himself, removing the blinders, to enable them to see him in the Hebrew Bible. He continues in verses 15–16: "Yes, till today, whenever Moshe is read, a veil lies over their heart. 'But,' says the Torah, 'whenever someone turns to ADONAI, the veil is taken away.'" Relative to the resistance of some, David Stern notes it is descriptive and "[t]here is no criticism here against Jews ethnically, racially, biologically, culturally, nationally as a people, or even religiously, in respect to other aspects of Judaism,"[16] much as it is that many of our Jewish friends simply do not understand the Jesus connection to the Hebrew Bible.

Sha'ul's referencing the Hebrew Scripture as the "Old Covenant," i.e., from the Greek *he palaia diatheke,* is said to be the first example of any such usage. The later writer of Hebrews, for his part, did not focus on the term, but opted instead for "the first covenant," i.e., *he prote diatheke.*[17] It may well be that for Rabbi Sha'ul, being "old" attends to it going back in time, more so than it being antiquated for religious purposes. That this is most surely his understanding and explains why he frequently employed the "Old Covenant" for pedagogical purposes when unpacking the "New Covenant," along with that he lived within its parameters himself. The term was not used for disparaging purposes. In any case, Sha'ul noted that many of his contemporaries do not see the Messianic picture in sacred literature.

---

16. Ibid., p. 499.

17. Victor Paul Furnish, *Ibid.,* pp. 208-209.

Many well intended non-Jewish believers slight Jews for not perceiving Jesus Christ in the Hebrew Scriptures. Credence for the critique is garnered based on the passage. After two-thousand years of church history, most Messianic Jews do not find it surprising that the better part of our people does not see behind the veil and perceive Yeshua to be the Messiah, much as we are surprised that our non-Jewish, Spirit-empowered Christian friends read the Old and New Testaments and do not see the Jews therein.

Hard-heartedness and lack of perception is less a problem with Jewish nature as it is with human nature, overall. Being "born again," and receiving the *Ruach HaKodesh,* i.e., the Holy Spirit, came to Sha'ul on the heels of a radical and personal experience. Renewed and empowered by that experience, Sha'ul could see with a new set of eyes: "Now, 'ADONAI' in this text means the Spirit. And where the Spirit of ADONAI is, there is freedom" (v. 17). That "freedom" opened many things, one of which is entrance into the Kingdom of God for women and men of non-Jewish extract, without their having to become Jews. When he closed in verse 18, he wrote to his mostly non-Jewish associates and said: "So all of us," note the "us," i.e., with non-Jews included— "with faces unveiled, see as in a mirror the glory of the Lord; and we are being changed into his very image, from one degree of glory to the next, by ADONAI the Spirit."

Ancient rabbis, in *b. Ber.* 7[a], understood the transformation of Moses' face to have been a divine reward for turning his face away from the vision of God.[18] According to Sha'ul, Jews and Gentiles alike, because of Yeshua's agency, see God's glory. That, and the fact that the Lord accomplishes his purposes for and through all humanity now, through the Spirit, is for Sha'ul of greater significance than the writing of the First Covenant itself.

____

18. Alan J. Avery-Beck, p. 320.

2 CORINTHIANS 4

Sha'ul thanked God for the empowerment to advocate for the New Covenant. "God has shown us such mercy (κάλυμμα, "mercy") that we do not lose courage as we do the work, he has given us" (v. 1). People can and do indeed become discouraged in doing ministry. In North America, one in four ministers are fired and of seminary graduates, only 30% retire as ministers. Many are tossed around within ministry and eventually tossed out; many opt out. People can be difficult, and ministry can be tough; the abysmal statistics are telling. Sha'ul did *not* lose courage," however. Discouragement gives heed to breathing courage out, whereas encouragement speaks of breathing encouragement in. Sha'ul was oxygenated by the *Ruach HaKodesh*, the Holy Spirit, and was thankful for both his assignment and the enablement to carry on with it, even though he was perennially maligned and undermined—as many ministers are today.

As noted above, his critics in Corinth accused him of being incompetent and less than honest. By way of response, he said in verse 2: "[W]e refuse to make use of shameful, underhanded methods (κρυπτὰ τῆς αἰσχύνης, "hidden things of shame"), employing deception or distorting God's message. On the contrary, by making clear what the truth is, we commend ourselves to everyone's conscience in the sight of God"—as per his points in chapter 3.

Returning to the veil motifs mentioned previously, he offered a twist: "So if indeed our Good News is veiled, it is veiled only to those in the process of being lost" (v. 3) His negatively inclined interlocutors weren't going to be persuaded by his arguments, because their minds were previously made up, veiled (i.e., shut down). Trying to reason with someone who refuses to reason is like trying to give medicine to a dead man: it does not work. For him, his disbelievers and critics "do not come to trust because the god of the *'olam hazeh'* i.e., "this world" has blinded their minds, to prevent them from seeing the light shining from the Good News about the glory of the Messiah, who is the image of God" (v. 4). Much as there is a Holy Spirit, there is a nefarious, i.e., not-so-holy spirit, one at work in the world, wrapping itself around people's minds and preventing them from seeing.

His critics claimed Sha'ul was egotistical and wrapped up in himself. For his part, in verses 5–6, he said:

> What we are proclaiming is not ourselves, but the Messiah Yeshua as Lord, with ourselves as slaves (δούλους, "servants") for you because of Yeshua. For it is God who once said, 'Let light shine out of darkness,' who has made his light shine in our hearts, the light of the knowledge of God's glory shining in the face of the Messiah Yeshua.

Notice it took God "[making] his light [to] shine in hearts." Absent mercy and divine initiative, the god of this world inhibits individuals from seeing how God so loved the world that he came into it to save it—from the Adversary; spiritual warfare is alluded to.

In verse 7, Sha'ul was mindful of his weakness and God's strengths: "[W]e have this treasure (θησαυρὸν) in clay jars, so that it will be evident that such overwhelming power comes from God and not from us." He was keenly aware of his weakness and God's strengths, much as he was of his personal struggles as an emissary of this emerging new Kingdom. He went on to say: "We have all kinds of troubles (θλιβόμενοι, "being hard pressed"), but we are not crushed (στενοχωρούμενοι, "being crushed"); we are perplexed (ἀπορούμενοι, "being perplexed"), yet not in despair (ἐξαπορούμενοι, "despairing")," and followed in verse 9–12 with:

"[We are] persecuted (διωκόμενοι, "being persecuted"), yet not abandoned (ἐγκαταλειπόμενοι); knocked down (καταβαλλόμενοι, "struck down"), yet not destroyed (ἀπολλύμενοι, "being destroyed").

We always carry in our bodies the dying of Yeshua, so that the life of Yeshua may be manifested in our bodies, too. For we who are alive are always being handed over to death for Yeshua's sake, so that Yeshua's life also might be manifested in our mortal bodies. Thus, death is at work in us but life in you." "This is why we do not lose courage (ἐγκακοῦμεν, "lose heart")," said he in verse 16, "[t]hough our outer self is heading for decay, our inner self is being renewed (ἀνακαινοῦται) daily." Believing, as he did, that "our light and transient troubles are achieving for us an everlasting glory," in verse 17, in verse 18 he could close with: "We concentrate not on what is seen but on what is not seen, since things seen are temporary (πρόσκαιρα), but things not seen are eternal (αἰώνια)."

2 CORINTHIANS 5

In chapter 4, Sha'ul likened the Spirit's presence in believers to a treasure deposited in an earthen vessel. In verse 5:1, he used another analogy: a tent. "We know that when the tent (αἰώνια) which houses us here on earth is torn down, we have a permanent building from God, a building not made by human hands, to house us in heaven." Sha'ul vexed by his present momentary troubles, as noted previously; but in verses 2–4 he was in a restless state as he anticipated the future. "For in this tent, our earthly body, we groan (στενάζομεν) with desire to have around us the home from heaven that will be ours. With this around us we will not be found naked. Yes, while we are in this body, we groan with the sense of being oppressed (βαρούμενοι, "being burdened"): it is not so much that we want to take something off, but rather to put something on over it; so that what must die may be swallowed up by the Life."

With the promise of a new life in a resurrected body, one would not be surprised to hear him looking forward and beyond the grave—when his life finally runs its course. As we shall see later, Sha'ul's critics made much of his ailments and his unimpressive human form. He, to put it bluntly, wasn't much to look at. Years of hardships on the road had taken a toll on this older man. That, coupled with his having less-than-clear vision in the first place, enabled his detractors to question his spiritual power and apostolic calling. Believing that Spirit-inspired emissaries should be specimens of bodily health and perfection—as evidence of the Spirit's being at work in and through them—Sha'ul was found wanting. The fact that he "groans" in his mortal body was of little consequence to him, though. He contended in verse 5: "God who has prepared us for this very thing... has given us his Spirit."

It mattered not to Sha'ul if he was a less than perfect human specimen, or if others cast aspersions on him for that and for other reasons. He said: "[W]e are always confident (Θαρροῦντες)—we know that so long as we are at home in the body, we are away from our home with the Lord; for we live by trust, not by what we see. We are confident, then, and would much prefer to leave our home in the body and come to our home with the Lord" (vv. 6–8).

The body was but a "tent" for Sha'ul. His objective while in his body had less to do with perfecting it than it did with seeking the world that exists beyond it. "Whether at home [in the body] or away from home, we try our utmost to please him," was his word in verse 9. His reasoning was made clear in verse 10, where he said: "[W]e must all appear before the Messiah's court of judgment (βήματος), where everyone will receive the good or bad consequences of what he did while he was in the body." A sobering thought, is it not?

In verse 11, he said "it is with the fear (φόβον) of the Lord before us that we try to persuade people." The "fear" noted has more to do with reverence than it does with panic. The author was less concerned about others' opinions of him than he was God's, mindful that, in the future, God will render judgment—and mete out rewards in accordance with his ultimate decisions. Sha'ul knew that God knew him for what he really was, in verse 11 he said to the Corinthians: "...God knows us as we really are; and I hope that in your consciences (συνειδήσεσιν) you too know us as we really are." That said, he again was inclined to be a bit defensive, saying in verse 12: "We are not recommending ourselves to you again, but giving you a reason to be proud of us, so that you will be able to answer those who boast about a person's appearance rather than his inner qualities." Sha'ul likened his message to "nonsense" in 1 Corinthians 1:21 (See 1 Cor. 1:17-2:9) and did so again a bit later in 2 Corinthians 11:1ff. Now, in verse 13, in hyperbolic fashion, he pushed his self-deprecation further, likening himself to an insane person. "If we are insane (ἐξέστημεν, "if we are besides ourselves"), it is for God's sake; and if we are sane, it is for your sake." When in verse 13 he spoke of being "insane," or "beside himself" (as per the RSV), Avery-Beck believed Sha'ul is distinguishing himself from his critics, saying: "Paul's opponents may have derided him for an apparent lack of ecstatic experience (12:1,12); Paul answers by distinguishing between being beside ourselves (lit. "we are ecstatic") and being in our right mind, and, gave pride of place to lucid speech, which was common among ancient rabbis, as per *b. B. Kamma* 80b; *b. Sanh.* 24b; *b. Arak.* 2b." (Alan J. Avery-Beck, p. 322).

Rabbi Sha'ul said: "Call me a madman. I don't care." In his own words, it was uttered like this: "For the Messiah's love has hold of us, because we are convinced that one man died on behalf of all mankind... in order that those who live should not live any longer for themselves but for the one who on their behalf died and was raised" (verses 14–15). Life, for Sha'ul, was a life in the service of Israel's Messiah—despite that many were unimpressed by the Messiah, himself.

Sha'ul's biographer, Luke, noted it was his habit to frequent synagogues and "reason from the Scriptures" that Yeshua was the Messiah (cf., e.g., Acts 17:1ff). The premium there was on cogent biblical exposition. When giving voice to the Messiah's death, burial and resurrection in the New Covenant corpus, Isaiah 53 is the most often quoted Old Covenant text. According to Isaiah 53:2–3, the Messiah wasn't much to look at personally. The text reads: "He was not well-formed or especially, handsome; we saw him, but his appearance did not attract us... he was despised; we did not value him." Mindful of this, Sha'ul said in verse 16: "From now on, we do not look at anyone from a worldly viewpoint. Even if we once regarded the Messiah from a worldly viewpoint, we do so no longer."

The cross was understandably looked at pejoratively. No more in this case—at least not Yeshua's cross. According to Sha'ul, individuals would not only do well to look at the Messiah's sufferings and subsequent crucifixion with a new set of eyes, but they would similarly do well to re-think the way they assess the afflictions of those who follow him. "[I]f anyone is united with the Messiah, he is a new creation—the old has passed; look, what has come is fresh and new" (v. 18)!

Individuals would do well to not make too much of the fact that Sha'ul wasn't much to look at, physically. He was an emissary/apostle, and problems with his physical condition and public appearance are not disqualifiers—later, in fact, he will note that his lackluster condition was, in fact, a qualifier—and he will make his infirmities his boast. "Messiah has reconciled us to himself and has given us the work of that reconciliation," was his message in verse 18, and "we are ambassadors of the Messiah; in effect, God is making his appeal through us," Sha'ul said in verse 20.

2 CORINTHIANS 6

While Sha'ul wanted to be appreciated as a laborer, he also wanted the Corinthians who were loyal to him to be construed as co-laborers with him. "As God's fellow-workers, we also urge you not to receive his grace and then do nothing (εἰς κενὸν, 'in vain') with it." God helps believers fulfill their destinies (cf. v. 2). His point here recalls Yeshua's parables, especially the Parable of the Talents, in Matthew 25:1-44, esp. vv. 14-30.

That many do nothing with the grace offered was noted by The Billy Graham Evangelistic Association. They noted that of those who came forward at evangelistic rallies, only 2.5% will be found in a church six months later. Here, Sha'ul wanted to facilitate their growth in faith and not hinder them. In that regard he said: "We try not to put obstacles (προσκοπήν) in anyone's path," in verse 3, and followed with: "so that no one can find fault with the work we do." Individuals were, in fact, looking for fault in the man—e.g., in Sha'ul personally, partly by, in 3:1ff, claiming he was showy and too self-commending. His response was, "We try to commend ourselves in every way as workers (διάκονοι, "servants") for God by continually enduring troubles (θλίψεσιν, "tribulations"), hardships (ἀνάγκαις), calamities (στενοχωρίαις, "distresses"), beatings (πληγαῖς), imprisonments (φυλακαῖς), riots (ἀκαταστασίαις), overwork (κόποις), lack of sleep (ἀγρυπνίαις, "watchings") and food (νηστείαις "fastings")" (vv. 4–5). This list pales in comparison to the one that will follow (cf., 11:1ff). After noting that what he endures for the message commends him as a faithful messenger of it, in verses 6–7, he spoke of his heart for the work: "We commend ourselves by our purity (ἀγνότητι), knowledge (γνώσει), patience (μακροθυμίᾳ) and kindness (χρηστότητι); by the Ruach HaKodesh; by genuineness of love and truthfulness of speech; and by God's power." He will return to the physical afflictions associated with the ministry, and their toll on his body in a few chapters.

Though weakened physically by his trials, Sha'ul made much of the power at work in and through him as he finished his letter. He will speak of the "righteous weapons" he possessed in 7. He tells them, specifically, how he was going to use them, too, later. Though he had an arsenal of weapons, granted he looked weak in the eyes of some. In verse 9 he noted he is "dishonored (ἀγνοούμενοι, "being unknown")"... and that he is a "worker headed for death (ἀποθνήσκοντες, "dying")." There was not much to feel good about, at one level. Though having a reason to be dejected as a result of his less-than-perfect circumstances, in verse 10 he said: "[though] having reason to be sad (λυπούμενοι, "sorrowful"), yet [we are] always filled with joy (χαίροντες, "rejoicing"); [though some consider us as] having nothing, yet [we see ourselves as] having everything!" To quote his point in 5:16, he did not look at things from a human point of view, but rather a spiritual one.

Sha'ul was not just emoting. Giving voice to the extent of his sufferings—for the sake of the Gospel and for their sakes—was a way of eliciting their affections. In verse 11, it is telling in that regard: for its emotion, for its drama, and for its rhetorical purposes. "Dear friends in Corinth! We have spoken frankly to you; we have opened our hearts wide." See also verse 13 for the same expression. The author is not a cardiologist, of course. When he spoke of "opening the heart" he was employing a poetic expression, denoting he had taken the liberty to make his feelings known. His ability to do so was precipitated by his realization that the community was being supportive of him at the time of 2 Corinthians' writing—something not at all apparent when he wrote 1 Corinthians. The situation, as we will see in chapter 7, changed by the writing of 2 Corinthians. He knew at this time that the better part of the community was now supportive of him—but not all. After speaking to the majority, he turned his attention to the recalcitrant minority and let them have it. More on that below.

As he opened his heart to them, in verse 13, he asked them to "open wide your hearts too." After beseeching them to be aligned with him, he beckoned them to separate from the smaller faction(s) in their midst that eroded his authorization, which had a corrosive effect on the community. In verses 14–15 he thundered: "Do not yoke yourselves together (ἑτεροζυγοῦντες, be 'unequally yoked')" in a team with unbelievers. For how can righteousness and lawlessness be partners? What fellowship does light have with darkness? What harmony can there be between the Messiah and B'liya'al? What fellowship does light have with darkness?" and with "idols" in verse 16?

The inability of light and darkness to adhere, one with another, is attested in nature. The sectaries at Qumran, the ancient Essene sect who penned the Dead Sea Scroll, made much of the principle that the "Sons of Light" needed to disassociate from the "Sons of Darkness" (cf., 1QM, *passim*). As well, the Rabbi from Tarsus made the same point, using the same language. The name, B'liya'al, employed was a name for the devil, referenced in the Hebrew Bible, and attested in Jewish and Christian literature. Though the difference between him and the Messiah is night and day, the problem is that the Prince of Darkness often appears as an Angel of Light—a point he will accentuate later in 2 Corinthians 11:14 and apply to the false teachers who had been undermining him. He carried on with his rhetorical flurry, quoting the Hebrew Bible in verses 17–18 saying: "Therefore ADONAI says, 'Go out from their midst; separate (ἀφορίσθητε) yourselves; don't even touch what is unclean. Then I myself will receive you. In fact, I will be your Father and you will be my sons and daughters,' says ADONAI-*Tzva'ot.*"

2 CORINTHIANS 7

Using fraternal language, Sha'ul referred to his readers here as "dear friends," in verse 1. He again beckoned his "friends" to disassociate from his enemies, i.e., the recalcitrant minority in Corinth who were not paying him any mind. After saying "let us purify ourselves from everything that can defile either body or spirit," in verse 1, i.e., to get away from the defiling influences (i.e., in his context contentious false teachers who have been undermining him), he again beckoned them to open their heart to him in verse 2. "Make room (Χωρήσατε) for us in your hearts—we haven't wronged (ἠδικήσαμεν) anyone, we haven't corrupted (ἐφθείραμεν) anyone, we haven't exploited (ἐπλεονεκτήσαμεν) anyone." This was emotion-laden language. His emphatic statement in verse 2 that he and his associates had not "wronged," "corrupted" or "exploited" anyone prompted the realization that he and they were accused of just that. As he will go on to disclose in a moment, he wrote 2 Corinthians realizing the better part of the community had reconciled with him and had already begun disassociating from the bad lot among them. As of this writing, he could say in verse 4, "I am very confident in you," "I am proud of you" and "you have filled me with encouragement" (παρακλήσει)—despite "of all our troubles." He could not speak in the same manner when he wrote 1 Corinthians.

Related to the "troubles" he experienced that were already mentioned a few times in the letter, he shared some specifics and noted their principal resolution. He, in verse 5, for example, opened saying: "For indeed when we came into Macedonia, our bodies had no rest. On the contrary, we faced all kinds of troubles—altercations (θλιβόμενοι, 'being pressed') without, apprehensions (φόβοι, 'fears') within."

"Altercations" speak of conflicts with others; "apprehensions" speak of internal conflicts relative to people and circumstance. Relative to both, Sha'ul said something happened for the better, something that dispelled his negative disposition. "But God who encourages the downhearted, encouraged (παρεκάλεσεν, 'comforted') us with the arrival of Titus!" Previously, Titus was dispatched to Corinth. According to verse 6, prior to writing this letter he reconnected with Sha'ul, and brought word of the Corinthians having reconsidered their disparagement of Sha'ul and noted they were wanting to be reconnected with him now. In his own words, he said in verse 7: "[I]t was not only his [i.e., Titus'] arrival which encouraged us, but also how encouraged (παρακλήσει) he was about you, as he told us how you long[ed] (ἐπιπόθησιν, "earnest desire") to see me, how distressed (ὀδυρμόν, "mourning") you are over my situation, how zealous (ζῆλον) you are in my defense—this news made me even happier!"

Sha'ul was thrilled to discover the congregation was longing to see him, distressed over his circumstance and zealous in defense of his position, refreshing, to be sure. Against that backdrop, he referred to his previously written, corrective letter, and said in verse 8: "If I caused you pain (ἐλύπησα, "grieved") by my [previous] letter, I do not regret it. Even if I did regret it before—for I do see that letter did distress you, though only for a short time." Human nature being what it is, there is always a risk when someone rebukes another. The party on the receiving end can—and often does—take umbrage and, as a result, then withdraws from the relationship— temporarily or permanently. Sha'ul was often abandoned by the communities he established (cf., 2 Tim. 1:15). In this case, the correction he delivered had its desired effect, prompting Sha'ul to say in verse 9: "Now I rejoice (χαίρω) not because you were pained, but because the pain led you to turn back to God." While, true, they inclined themselves toward Sha'ul (as just noted above), more importantly they did right by God by returning to him. In 9 he continued: "For you handled the pain in God's way, so that you were not harmed by us at all."

What is the author referring to when spoking of "God's way" in 9? When an individual is confronted with a shortcoming, with their missing the mark, they can either turn inward and bathe in a pool of emotional sorrow (and leave the matter there), or they can grieve, arise, straighten up, and change their course of direction. While repentance, itself, entails an understandable emotional component (i.e., a normal emotional response to the mishap), repentance, itself, is characterized by the grieving person taking hold of themselves and their circumstances, turning and changing their direction, thus altering their downward trajectory. The emotion, in and of itself, is not repentance—it is grief; repentance entails grief that leads to change—not just sulking.

Sha'ul said in verse 10: "Pain handled in God's way produces a turning (μετάνοιαν, 'repentance') from sin to God which leads to salvation, and there is nothing to regret in that! But pain handled in the world's way produces only death," i.e., mere emotional grief. Again, without turning and changing, when all is said and done, grief is non-productive. Titus told Sha'ul that the better part of the Corinthian community did it right, however, prompting him to say in verse 11: "For just look at what handling the pain God's way produced in you! What earnest diligence (σπουδήν), what eagerness to clear yourselves (ἀπολογίαν, 'reasoned defense'), what indignation (ἀγανάκτησιν), what fear (φόβον), what longing (ἐπιπόθησιν), what zeal (ζῆλον), what readiness (ἐκδίκησιν, 'vindication') to put things right! In everything you have proved yourselves blameless (ἁγνούς, 'innocent') in the matter." Thrilled as he was by the result, he returned to his initial rebuke and said in verses 12–13: "So even though I wrote to you, it was not for the sake of either the one who did the wrong or the one wronged, but so that before God you could see for yourselves how deep is your devotion to us. This is the reason we have been encouraged."[19]

---

19. See also 13b-16.

2 CORINTHIANS 8

For understandable reasons, chapters 8–9 seem out of place to some. Sha'ul's swift pivot to fundraising, though adjudged by some to be indicative of this section's being an interpolation by a later redactor, need not be seen as such for the following reason. Previously, in both this letter and in 1 Corinthians, he alluded to the fact that individuals questioned his honesty with money.[20] Worth noting is that the author is on much better footing with the Corinthians and now confident that the group is supportive of him. Thus, he can now more comfortably talk to them about bringing to fruition the financial gift he had previously arranged with them—and other congregations in the diaspora—and do so with an expectation of its being carried out.

He opened in verses 1–3 with: "Now, brothers, we must tell you about the grace God has given the congregations in Macedonia. Despite severe trials, and even though they are desperately poor (πολλῇ δοκιμῇ θλίψεως, "much proof of [financial] tribulation" and then βάθους πτωχεία, "deep poverty, their joy has overflowed in a wealth of generosity (ἁπλότητος). I tell you they have not merely given according to their means, but of their own free will they have given beyond (παρὰ) their means." The Greek word *charis*, i.e., "grace," was used many times in chapters 8–9. While some pride themselves in charismatic gifts, Sha'ul goes on to highlight an opportunity for them to be a gift themselves. He started off saying: Let me tell you about those Macedonians. The economy was so bad there. Employment was down and, with it, family income. Even so,

---

20. He addresses that matter more forcefully toward the close of this letter.

those Macedonians outdid themselves in their warmhearted sharing with the poor in Judea. Not only were they represented as being selfless in the matter, Sha'ul went on to say in verse 4 that "[t]hey begged (παρακλήσεως, 'entreated') and pleaded (δεόμενοι, 'imploring') with us for the privilege of sharing in this service for God's people." He represented that they were concerned they might not have the opportunity and begged for it. Continuing in verse 5, he said: "First they gave themselves to the Lord, which means, by God's will, to us." They sought God first, to ascertain what he would have them do. The fact that he was on better footing with them was evidenced by the fact that he went on to play them a bit now, while doing so—and expecting them to know that he was.

The Olympics originated with the Greeks. City-states that had warred with each other historically were beckoned to come together and fight in sportsmen-like games. Wrestling, javelin throwing, boxing, foot racing, horse racing, fencing and the like are all sports that originally had military origins. This is all worth noting because Sha'ul began his fundraising in Corinth, which was in Achaia, by giving voice to how those in Macedonia had previously responded so positively. He, in effect, said: "Hey guys. You're not going to let those others up there to the north out-do you, are you?" He is tinkering with them, and they know it. It's all for a worthy cause, however, and because the letter writer and recipients are on better footing, it affords him an opportunity to speak this way.

Gracious as they were up north, according to Sha'ul, he figured he would pitch it to their competitors in the south, in verse 6: "All this has led us to urge (παρακαλέσαι, 'exhorted') Titus to bring this same gracious gift to completion among you, since he has already made a beginning of it." He, in effect, was pitting one Greek state against another: Corinth vs. Macedonia. Who will outperform whom in this contest? He blew stardust in their face in verse 7, saying: "Just as you excel (περισσεύετε) in everything—in faith, in speech, in knowledge, in diligence of every kind, and in your love for us—see that you excel in this gift too (περισσεύητε)." In verse 8 he said: "I am not issuing an order." How can he, really—he can't. He said: "I am testing the genuineness of your love against the diligence of others."

Jews have long placed a premium on *tzedakah*, i.e., "righteous charity." "Love," for that matter, in the Hebraic mind, derives from the Hebrew word *ahav*, and speaks to one doing good on behalf of another. It is less a feeling and more a search for something tangible. The question was: Will they do good?

After playfully working them over a bit, by noting how the poor, poor Macedonians poured themselves out, Sha'ul went on to speak of the Messiah, himself, reminding of his example of giving: "For you know how generous our Lord Yeshua the Messiah was—for your sakes he impoverished himself, even though he was rich, so that he might make you rich by means of his poverty" (v.9). That said, and not simply wanting to leave it having said it, he reminded in verses 10–11 that they already agreed to attend to this and had taken some steps: "A year ago you were not only the first to act, but the first to want to do so. Now it would be to your advantage to finish what you started, so that your eagerness in wanting to commence the project may be matched by your eagerness to complete it, as you contribute from what you have." Sha'ul is nudging them.

The Macedonians were represented as being poor and, in certain respects, giving from what they did not have (see verses 1–5). The Corinthians, by contrast, were simply asked to give from what they had in verse 11. He noticed this in verse 12 and made a point that giving is more about attitude than it is amount: "For if the eagerness to give is there, the acceptability of the gift will be measured by what you have, not by what you don't have." He said, in verse 13, "it is not that relief for others should cause trouble for you, but that there should be a kind of reciprocity (ἰσότης, 'equality')," i.e., the giver gets something reciprocal in return for the gift. He rounded off that point, underscoring the principle of reciprocity and quoting the Hebrew Bible in support of it: "At present your abundance can help those in need; so that when you are in need, their abundance can help you—thus there is reciprocity. It is as the *Tanakh* says, 'He who gathered much had nothing extra, and he who gathered little had nothing lacking'"(vv. 14–15).

Speaking of "giving and receiving," the Corinthians kindly received Titus, who, subsequently went back to Sha'ul with word of their resolutions. Titus (in love with them, as he was) will return on his own initiative this time, along with another—for the purpose of receiving the offering. In his words:

> Now I thank God for making Titus as devoted to you as we are; for he not only responded to our urging, but being so devoted, he is coming [back] to you [shortly] on his own initiative. And with him we are sending the brother whose work for the Good News is praised in all the congregations; not only that, but he has also been appointed by the congregations to travel with us, so that the way we administer this charitable work will bring honor to the Lord and show our eagerness to help. (vv. 16–19)

His reasoning followed in verses 20–24:

> Our aim in this is to show that our conduct in dealing with these substantial sums is above reproach; for we take pains to do what is right not only in the sight of God but also in the sight of other people. With these two we are sending another brother of ours, one whose diligence we have tested many times in many ways, but who is now even more diligent because of his great confidence in you. As for Titus, he is my partner who works with me on your behalf; and the other brothers with him are emissaries of the congregations and bring honor to the Messiah. So, the love you show these men will justify our pride in you to them, and through them to the congregations that sent them.

Professor David Lowery observed: Sha'ul "scrupulously worked to avoid bringing any disrepute on his name through charges of mismanagement or avarice" (2 Cor. 8:20; cf., 12:17-18), "2 Corinthians," in *The Bible Knowledge Commentary* (Wheaton: Victor Books, 1984), p. 574.

Sha'ul is going out of his way to ensure the funds will be handled honorably by honorable people.

Referencing the aforementioned ministry team, Avery-Beck opined:

> The sending of Titus and two brothers (vv. 18, 22–23) might indicate that the collection is modeled on the Temple tax (Ex. 30:13–15), the delivery of which, according to Philo, *Spec. Laws* 1:76–78... was carried out by "sacred ambassadors selected on account of their virtue." (Alan J. Avery Beck, p. 325.)

His need to "take pains" and show that his conduct is "above reproach," and to add yet another level of accountability by sending yet another to accompany the gift, attests to the precariousness of leadership, in general, and the need to be ever so sensitive in managing donated monies in non-profit corporations, in particular.

2 CORINTHIANS 9

Though Sha'ul was on shaky ground with those who charged him with financial improprieties, he wrote 2 Corinthians knowing they were in the minority. Armed with this knowledge, he wrote this letter presuming their compliance with the pre-arranged offering, in verse 1, and said: "There is really no need for me to write you about this offering for God's people." That said, he went on to play the Corinthians against the Macedonians, still yet again. Whereas in chapter 8, the Macedonians were the heroic givers (mentioned to spur the Corinthians on in their philanthropy), in verse 2, Sha'ul said the Macedonians were spurred on themselves, when he shared with them word of the Corinthians' largesse. He said: "I know how eager (προθυμίαν, 'ready') you are, and I boast[ed] (καυχῶμαι) about you to the Macedonians. I tell them, 'Achaia has been ready since last year,' and it was your zeal that stirred up most of them." Given that this statement, along with the one in 8:1ff are in such proximity, there is no reason to think the Corinthians, when hearing it, would not have smiled, knowing that Sha'ul was playfully prodding them.

That it was for a good cause, and not an extension of a manipulator's endeavoring to get the better of them for his own purposes (as had been charged by some), Sha'ul again reminded them that a variety of esteemed "brothers" would attend to the monies—and not him. "But now I am sending the brothers so that our boast about you in this regard will not prove hollow," he said in verse 3. He pressed them further, with an understanding that they would smile when they heard it, much as he was snickering when he said it. In 3-4 he said: I am doing this "so that you will be ready, as I said [to the Macedonians] you would be. For if some Macedonians were to come with me and find you unprepared, we would be humiliated at having been so confident—to say nothing of how you would feel." He said he was doing it so they would not be embarrassed. While that may be, most surely, they knew what he was up to. Claiming to be thinking of their interests in verse 5, he wrote, "So I thought it necessary to urge these brothers to go on to you ahead of me and prepare your promised gift in plenty of time; this way it will be ready when I come and will be a genuine gift, not something extracted by pressure."

Though he spoke of not exacting money by "pressure," he most assuredly was gently applying some here, with the best of intentions. Returning to the important issue of reciprocity addressed previously, to underscore that it is in their best interests to give, he recited a text that was often quoted from the Hebrew Bible, opening in verse 6 with: "He who plants sparingly also harvests sparingly." With this he administered a Jewish maxim. The expression "measure for measure" (or *midda k'negged midda*) is an oft-quoted Jewish dictum. In effect, it enforces the notion that a person gets what they give. The biblical text cited comes from "Parashah T'rumah," in *Sh'mot* (Exodus) 25:1ff. "T'rumah," meaning "contribution" is a fitting title for a passage where resources for the *Mishkan* (the Tabernacle) were asked for and received. Therein, offerings were to be given "from the heart" (v. 2). With the famous Torah passage in mind, in verse 7, Rabbi Sha'ul said: "Each should give according to what he has decided in his heart, not grudgingly (λύπης, out of 'regret') or under compulsion (ἀνάγκης, 'necessity'), for God loves a cheerful (ἱλαρὸν) giver." Though it is true God loves a cheerful giver, Sha'ul was happy to take an offering even from those who weren't particularly happy. In asking for it, in verses 8–9, he held out a promise and buttressed it with a quote from the Hebrew Bible: "Moreover, God has the power to provide you with every gracious gift in abundance, so that always in every way you will have all you need yourselves and be able to provide abundantly for every good cause—as the *Tanakh* says, 'He gave generously to the poor; his *tzedakah* (charity) lasts forever.' He reiterated his point in verses 10–12: "He who provides both seed for the planter and bread for food will supply and multiply your seed and increase the harvest of your tzedakah. You will be enriched ($\pi\lambda o\upsilon\tau\iota\zeta\acute{o}\mu\epsilon\nu o\iota$) in every way, so that you can be generous ($\dot{\alpha}\pi\lambda\acute{o}\tau\eta\tau\alpha$) in everything. And through us your generosity will cause people to thank God, because rendering this holy service not only provides for the needs of God's people, but it also overflows in the many thanks people will be giving to God." Sha'ul prodded them a bit, true; still, it really is a "holy service."

The preceding passages are often cited when offerings are taken in and for local congregations, for the specific needs of the congregations. Understated in all the above is the fact that, by contrast, the offering considered in 2 Corinthians 8–9 was a mission's offering—and not for utilization locally: in this case it was a gift for Messianic Jews, in Jerusalem. The idea of getting behind Israel is foreign to many Christians today, as is the idea of supporting Messianic Jewish people and experience in Jerusalem— and in the world, at large. In verse 13, Sha'ul said: "In offering this service you prove to these [Jewish] people that you glorify God by actually doing what your acknowledgement of the Good News of the Messiah requires, namely, sharing generously with them and with everyone."

The "requirement" noted above, was similarly and explicitly attested to in Romans 15:25–27, which was written a bit later. With the money already collected from those in Macedonia and Achaia, Sha'ul wrote the Romans and said:

But now I am going to Yerushalayim [Jerusalem] with aid for God's people there. For Macedonia and Achaia thought it would be good to make some contribution to the poor among God's people in Yerushalayim. They were pleased to do it, but the fact is that they owe it to them. For if the Gentiles have shared with the Jews in spiritual matters, then the Gentiles clearly have a duty to help the Jews in material matters.

"Sharing generously with [Jews]" in verse 13, was followed by verses 14–15: "And in their [reciprocal] prayers for you they will feel a strong affection for you because [they will acknowledge their grafted in status, and, cognizant of you, will be reminded] of how gracious God has been to you. Thanks be to God for his indescribable gift!"—both the gift that you give and the gift that you are.

2 CORINTHIANS 10

At this time, Sha'ul changes his tone and gets a bit more militant—a disposition that he maintains to the end of the letter. Energized by the realization he enjoyed the confidence of the better part of the Corinthian community, Sha'ul got to and through his financial appeal, in chapters 8–9, with verve and vitality to spare. That attended to, he then turned his attention to judge the recalcitrant minority in Corinth. Given the wide circulation of the "separation of church and state" doctrine in today's economy, the notion of judging is not going to comport with the sensibilities of modern readers. In Sha'ul's day, however, local Jewish communities had their respective *Beit Dins*, i.e., tribunals called to decide in legal cases among Jews in the community, and so the idea of his "judging" would not have been seen as out of place.

Albeit there was the Great Sanhedrin (court) in Jerusalem, there were lesser tribunals in synagogues scattered throughout the Greco-Roman world. Not wanting to concern themselves with petty disputes among Jews, the Romans gave binding authority to community elders to hear and settle various civil and criminal matters. Previously, in 1 Corinthians 6:1ff, Sha'ul opened with "How dare one of you with a complaint against another go to court before pagan judges and not before God's people?" He followed up then in verses 4–6, hammering that point, as well: "Why do you put them [i.e., court cases] in front of men who have no standing in the Messianic Community [i.e., before Gentile judges]? I say, shame on you! Can it be that there isn't one person among you wise enough to be able to settle a dispute between brothers? Instead, a brother brings a lawsuit against another brother, and that before unbelievers!" Someone who speaks this way is living in a thought-world unlike our own; for, there indeed is no one vested with authorization to address civil and criminal matters in congregations today, as yesterday.

There is a tractate in the *Mishnah* (and *Talmud*) called *Gittin* that deals with legal issues associated with divorce. In 88 it says: "In every place where you find pagan law courts you must not use them, even if their laws are the same as the laws of Israel" (David Stern *Jewish New Testament Commentary*, p. 450). It was different yesterday, however. In vv. 2-3 he says: "Don't you know that God's people are going to judge the universe? If you are going to judge the universe, are you incompetent to judge these minor matters? Don't you know that we will judge angels, not to mention affairs of everyday life?"

Sha'ul opens in 2 Corinthians 10:1 with: "Now it is I myself, Sha'ul, making an appeal to you with the meekness and forbearance that come from the Messiah." He, the trial judge, is maintaining his remaining reserved, at the moment. He is speaking to those loyal to him. In verse 1 he noted how some mistakenly take his meekness, when present, as timidity and misconstrue his firmness in his letter writing as bullying: "I who am considered timid (ταπεινὸς, 'humble') when face-to-face with you, but intimidating (θαρρῶ, 'bold') from a distance." He then said in verse 2 that he was more than willing to take on his accusers but preferred not to have to: "But I beg you not to force me to be intimidating when I am with you, as I expect to be toward some who regard us as living in a worldly way (κατὰ σάρκα περιπατοῦντας, 'walking according to the flesh')."

Sha'ul was something of a beaten man physically, and admittedly not much to look at—as he will explicitly note in the very next chapter. He maintained, however, in verses 3–5 that he was still very strong:

> For although we do live in the world, we do not wage war in a worldly way; because the weapons we use to wage war are not worldly. On the contrary, they have God's power for demolishing strongholds. We demolish arguments and every arrogance that raises itself up against the knowledge of God; we take every thought captive and make it obey the Messiah.

Though he preferred to be gentle, he represented himself as being able and willing to fight, if necessary. Expecting his loyalists in Corinth to rally behind him now, in verse 6, he referenced their compliance with "becom[ing] completely obedient," and, with that assured, he pivoted and said: "then we will be ready to punish (ἐκδικῆσαι, 'avenge') every act of disobedience (παρακοήν)"—and there, indeed still, were residual acts of disobedience.

David Stern observed how Sha'ul "makes use of irony [in this text], even sarcasm, as he ridicules his opponents, especially the 'super-emissaries' (11:5; 12:11) who are actually 'pseudo-emissaries' (11:13)." (*Jewish New Testament Commentary*, p. 513.)

In a somewhat defensive tone—though he really is just badgering his foes—he continued in verse 7: "You," i.e., the contentious sorts, "are looking at the surface of things. If anyone is convinced that he belongs to the Messiah, he should remind himself that we belong to the Messiah as much as he does." In effect he is saying: "If you think you've got something going with the Lord, fair enough: I've got something going, too." He continued in verses 8–9: "For even if I boast a little too much about the authority the Lord has given us—authority to build you up, not tear you down—I am not ashamed. My object is not to seem as if I were trying to frighten (ἐκφοβεῖν) you with these letters." This is what some of his detractors are saying. In verse 10 he noted: "Someone says, 'His letters are weighty and powerful, but when he appears in person, he is weak, and as a speaker he is nothing.'" In verse 1 he alluded that some of his detractors in Corinth alleged he was mightier with his pen than he was with his presence. He called them out in verse 11, warning: "Such a person should realize that what we say in our letters when absent (ἀπόντες), we will do when present (παρόντες)."

As noted above, the Corinthians had slipped into comparing and classifying teachers when he first wrote them (cf., 1 Cor. 1:10–16); but, by the time of the writing of 2 Corinthians, the situation had been amended, though not entirely. Some of the haughty, false teachers in Corinth had not vacated their position, and so Sha'ul carried on with his corrective in verse 12: "[Unlike some among you] we don't dare class or compare ourselves with some of the people who advertise themselves. In measuring themselves against each other and comparing themselves with each other, they are simply stupid (οὐ συνιᾶσιν, "not understand[ing]")." Sha'ul did not abide celebrating religious personalities and diversifying into petty religious tribalism. He did, however, compare himself on one count. Unlike the false teachers who entered his domain in Corinth, sometime after he had established it, he said in verse 13 that: "We will not boast (καυχησόμεθα) about what lies outside the area of work which God has given us; rather, we will boast within our assigned area, and that area does reach as far as you." He underscored that the false emissaries/apostles were not really emissaries/apostles, at all.

They are not out in the world building anything; rather, they simply entered a house that Sha'ul built and, for a fee (as we shall see), began undermining Sha'ul, by casting another vision for what it means to walk in the footsteps of Israel's Messiah. Unlike the interlopers bent on undermining him, Sha'ul said in verse 14–16: "We are not overextending (ὑπερεκτείνομεν) our boasting as if we had not reached as far as you; for we did come all the way to you with the Good News of the Messiah. We do not boast about the area in which others labor (ἀλλοτρίοις κόποις); but our hope is that as your trust grows, we will be magnified in your midst in relation to our own area of work, so that we can go on to do even more, namely, to proclaim the Good News in regions beyond you. Our hope is not to boast about the work already done by someone else." Having differentiated himself from the others on this score, he rounds off the point in verses 17–18 saying: "So, let anyone who wants to boast, boast about ADONAI; because it is not the one who recommends himself (ἑαυτὸν συνιστάνων, 'himself promoting') who is worthy of approval, but the one whom the Lord recommends (συνίστησιν)."

2 CORINTHIANS 11

Sha'ul was just getting started in chapter 10. With his nemeses in full view, he went on to give full vent to his pent-up, righteous indignation. He opens in verse 1: "I would like you to bear with me in a little foolishness (συνίστησιν) —please do bear with me!" He used the word *aphrosyne*, i.e., "foolishness," as opposed to having a moderate and sober disposition. He, in effect, was saying: "I need you to bear with me for a second. I'm going to shoot straight, ramp it up, and it's going to sound a bit rough" …. He continued in verse 2: "For I am jealous (ζηλῶ) for you with God's kind of jealousy; since I promised to present you as a pure virgin in marriage to your one husband, the Messiah." He likened himself to a father who had raised a daughter and who, among other things, had wanted to present her to a future husband in perfect condition. Thus inclined, he reported being disturbed in verse 3: "I fear (Φοβοῦμαι) [now, however,] that somehow your minds may be seduced (φθαρῇ, "corrupted") away from simple and pure devotion to the Messiah, just as *Havah* [Eve] was deceived by the serpent and his craftiness." He alighted upon his astonishment at discovering the young woman he tenderly raised seemed to have disregarded his instruction and, was now, preferring the guidance of others. "For if someone comes and tells you about some other Yeshua than the one, we told you about," he said in verse 4, "or if you receive a spirit different from the one you received or accept some so-called 'good news' different from the Good News you already accepted, you bear with him well enough!" Havah was deceived by the serpent's schemes. Having reminded them of that, he castigated individuals for abiding by the deceitful notions, not to mention the insults to his person perpetrated by those who wanted to undermine him.

In 10:12 he said he wasn't inclined to "compare" himself with "some of the people who advertise themselves," i.e., the other teachers who came to Corinth after his departure. In 11:5, however, he seemed to backtrack and do just that: "For I don't consider myself in any way inferior (ὑστερηκέναι) to these 'super-emissaries' ('Υπερλίαν ἀποστόλων, "most eminent apostles")." Mindful of their claiming to be better than him, Sha'ul pushed back and said these slick religious "super-stars" don't have anything on him. Listening to their critique of his straightforward style, he retorted in verse 6: "I may not be a skilled speaker, but I do have the knowledge (γνώσει); anyhow, we have made this clear to you in every way and in every circumstance."[21] Sha'ul, as we know, did in fact have an advanced academic pedigree—more so than the originals who first followed the Lord from Galilee; he, however, was not ostentatious, and preferred direct speech over needless verbosity. Having addressed their critique of his style, Sha'ul went on to compare himself to his nemeses on another matter—money.

"Did I sin in humbling myself so that you could be exalted, in proclaiming God's Good News to you free of charge (δωρεὰν)?" was Sha'ul's rhetorical question in verse 7. In verses 7–12, he reminded his hearers that he asked nothing from them. For rhetorical purposes, he asked if that was a sin; it isn't, of course. Later, in 12:12, for the same purposes, he apologized for not burdening them financially. A trained orator, Sha'ul employed a genre called "irony." He was being hyperbolic, for effect, and his readers understood that. Avery-Beck (p. 328) showed that "Greco-Roman philosophers viewed craftsmen as debased, but rabbis did not." He went on to say, by way of contradistinction, rabbinic literature extols the virtues of those who work with their hands, evidenced in *b. Ber.* 58; *b. Moed Qat.* 13 and *b. Arak.* 10. Sha'ul's Gentile critics might have looked skeptically at him because of his "blue collar," side bar

---

21 . Recall 1 Corinthians 2:1 where he made a spirited defense for his simple approach to communication.

vocation, thinking it beneath the station of intellectual luminaries. Pharisees, in Jewish culture, were more popular than Sadducees, precisely because they worked with their hands. Sha'ul made the Corinthians' disparagement his boast.

In verse 8, he hyperbolically said: "I robbed (ἐσύλησα) other congregations by accepting support from them in order to serve you." He did not "rob" them, of course. His tone was ramped up so his listeners would understand he was speaking this way for an effect. Sha'ul did not steal from other congregations, but he did solicit personal financial support from them. In verse 9 he reminded: "When I was with you and had needs, I did not burden (κατενάρκησα) anyone: my needs were met by the brothers who came from Macedonia. In nothing have I been a burden to you, nor will I be." He explained that he was helped along by Macedonians. For a reason he disclosed here, however, he opted not to accept support from the Corinthians.

> The truthfulness of the Messiah is in me, so that this boast concerning me is not going to be silenced anywhere in Achaia. Why won't I ever accept your support? Is it that I don't love you? God knows I do! No, I do it—and will go on doing it—to cut the ground from under those who want an excuse to boast that they work the same way we do, he said in verses 10–12. In verse 12 he further explained he wanted to distinguish himself from others whom he sarcastically referred to as "super-apostles" by, among other things, underscoring that unlike them, he didn't ask the Corinthians to personally support him financially. He was reiterating an issue he had brought up previously.

In 1 Corinthians 9:6 he forcefully put forth that he and Bar Nabba (i.e., Barnabas) are "required to go on working for our living?" It was a self-requirement, however, that they choose to do so. He wanted to use their doing so to again counter the new teachers in Corinth who were undermining them and lording it over the constituents there—and leaning on them for financial support. More on that later.

"Did you ever hear of a soldier paying his own expenses (ὀψωνίοις)?" he asked in verse 7, fully knowing that soldiers were paid by the empire. Sha'ul was making the point that the faith community can pay ministers. He followed with: "[Did you ever hear of] a farmer planting a vineyard without eating (οὐκ ἐσθίει, "not does eat") its grapes?" The answer is no because the farmer is entitled to the product of his labor. Sha'ul then asked another pointed question: "Who shepherds a flock without drinking (οὐκ ἐσθίει, "not does drink") some of the milk?" The answer was: he does—but he's not playing his hand quite yet. He quoted the Torah in 1 Cor. 9:9: "for in the *Torah* of Moshe it is written, 'You are not to put a muzzle on an ox when it is treading out the grain,'" and then explained his point more fully in verses 9–12:

> If God is concerned about cattle, all the more does He say this for our sakes. Yes, it was written for us, meaning that he who plows, and he who threshes should work expecting to get a share of the crop. If we have sown spiritual seed among you, is it too much if we reap a material (σαρκικὰ) harvest from you? If others are sharing this right to be supported by you, don't we have a greater claim to it? But we don't make use of this right. Rather, we put up with all kinds of things so as not to impede in any way the Good News about the Messiah.

Later in 2 Corinthians, Sha'ul pressed the point about his working among them for free much further, to differentiate himself from the false teachers who were both undermining his religious authority and exploiting the Corinthians for their financial gain.

Money is a thorny issue—then and now; and, in 1 Corinthians 16:1–4, he gave heed to arrangements he had previously made for its collection and distribution. In verse 1, he spoke of "the collection being made for God's people" and said: "you are to do the same as I directed the congregations in Galatia to do."[22] Sha'ul's congregations in the *Galut* (i.e., those outside Judea) were constituted both by Jews and non-Jews. As a show of solidarity with the Jewish people, Sha'ul beckoned his non-Jewish associates to lay aside monies that, in turn, were to be sent to Yerushalayim as a gift to the Messianic Jewish believers there (See v. 3 below). The offering noted in 1 Corinthians was addressed in much more detail in 2 Corinthians, chapters 8–9. As for its specifics, he is on record saying: "Every first of the week (μίαν σαββάτου), on *Motza'ei-Shabbat*, each of you should set some money aside, according to his resources, and save it up; so that when I come, I won't have to do fundraising" (v. 2). This offering for Jewish believers was to be collected *Motza'ei-Shabbat* (i.e., gathered after the Sabbath). By Jewish reckoning, this would be on the first day of the week (See *Complete Jewish Study Bible*, p. 1652), what we would call Sunday.[23] However, it actually begins Saturday night by biblical reckoning, where a new day begins just after sundown.

The offering was to be gathered over time, and because the sum would have been rather large, Sha'ul wasn't minded to handling it himself. In verse 3 he said: "[W]hen I arrive, I will give letters of introduction to the people you have approved, and I will send them to carry your gift to Yerushalayim," and then in verse 4 "If it seems appropriate that I go too, they will go along with me." He attempted to engender confidence in its handling by assuring it will be safeguarded and managed by individuals of their choosing, who enjoy their confidence.

Previously, in 2 Corinthians 8:16–17 he mentioned Titus' involvement, saying: "...he is coming [to Corinth] on his own

---

22. For a detailed example of Sha'ul's fundraising for the Judean brethren, see Rom. 15:25-27.
23. Interestingly, it's in effect a Sunday offering by today's standard.

initiative (αὐθαίρετος, "of his own accord")." In verses 18–19, he referenced another brother chosen to come help on the basis of his sterling reputation: "And with him we are sending the brother whose work for the Good News is praised (ἔπαινος) in all the congregations; not only that, he has also been appointed by the congregations to travel with us, so that the way we administer this charitable work will bring honor to the Lord and show our eagerness to help." He continues in verses 20–21 saying: "Our aim in this is to show that our conduct in dealing with these substantial sums is above reproach; for we take pains to do what is right not only in the sight of God but also in the sight of other people." He mentioned another brother sent to help in verse 22.[24] Money matters are sensitive, and Paul is on record by approaching those matters with understanding of the precariousness associated with collected monies.

Interestingly, for reasons that surface again in 2 Corinthians, some alleged he was stealthily taking money from the Corinthians. They besmirched his character, alleging he raised offerings in Corinth, for believers in Judea, but he, in fact, was taking money for himself. Being remunerated financially was a right he chose not to exercise. To illustrate and buttress the point, various industries evolved in Jerusalem to assist Temple priests receive remuneration for services rendered while working there. The hides of sacrificial animals offered went to tanneries, providing priests with some revenue in return for services provided. Other parts of sacrificial animals were eaten by priests as another form of payment. Waste product, e.g., blood, entrails and the like, were gathered up and sold as fertilizer, with monies returning to the priests in exchange for services carried out at the Temple site. Common knowledge then— though not commonly known now—Sha'ul stated emphatically in

---

24. It didn't assuage the aggravations of his critics, however. Later, in 2 Corinthians he wards off those who say he deceived them and he's tapping into the monies for his own purposes.

verse 13: "Don't you know that those who work in the Temple get their food from the Temple, and those who serve at the altar get a share of the sacrifices offered there?"

He applied the principle to himself, though he deprived himself of its employment. In 1 Corinthians 9:14 he made his application:

> In the same way, the Lord directed that those who proclaim the Good News should get their living from the Good News." Note the conjunction, "but" in verse 15, and what follows in verses 16–18: "But I have not made use of any of these rights. Nor am I writing now to secure them for myself, for I would rather die than be deprived of my ground for boasting! For I can't boast merely because I proclaim the Good News — this I do from inner compulsion: woe is me if I don't proclaim the Good News! For if I do this willingly, I have a reward; but if I do it unwillingly, I still do it, simply because I've been entrusted with a job. So then, what is my reward? Just this: that in proclaiming the Good News I can make it available free of charge, without making use of the rights (κέχρημαι οὐδενὶ τούτων, "have not used these [rights]") to which it entitles me.

Lander (p. 301) believes Sha'ul is alighting upon the rabbinic principle: *sekhar mitzvah*, i.e., "the performance of a divine imperative is its own reward" (*m. Avot* 4.2). In any case, Sha'ul had rights he chose not to exercise.

In 2 Corinthians 11, Sha'ul spoke of "pseudo-emissaries"— fakes! —in verse 13. He said: "they tell lies about their work and masquerade (μετασχηματιζόμενοι) as emissaries of the Messiah." For rhetorical purposes, he followed up expressing little-to-no alarm, saying in verse 14: "There is nothing surprising in that, for the Adversary himself[25] masquerades (μετασχηματίζεται) as an angel of light." The appellation "Lucifer" has its roots in this verse. It comes

---

25. Already alluded to in v. 3.

from a Latin epithet meaning "light bearer," and gives attention to the passage in Isaiah 14:12 where the prophet spoke of the "morning star," i.e., the rising son that displaces the darkness. Individuals think he was displacing the darkness when, in truth, he was expanding the influence of his darkness. Lucifer is said to deceitfully peddle his influence, and Sha'ul furthered in verse 15: "so it's no remarkable thing if his workers masquerade as servants of righteousness. They will meet the end their deeds deserve,"

Sha'ul introduced this embellished flurry in verse 1, begging permission to parrot a "little foolishness." In verse 16 though, he said: "I repeat don't let anyone think I am a fool." He previously disembarked upon how his boastful nemeses underestimated his foolish speech and unimpressive presence. Though not wanting to be understood as a fool, he went on to beg permission to sound like one for a moment, in verses 16–21, in advance of his tendering a foolish boast in verse 22–33—the contents of which are worthy of much reflection. In verse 19 he castigated them saying "you yourselves... gladly put up with fools!" (ἀνέχεσθε τῶν ἀφρόνων, 'you bear with fools') and in verse 20 that "You put up with it if someone makes slaves (καταδουλοῖ, 'enslaves') of you, exploits (κατεσθίει, 'devours') you, takes you in, puffs himself up, slaps (δέρει, 'strikes') you in the face." He was giving heed to some abiding false teachers who were taking advantage of them. Mindful of that, he now said in effect, they put up with foolishness, fine— put up with mine now.

Sha'ul went on to compare himself to those who had been undermining him. "Are they Hebrew speakers?" he asked in verse 22; "So am I," was his response. "Are they of the people of Isra'el?" he continued; "So am I," was his response again. "Are they descendants of Avraham?" he asked; "So am I" was his answer, once again. In verse 23 he further inquired: "Are they servants of the Messiah?" By way of response, he critically reflected on his response and said: "I'm talking like a madman!" (παραφρονῶν, 'beside myself') and followed by saying "I am a better one!" He went on further: "I've worked much harder, been imprisoned more often, suffered more beatings, [and] been near death over and over." The false teachers commend themselves to the Corinthians based on their eloquent religious speech (1 Cor. 2:1ff) and ecstatic spiritual jargon (1 Cor. 11–14). For his part, Sha'ul justified his simple speech, noted he has ecstatic speech (1 Cor. 14:17) and revelations (2 Cor. 12:1–6), as well, but saved the better part of his commendation for his sufferings.

For Sha'ul, the proof of his ministry was the price he paid for it personally. To make it clear, he continued in verses 24–27, saying:

> I received forty lashes less one... Three times I was beaten with rods. Once I was stoned. Three times I was shipwrecked. I spent a night and a day in the open sea. In my many travels I have been exposed to danger from rivers, danger from robbers, danger from my own people, danger from Gentiles, danger in the city, danger in the desert, danger at sea, danger from false brothers. I have toiled and endured hardship, often not had enough sleep, been hungry and thirsty, frequently gone without food, been cold and naked.

Sha'ul used his sufferings as a double-edged sword.

On one side, he used his sufferings as proof of his love for the Lord, for the Corinthians, and for his ministry; on the other, the aggregate effect of his physical sufferings explained why he did not present to the Corinthians as a perfect specimen of physical health. Re-read the list of sufferings in verses 24–27. An older man at the time of the writing, who would begrudge the author being a bit war-torn physically? He will go on to develop that assessment in the next chapter. He finishes off his list of physical distresses by talking about the emotional stress he was under in his ministry. "And besides these external matters," he said in verse 28: "there is the daily pressure (ἐπίστασίς) of my anxious concern for all the congregations." Boldly, in verses 29–30, he followed: "Who is weak without my sharing his weakness... If I must boast, I will boast about things that show how weak (ἀσθενεῖ) I am." The rabbis spoke of God's *yisurin shel'ahav*, i.e., "chastisement of love," what we would call "trials" today. Lander speaks of the "suffering of the righteous" here (*Gen. Rab. 40.3*; *b. Ber. 5a-b*), p. 303.

Sha'ul's biographer, Luke, gave a window's view into his entrance to the Messianic fold, in Acts 9:1ff. In verses 15–16 of that chapter, and in response to questions raised about Sha'ul's past, a prophetic word was given over Sha'ul: "[This man] is a chosen instrument to carry my name to the nations... I will show him how much he will have to suffer on account of my name." In 2 Corinthians 11, Sha'ul gave his readers a glimpse into those sufferings. Anticlimactic, he finished his list of sufferings in verses 31–33, by noting an incident that pales in intensity in comparison to the list just noted.

"God the Father of the Lord Yeshua — blessed be he forever — knows that I am not lying! When I was in Dalmanuta, the governor under King Aretas had the city of Dalmanuta guarded to arrest me; but I was lowered in a basket through an opening in the wall and escaped his clutches." Sha'ul referred to an earlier-in-life ministry escape noted in Acts 9:19–25—not itself a major source of suffering, but to underscore how, at the very outset, he knew that his life would be checkered by trials and great escapes.

2 CORINTHIANS 12

The emissary who was ramping up in chapters 10–11 hadn't lost any steam by the time he got to this next chapter. Relative to the "madness" and "boasting" he talked about previously, in 12:1 he informed them that he was not done yet. "I have to boast," he said; "There is nothing to be gained by it, but I will go on to [give voice to] visions (ἀσθενεῖ) and revelations (ἀποκαλύψεις) of the Lord" [I have had]. Truth is, there is something to be gained by it—or why say it? Sha'ul, himself, derived no benefit, true; however, he is hoping to get utility out of the story that follows in verses 2–4, for reasons that will be considered immediately below.

> I know a man in union with the Messiah, who fourteen years ago was snatched up to the third heaven; whether he was in the body or outside the body I do not know, God knows. And I know that such a man—whether in the body or apart from the body I do not know, God knows—was snatched [26] into *Gan 'Eden* and heard things that cannot be put into words, things unlawful for a human being to utter.

In verse 2 he said, "I know a man," all his readers—both then and now—understand that he is, in fact, the man. Avery-Beck (p. 329) sees "the oblique self-reference" as "following the apocalyptic convention of anonymous authorship....In rabbinic anecdotes, narrators often refer to themselves in third person as "that man" (cf., e.g., *b. Moved Qat* 17a). In verse 2 that man was "snatched up to the third heaven"—a figure of speech denoting an unknown level in

---

26. The Greek used here, *harpazo*, is the same word employed in 1 Thess. 4:17 to denote what's called the "rapture."

heaven; and then, in verse 4, he said the man was "snatched to *Gan 'Eden*"[27] and "heard things he cannot put into words." This "chosen instrument," laid siege to the claim that he, himself, had an intense, spiritual experience. Here, too, Avery-Beck is helpful: "Paradise... according to mystical Judaism (see e.g., *Ex. Rab.* 25.7–8; 45:6, and esp. *b. Hag.*14) [is where] one obtains a vision of God."[28] Sha'ul indicates that he was seen and heard from Heaven—and thus is not inferior to the ecstatic prophet-ladies who were critical of him and claimed to be better than him.

Some might say Sha'ul was "out of his mind" and they are entitled to their opinion. Irrespective, the language comported with Jewish views. Why did he opt to talk about his trip to Paradise now? Why here? The alleged super-emissaries who were dismissive of Sha'ul claimed they were more spiritually elevated than he was. As noted above, 1 Corinthians was awash in correctives on spiritual gifts, the giving of prophetic words, and the need for prophets to be accountable. He straightened it out there and then, and now he wanted to clarify more of his own position and experience relative to spiritual experiences. Though Sha'ul was less showy and less fantastic in his approach to ministry as the false ministers, he went on record insisting he, indeed, had spiritual experiences. In verse 6 he said: "because of the extraordinary greatness (ὑπερβολῇ, 'surpassingness') of the revelations (ἀποκαλύψεων), I refrain [from speaking in detail], so that no one will think more of me than what my words or deeds may warrant."

That said, in verse 7, he pivoted away from his elevated spiritual experience(s) and informed: "Therefore, to keep me from becoming overly proud, I was given a thorn (σκόλοψ) in my flesh, a messenger (ἄγγελος) from the Adversary to pound away at me, so that I

---

27. *Gan'Eden* harks to Gen. 2:8. It is referred to as "paradise," from the Greek word *paradeisos*.
28. Alan J. Avery-Beck, p. 330.

wouldn't grow conceited (ὑπεραίρωμαι)." The nature of the "thorn in the flesh" has been the object of some consideration by scholars. It is adjudged best to understand that Sha'ul had a noteworthy and unrelenting physical affliction, poor eyesight. Sha'ul spoke of his poor vision in Galatians 4:13–15. In verse 13 he noted explicitly: "I was ill," and in verse 14 "even though my physical condition must have tempted you to treat me with scorn, you did not display any sign of disdain or disgust. No, you welcomed me as if I had been an angel of God, as if I had been the Messiah Yeshua himself!"

In verse 15 he went on to say: "I bear you witness that had it been possible, you would have gouged out your eyes and given them to me." These earlier texts, coupled with the fact that he used scribes to write his letters, gives credence to the notion he had an enduring physical problem with his eyes. That issue, along with enduring so much physical trauma over the years, the aging man's body was less than perfect, which prompted his critics to say he was spiritually deficient. They reasoned, if he were an emissary of the New Covenant, surely the Spirit's miracle-work would be manifest in him and fix all that.

Relative to his affliction(s), Sha'ul said in verses 8–9:

> Three times I begged the Lord to take this thing away from me; but he told me, 'My grace (χάρις) is enough for you, for my power (δύναμις) is brought to perfection in weakness (ἀσθενείᾳ).' Therefore, I am happy to boast about my weaknesses, in order that the Messiah's power will rest upon me.

When we ask the Lord for something, we do best to realize that sometimes the answer is, "No!" In this case, the weakness in his body was construed by Sha'ul as a mechanism to keep him humble—and thus powerful (cf., v. 7). He made peace with his less than perfect condition—though some others apparently had not— and said in verse 10: "Yes, I am well pleased with weaknesses (ἀσθενείαις), insults (ὕβρεσιν), hardships (ἀνάγκαις), persecutions (διωγμοῖς) and difficulties (στενοχωρίαις) endured on behalf of the Messiah; for it is when I am weak that I am strong." C. S. Lewis once said: "Humility isn't thinking less of yourself; rather, it is thinking of yourself less." After giving voice to a hefty amount of self-disclosure, he backed off thinking and talking about himself. He hit the brakes on revealing more about himself and hit the throttle on attacking the false teachers in Corinth—as he finished up his letter.

In verse 11, he hit himself and them hard: "I have behaved like a fool, but you forced me to do it—you who should have been commending (συνίστασθαι) me." His point in his argument was that he shouldn't have needed to commend himself and his ministry to them in this letter; rather, they should have taken a stand for him all along.[29] Sha'ul battled on in verse 11: "For I am in no way inferior (ὑστέρησα, 'was I inferior') to the 'super-emissaries' (Ὑπερλίαν ἀποστόλων, 'most eminent apostles'), even if I am nothing." The "super-emissaries" claimed they were more spiritual and had more spiritual power than the semi-blind, aging, weak Sha'ul. He had already owned his weakness. He understood his overall condition was the result of years of abuses on the road—e.g., beatings, imprisonments, shipwrecks and the like. He knows God delivered him from many distresses, and he understands that his eye problems remained to keep him humble.

With personal difficulties aside, he contended in verse 12: "The things that prove I am an emissary—signs, wonders and miracles— were done in your presence, despite what I had to endure." Miracle-working was, indeed, the authenticating criterion for apostolicity. When tendering a history of Sha'ul's travels, his biographer, Luke, frequently alighted upon the miracles performed through him—

---

29. They hadn't. Happily, however, they came together and made a start of it by the time of this writing.

noting in the Acts of the Apostles that they were identical to those performed through Kefa/Peter. Though Sha'ul was less than perfect in his physical body, he forcefully contended that the Ruach/Spirit was at work in and through him spiritually.

Having countered his critics with his diatribe, he gave one parting shot in verse 13: "Is there any way in which you have been behind (ἡσσώθητε, 'inferior') any of the other congregations, other than in my not having been a burden to you? For this unfairness (ἀδικίαν, 'wrong'), please forgive me (χαρίσασθέ μοι)!" As a counter to the false teachers who were bleeding the Corinthians financially, he finished his response and critique by sarcastically apologizing for not being a financial "burden" to them, i.e., for not taking any money from them.

In 1 Corinthians 11, Rabbi Sha'ul addressed the issue of out-of-control women—super-spiritual, prophetess types. In that verse, he previously picked up on a marriage motif and began speaking about the nature of the covenant relationship between a married man and married woman. This was not to be a marriage lesson, however.[30] In 1 Corinthians 11:3 he said: "But I want you to understand that the head of every man is the Messiah, and the head of a wife is her husband, and the head of the Messiah is God." Plato, and Philo later, saw the "head" as the most divine part of the human body. See Philo, *On Creation* 119; Plato *Tim.* 45a, *Leg.* 12.942e. The notion of "God's glory resting on the men's heads like a crown" was axiomatic in Sha'ul's day. See Psalms 8:5 (LXX 8:6); *Bar.* 5.2; 4Q491 frag. 11; *1 Enoch* 62:15-16; *b. Ber.* 17b; *b. Sanh.* 111b; *b. Meg.15b.* (Shira Lander, p. 304.) Sha'ul descended upon the

---

30. Though he does say "For a man indeed should not have his head veiled, because he is the image and glory of God, and the woman is the glory of man (v. 7). For man was not made from woman, but woman from man (v. 8); and indeed man was not created for the sake of the woman but woman for the sake of the man" (v. 9), *his principle point is to take on women who are not under authority,* e.g., some independent prophetess types in Corinth who are eroding his with the prophetic banter.

authority motif with it (i.e., 'headship'), and immediately pivoted to a consideration of prayer and then prophecy, which was really where he was going.

In verses 4–5, Sha'ul said: "Every man who prays (προσευχόμενος, 'praying') or prophesies (προφητεύων, 'prophesying') wearing something down over his head brings shame to his head, but every woman who prays or prophesies with her head unveiled (ἀκατακαλύπτῳ, 'uncovered') brings shame to her head—there is no difference between her and a woman who has had her head shaved." Some have slighted Jewish men who pray with a skull cap, a *yarmulke* (or *kippah*), based on the mandate to not pray with heads covered in verse 4. Happily, this misread is corrected in the *Complete Jewish Bible*, where it is rendered with "wearing something down over his head." The Halachic (rabbinic) dictum to "cover your head in order that the fear of heaven may be upon you" (*Shabbat* 156^{b}) was written much later. (See the *Complete Jewish Study Bible*, p. 1644 for more on the matter.) Rabbi Sha'ul was not critiquing Jewish approaches to Hebrew men and their piety, much as he was looking more deliberately at *women*. "For if a woman is not veiled, let her also have her hair cut short," was his follow up in verse 6, and then "but if it is shameful for a woman to wear her hair cut short or to have her head shaved, then let her be veiled." Rabbi Sha'ul wanted to get utility out of the necessity of women having a head covering while in prayer. What is unclear to some is as to why.

In verse 10, a women's veil was worn for the purpose of "demonstrating that she is under authority." Notions of dominance and submission were central in Greco-Roman culture. Though such notions seem anachronistic today, readers need to realize they are venturing into yesterday's world, and endeavor to give the literature a fair hearing within the culture and context within which it was written.

The interdependent nature of women and men, in and of itself, was less the issue in Sha'ul's writing as was the need for a structured relationship between the real 'head,' i.e., the Lord himself (cf. v. 3) and his conduit vessels, i.e., those who give voice in his Name. Women who prophesied ecstatically and independently of any designated authority, were found wanting—and this was his principal problem and point.

Recall the super-spiritual prophet-teachers noted in 1 Corinthians 1:12. At the letter's outset, Sha'ul noted there were those who claimed no adherence to human authorities. In his case, those authorities were himself, Apollos or Kefa (Peter). In Sha'ul's words, they, in effect, were saying: "I [only] follow the Messiah." After that, Sha'ul said he had no bone to pick with Apollos and Kefa. Kefa is not mentioned elsewhere in the Corinthian correspondence.[31] What were left were the independent, super-spiritual ones—women in this case.

Sha'ul's nemeses are here in view: independently minded, supposedly-prophetic women, who were uttering things—in the name of the Spirit—contrary to Sha'ul. Another woman named Chole, (cf. 1:11) a woman with means and influence, who was particularly loyal to Sha'ul, took issue with those ladies. She informed Sha'ul about them and the fight was on. Returning to his opening argument—which will extend into 1 Corinthians chapters 12–15—Sha'ul said in verses 10–12: "The reason a woman should show by veiling her head that she is under authority has to do with the angels. Nevertheless, in union with the Lord neither is woman independent of man nor is man independent of woman; for as the woman was made from the man, so also the man is now born through the woman. But everything is from God." The notion that

---

31. A subtle reference to individuals who, like Kefa, were more prone to subscribe to the conventions of then-traditional Jewish religious experience and understanding is to be noted. Sha'ul, himself, was Torah-observant; he, however, was much more liberal toward non-Jews than were his Jewish compatriots.

God was the source, author, and thus authority was an established dictum, and was not an invention of the emissary. The problem in Corinth was that some were acting independently of designated authority: a pushy woman—or women.

Sha'ul's cryptic utterance in verse 10 about women being veiled "because of the angels" has mystified interpreters—this one included. Lander thinks Sha'ul may be paying attention to Genesis 6:1ff and employing an expression used by the ancients: "...to avoid the 'watchers,'" the "watchers" being angels. See *1 En.* 6-11; *T. Naph.* 3.5; *Tg. Ps. -J* to Gen. 6:2. (Shira Lander, p. 304.) That aside, and thinking that to be sufficient, Sha'ul continued in verse 13: "Decide for yourselves: is it appropriate for a woman to pray to God when she is unveiled," i.e., independent of authority, what we call an authoritative "covering" today. He then made a point in verses 14–15 that would resonate decisively with his hearers in his day, though not necessarily with readers in our own day: "Doesn't the nature of things itself teach you that a man who wears his hair long degrades himself? But a woman who wears her hair long enhances her appearance, because her hair has been given to her as a covering." He was appealing to standards that had bearing in his own time, not our own. This author, for example, does not think males degrade themselves by having long hair—unless they do so to telegraph transgender impulses.

All said, an otherwise liberally minded Sha'ul drew a line in the sand in verse 16: "If anyone wants to argue about it, the fact remains that we have no such custom, nor do the Messianic communities of God." The uncharacteristic force with which he issued a challenge is telling, indicative, as it was of a primary concern. He simply did not abide pushy and misinformed unauthorized religious spokespersons who, in this case, happen to have been women.

In 1 Corinthians 11:1ff, Sha'ul took on the matter of women prophesying without veils. Later, in chapter 14, Sha'ul took the veil off the argument he was pressing and seemed to firmly suggest women should not talk in congregations at all. It wasn't a generalizable statement—one for all people and all times—much as it was him dealing with exigent circumstances in Corinth. After saying that in verse 35, he seemed to snarl in verse 36, with: "Did the word of God originate with you? Or are you the only people it has reached?" Granted these are difficult statements, but note what followed in verses 37–38: "...acknowledge that what I am writing you is a command of the Lord. But if someone does not recognize this, then let him remain unrecognized." Bold language, is it not?

These chapters close with verse 40: "Let all things be done in a proper and orderly way," which reminds the reader again what it means to be "proper." Taking the text in context, the "orderly way" in Corinth entailed religious proclamations uttered in accordance with apostolic guidelines. In the Corinthian case, the unauthorized women who were preaching improperly, and who were disorderly, were pressed to be silent and submitted. For a variety of reasons, at face value, this is a tough read for moderns. Working the text contextually gives it an important sense that would not otherwise be there.

Is Rabbi Sha'ul a misogynist? Is he game to silence women? Was this his culture? Flavius Josephus noted that Jewish women spoke publicly in civil matters in *Ant.* 13.405, e.g., and in synagogues, too. (*ClJ* 741). See Shira Lander, p. 310. Sha'ul sounds misogynistic; but sounds, like looks, can be misleading.

When we hear Sha'ul's voice in this passage—and it is his voice—it is little wonder why modern women (and men) have trouble coming to terms with the man and his message. How can the New Testament[32] be a credible source of instruction for modern people, some ask. It is indeed an exceptionally good question.

---

32. Where his writings are dominant.

Many say language like this may have resonated in the minds of first century hearers, but it simply does not fit the sensibilities of modern readers. Should we understand that Rabbi Sha'ul was against women's participation in religious services? He seems to have been but looks can be deceiving. If one reads him within the context of his specific situation the perspective improves greatly. Here is a better question—and note the nuanced differences in it— Is the truth in 1 Corinthians that women needed to be silenced, or is the truth for the Corinthians that *certain* women in Corinth had nothing substantive to contribute to what it meant to be religious and needed to be silenced? In other words, was the writer forcefully laying down a sacrosanct and universal truth about womenkind and religious practice to be upheld at all places and for all times, or was he forcefully dealing with a particular circumstance in Corinth? Believing Sha'ul to be more inclined to advocate for women than against them, and for the aforementioned textual reasons, it seems best to interpret him as dealing with specific misguided women in Corinth.[33]

Refuting prophetesses, who claimed he was spiritually weak and inadequate in 2 Corinthians, he underscored that—even with his weaknesses—he has the power and authority. In 2 Corinthians 12:14–15, he referenced his travel plans, saying: "Look, I am ready this third time to visit you; and I will not be a burden to you; for it is not what you own that I want, but you! Children are not supposed to save up for their parents, but parents for their children. And as for me, I will most gladly spend everything I have and be spent myself

---

33. It seems that some compelling prophetess types were sowing dissension, were upending households, and were giving credence to their wild ideas through the utterance of ecstatic prophesies. These women had no covering to speak of, i.e., they had absolutely no legitimate accountability or ministerial endorsement. It is best to understand that Sha'ul needed to silence them. Reading him this way comports with the congregational situation in first century Corinth, as can be ascertained from the literature written to and about it. We do well to not read the discipline, a corrective that was uttered in and for a specific situation, as being normative for all people, in all places and at all times.

too for your sakes. If I love you more, am I to be loved less?" He, again, defensively restated that he took nothing financially from the Corinthians, in verse 16, and that he didn't send anyone else to do so either in verses 17–18: "Let it be granted, then, that I was not a burden to you; but crafty fellow that I am, I took you with trickery! Was it perhaps through someone I sent you that I took advantage of you? I urged Titus to go and send the brother with him; Titus didn't take advantage of you, did he? Didn't we live by the same Spirit and show you the same path?"

After saying in verse 19 that he had been less about "defending" himself, and more about "speaking [the truth] in the sight of God," he said the letter was written with their "up building" in mind. Not content to leave their welfare in the hands of a dispatched letter and having noted previously of his plans to come their way,[34] in verses 20–21, he looked ahead to his pending visit—albeit with some angst.

> For I am afraid of coming and finding you not the way I want you to be, and also of not being found the way you want me to be. I am afraid of finding quarreling and jealousy, anger and rivalry, slander and gossip, arrogance and disorder.[35] I am afraid that when I come again, my God may humiliate me in your presence, and that I will be grieved over many of those who sinned in the past and have not repented of the impurity, fornication, and debauchery that they have engaged in.

---

34. See also 2 Cor. 13:1-4.

35. The Emissary's penchant for lists has been noted already. Here he speaks of "quarreling and jealousy, anger and rivalry, slander and gossip, arrogance and disorder." Other lists are found at Rom. 1:29-31; 13:13; 1 Cor. 5:10-11; 6:9-10, and Gal. 5:19-21.

2 CORINTHIANS 13

One can feel the pent up and cascading energy building in the previous chapters. At the close, he reigns it in a little bit by commenting matter-of-factly: "This will be the third time that I have come to visit you." Confident as he is at the time of the writing, and emboldened as he has been in the later part of this letter, he pressed on with verve: "Any charge (ῥῆμα, 'matter') must be established by the testimony of two or three witnesses." He simply was not afraid of a conflict. "To those who sinned in the past and to the rest I say," in verse 2, "…if I come again, I will not spare you (οὐ φείσομαι, 'not spare anyone')." That he had the super-spiritually inclined and false teachers in mind was tacitly inferred in verse 3, with: "since you are looking for proof (δοκιμὴν) of the Messiah speaking in me." Aware of his personal and bodily imitations, some claimed that Sha'ul was lackluster in the arena of miracle power. Forcefully, he said those who want proof of his religious authority were going to experience it. In 3–4 he continued: "He [i.e., the Messiah] is not weak in dealing with you, but he is powerful among you. For although he was executed on a stake in weakness, now he lives by God's power." His point was this: Yeshua looked weak in the body—particularly on the cross, but it was for a reason and only for a season. He continued with: "And we too are weak in union with him, but in dealing with you we will live with him by God's power," saying, in effect, as it was with Yeshua so it will be with him.

Rabbi Sha'ul was undaunted and unafraid. He believed some of them should have trepidation, however. In verse 5 he beckoned: "Examine (πειράζετε) yourselves to see whether you are living the life of trust. Test yourselves. Don't you realize that Yeshua the Messiah is in you? —unless you fail to pass the test (δοκιμάζετε).” He previously exhorted them to examine themselves in 1 Corinthians 11:28–32, but with different circumstances in mind then.

As they reflected on their affairs, Sha'ul said in verse 6: “I hope you will realize (γνώσεσθε, 'you will know') that we are not failures (ἀδόκιμοι, 'unapproved')”—as some among them alleged. He continued in verse 7 that “...[w]e are not concerned with our appearing successful, but with your doing what is right, even if we appear to be failures (ἀδόκιμο ὦμεν, 'unapproved [we] might appear').” Though made to look like a failure in the eyes of some, Sha'ul set the record straight. Sha'ul said in verse 10 that he would rather write a straightforward, and possibly-hard-to-read letter now, than have to be direct in their presence: “I write these things while away from you, so that when I am with you I will not have to use my authority to deal sharply (μὴ ἀποτόμως, 'not with severity') with you, for the Lord gave it to me for building up and not for tearing down.”

Finally, he closed in verse 11 with *shalom*! and he then followed with a gentle exhortation: “Put yourselves in order, pay attention to my advice, be of one mind, live in shalom—and the God of love and shalom will be with you.” That said, as is common for him, he beckoned them to “Greet one another with a holy kiss,” in verse 12, followed by a note that “all God's people send greetings to you,” in verse 13.

After his tender good-bye, Rabbi Sha'ul offered a final benediction in verse 14, one that echoes what would later be worked into a trinitarian formulation[36]: “The grace of the Lord Yeshua the Messiah, the love of God and the fellowship of the Ruach HaKodesh be with you all.”

---

36. It will be approximately 150 more years till the word "Trinity" will come into vogue. A reference here to the Son, the Father and the Holy Spirit gives credence to the doctrine in the Rabbi from Tarsus' lips.

ABOUT THE AUTHORS

Dr. Yosef Koelner was born in Chicago and raised in an Orthodox Jewish home. His extended family is among the *Chalutzim* (Pioneers), the early settlers of Israel.

His education includes a BA in Spanish and Latin American Studies from Illinois State University; a Master of Ministry, with a concentration in Jewish studies from Messiah Biblical University; a MA in Jewish Studies from Gratz College, as well as a Doctor of Practical Ministry from Wagner Leadership Institute.

His ministry spans four decades — Rabbi of Temple Aron HaKodesh for 28 years and Rabbi Emeritus of Kehilat Bet Avinu, both in the Fort Lauderdale area. Fluent in Spanish, he travels extensively throughout Latin America presenting seminars on Jewish subjects.

Dr. Jeffrey Seif has 30+ years of experience as a Bible college and seminary professor. He graduated Southern Methodist University with Master of Theological Studies and Doctor of Ministry degrees. He also holds a master's degree in applied criminology and Police Management from Cambridge University— and is currently a doctoral student at Cambridge. He has recently been appointed executive director of the Union of Messianic Jewish Congregations.

Prof. Seif has authored many books and appears weekly on television, on *Our Jewish Roots*.

The Lives and Ministries of ELIJAH and ELISHA
PRAYING LIKE A JEW JESUS
His Names Are Wonderful
Barbara D. Malda   Come and Worship
Under THE FIG TREE   PATRICK GABRIEL LUMBROSO
Under THE VINE   PATRICK GABRIEL LUMBROSO
Making Eye Contact with God
You Bring the Bagels I'll Bring the Gospel   RUBIN
THE WORLD TO COME   LEMAN
Psalms & Proverbs   David H. Stern
MESSIANIC JUDAISM   STERN
GOD's APPOINTED CUSTOMS   KASDAN
GOD's APPOINTED TIMES   KASDAN
Passover
GATEWAYS TO TORAH   RABBI RUSSELL RESNIK
CREATION TO COMPLETION   RESNIK
Is Christ Really The End of The Law?
The Return
To the Ends of the Earth
On The Way to Emmaus   Dr. Jacques Doukhan
YESHUA
JEWISH NEW TESTAMENT COMMENTARY
MATTHEW PRESENTS YESHUA, KING MESSIAH   KASDAN

Printed in the United States
by Baker & Taylor Publisher Services